'WE'RE NOT GOING TO WEMBLEY'

THE STORY OF SHEFFIELD UNITED'S PREMIER LEAGUE PROMOTION SEASON

DANNY HALL

VERTICAL
editions

www.verticaleditions.com

Main cover image by Simon Bellis/Sportimage. Additional
front/back cover images by Tyrone Hoyland, Ian Manewell,
Eoin Doyle, Richard Markham, Remi Ogunbona and Matt
Waterhouse. Front matter illustration by Tom Bradshaw
(prints available from www.tombradraw.com)

First published in the United Kingdom in 2019 by Vertical
Editions, Unit 41 Regency Court, Sheffield, S35 9ZQ

www.verticaleditions.com

ISBN 978-1-908847-14-0

A CIP catalogue record for this book
is available from the British Library

Printed and bound by Jellyfish
Print Solutions, Swanmore, Hants

'Overall, I found myself with the same goose pimples reading 'We're not going to Wembley' as I did watching United throughout the promotion campaign. A wonderful record of a wonderful season'
- *'Dem Blades' annual*

'A treasure from one of the most memorable seasons in United's history... a page-turning thriller which will grip Blades fans. Another riveting must-read'
- *View from the John Street*

'This is a heartwarming tale of proper footballers playing and behaving in the right way, thereby becoming more closely connected with supporters than I'd guess at any other club in the country. This book truly lifts the lid on the story of the Blades' promotion to the Premier League'
- *Alan Biggs*

Contents

Acknowledgements

Where to start? There are so many people to whom I owe a debt of gratitude for the book you hold in your hand today - not least you for taking the time to (hopefully) read it. I was genuinely overwhelmed by the reception to my first book, *He's one of our own*, which gave me the drive and ambition to preserve the memorable 2018/19 season in print, and I just hope I've done it justice. There are too many people to name individually, so I'd like to give my sincere thanks to *everyone* who contributed to this book in any way, be it agreeing to or helping set up an interview, contributing a photograph, or penning a chapter. United's manager and players were newly confirmed as Premier League ones, yet still graciously gave up their time for this book. One of them even insisted on paying for our coffees!

I must, too, express my gratitude, in no particular order; to Chris Wilder for agreeing to provide the foreword for the book; to my editor at *The Star*, Nancy Fielder, for her permission; and to Karl Waddicor, my predecessor as publisher at *Vertical Editions*, for his guidance. This project, though, wouldn't have been at all possible without the constant support of my wonderful fiancé, confidante, sounding board, counsellor and occasional Transit van driver, Natalie. That old saying, 'behind every good man there is a great woman', is half true - except, in this case, she is right by my side, every step of the way.

Danny Hall, July 2019

Foreword

What a time to be a Blade. To have the experience against Ipswich Town at the last home game of the season, when we took a huge leap towards promotion, and then celebrate with my players the following day… it was a truly memorable occasion, and a humbling one, as well. To be with the boys and my family, to see us back in the Premier League... truly incredible. The Ipswich game was one of the greatest days of my life, and I should imagine that's the case for the majority of my generation of Blades fans as well.

A lot was spoken about the way we play and the defensive efforts and desire to keep the ball out of our net, and to keep 21 clean sheets over the course of the season is amazing. But I'm so proud of the way we took the game to opponents. When we first walked through the door we had to reconnect the supporters with the club and play in a way that enthused them. Give them something for them to hang on to. And they've certainly done that!

We always wanted to be within touching distance of promotion around Christmas, and our away form from there was incredible. We all looked at the fixture list and saw Aston Villa, West Brom, Leeds, Sheffield Wednesday, Norwich, Birmingham City... tough places to go. We had a couple of dips and setbacks, a couple of hurdles to get over. But to get over them and come back the way we did speaks volumes about the club, and most importantly about the players.

They're a humble group; if they weren't, they wouldn't be for me. I've said a few times that I'd chop their legs off if they weren't humble, and it's important that they go and have a beer and enjoy themselves when we achieve something. I've always been a big believer in that because you never know when the next opportunity to celebrate is going to come along. We used to do it in the early days, on coaches back from Alfreton and Halifax, and I've done that since; at Oxford, Northampton and obviously United. I'm not embarrassed by that at all - I think the media coverage of our celebrations went down well with proper football people!

The players enjoy being part of a group, but they're always part of a group. They have to work hard and compete; out-run and out-fight the opposition but then also out-think and out-play. And they've done that, with the support of Alan Knill and my staff who have given us huge backing. It's not easy celebrating like we do at times. It's a tough gig! It was tough when we came out of League One, when we gave it a good go for about six weeks. This time it was a bit more condensed and intense! But why not? I think we've been a breath of fresh air in how we went about our business in the Championship. It's no slight on how other clubs go about it but we've worked hard on the training ground and recruitment has been key. It always is. Add that to the togetherness we have shown, and the way we've attacked the division... I truly believe we deserve our success.

We realise and recognise though that it's not just about what happens on a Saturday afternoon. It's a group effort, from the commercial team to the staff up at Shirecliffe; from the youth teams up to the boardroom. There's a huge connection and it's fabulous to see. This can be a difficult club to follow at times, with what has happened in our history, and to reward supporters with days like we've had is brilliant. It's put us back on the football map; not just in the city and the county, but nationwide as well.

There are fabulous stories like that all the way through the group and it'll be a fabulous experience for everyone at our football club. We had a lot of pelters to deal with while we were in League One and now we have to enjoy this time, too. For me, it's undoubtedly the pinnacle of my career. Obviously I have a huge connection with the club, through family and friends and pals I went to school with. I'm immensely proud to have played for the club, and then take on the big job - even though it comes with a huge responsibility. But there's a pride that comes with that, too.

Throughout the season I heard people saying 'X and Y deserve to go up' but to be honest, I don't get that. The teams that deserve to go up over a season will be the ones who finish in the top two, and then the best team in the play-offs will go up as well. Maybe the cups are a little bit different but the best team in the Premier League won the title, as well. It's the same in every division. It's an accumulation of points over a long, hard season; through sunshine and a little bit of wet weather. And in the second half of the season, when the pressure was really on, to average well over two points per game really shows how well the players did. So, more than anything, I'm delighted for them.

They stuck together through thick and thin over a really good season and maintained their form and belief and desire in a relentless and ruthless league. To finish where we did, ahead of some powerful football clubs and in the manner we did, we deserve every plaudit that comes our way. It's been an amazing experience all the way through and the scenes after promotion will live in the memory forever. Not just for me, but for everyone connected with the club.

I've spoken before about the great teams in Sheffield United's history leaving a legacy behind them and the likes of Tony Currie and Len Badger, from the legendary 1970/71 side which is the best in my lifetime, are still watching and supporting us. Now, we're right up there with them and I can't really ask for any more than that. I am proud to be the manager of this team. Our fans have driven the players on all season to produce their best performances, just as the support of my family, friends and especially my wife, Francesca, has enabled me to do the job to the best of my ability. That means so, so much to me personally. A lot is spoken about city rivalry but the city is certainly ours at the minute, and hopefully this book will serve as a lasting reminder of our journey over the last few seasons.

Chris Wilder, Sheffield United manager

Prologue

April 28, 2019. Moments earlier, Bramall Lane had become the Premier League's newest football stadium and at the back of the John Street stand, the party was just getting started. It didn't take long for it to get into full swing, though, and it didn't show any signs of slowing down for the hours and days that followed. The venue often changed, but the theme remained very much the same. Sheffield United were back in the top flight of English football.

The booze-drenched floors of the Lane's International Bar glistened in the sunlight that poured through the windows on this most beautiful of beautiful Sunday afternoons, and the walls seemed to shake as the volume of the music was cranked higher and higher. This was, in some ways, the calm after the storm, which came earlier in the afternoon when Leeds, knowing they had to beat Aston Villa to delay United's promotion party, failed to do so. United's players and staff, on the brink of making history at this proud football club, gathered at Bramall Lane to watch.

Some looked on nervously, others were more relaxed - confident that the job was done. A couple of hours later, it was; the shrill of the full-time whistle at Elland Road sparking scenes that will live long in the memory for everyone fortunate enough to witness them. Beer spray flew everywhere, Kean Bryan's dreadlocks bounced out of control; top-flight footballers were perched precariously on chairs, tables and the shoulders of teammates. Then, the chant erupted and never seemed to end.

We, are, Premier League… say we are Premier League!

Covering this club from the day Chris Wilder walked through the door has produced so, so many pinch-yourself moments, but this was on another level. Skipper Billy Sharp showed off his party-piece by standing on his head, on a bench near the bar; Mark Duffy was showered with beer as soon as he arrived to join the celebrations. Defender Richard Stearman later wrote himself into Blades folklore, and coined a new verb, by getting

'*Stearmaned*' throughout the day and well into the night. United's players had followed their manager's lead all season and so when the time came to drink in their successes, they didn't let Wilder down then either.

For others lucky enough to be at the party, though, it was a time for some quiet reflection. As '*Sweet Caroline*' boomed over the speakers and Wilder's wife, Francesca, prepared to dance another lap of the room, I remember aimlessly wandering down to the front of the John Street stand and found myself, suddenly, in the seat from which I first watched the Blades. Falling in love - at the risk of showing my age - with early heroes such as Vas Borbokis and Jan Åge Fjørtoft, with his exotic name and aeroplane celebration which, to this wide-eyed seven-year-old boy, he seemed to wheel out in every single game he played.

From there, and various other vantage points inside Bramall Lane before I was fortunate enough to make my way into the press box, I have witnessed exhilarating promotions and the gut-wrenching feeling of relegation; huge cup wins against illustrious opposition, and a soul-crushing, gut-churning derby-day defeat. When Wilder says that the lows are a lot lower at this club, because it is in his blood, a small part of me can appreciate where he is coming from. But my word, when they do eventually come around... how high are the highs?

Towards the end of the promotion season, Wilder said in an interview that United 'is not a glory-hunting club' and, completely involuntarily, I found myself enthusiastically nodding in agreement. Boy, is that the truth! Even in my relatively short time following United, they have so often found a spectacular way to snatch defeat from the jaws of victory. Fortunately, I was far too young to comprehend the events of 1994, when United were relegated from the top-flight to a last-minute goal, in the final game of the season, having been well clear of the drop zone at one point on that day. In later years, as United's *unique* ways took hold of me, it all began to make perfect sense.

I've seen United go 3-0 behind in the first half of a play-off final and, somehow, felt confident they'd come back to win it; I've watched United score five goals, away from home, in a play-off semi-final and somehow *still* miss out on a trip to Wembley. Names of heroes and villains from bygone eras are etched on the brain; Woodward, Currie, Colquhoun. Stein, Hopkin, Tevez. All, in one way or another, woven in the fabric of United. For better or worse.

I thought about some of them on the day that United were officially promoted; the great players and the great battles this famous old ground had witnessed, and the ones that lay ahead. I wondered if my late grandad had watched cricket at Bramall Lane from a similar spot, before the beautiful old pavilion was demolished and Sheffield's proud cricketing history was all-but erased as Yorkshire moved up the M1 to Leeds. I thought about some of the characters I used to see at games, the little community at the front of John Street that my dad and I were, for a time, a small part of.

Some of them are still going strong - I see one every time I walk to Bramall Lane, selling programmes by the underpass - while some, sadly, have passed away. "In essence, football clubs are all the same," wrote United historian John Garrett in my first book, *He's one of our own*. "All have loyal fans, a football ground with (mostly) four sides, a pitch and floodlights." He's right. But the memories and characters, and that *connection* with your club, will always make it feel that bit more special than the rest.

This book was written in the shadow of a painting on my wall by the artist Bob Barker, called *'That's My Goal'*. It's a remarkable piece, with moody Sheffield clouds gathering over a floodlit Bramall Lane and a boy in a red-and-white No.10 shirt, stood outside The Cricketers pub with a ball under his arm. Looking at his very own theatre of dreams. The beauty of the painting is that that youngster could be you or I; it could be Wilder or Sharp, who grew up to live that boy's fantasy and more. It could be any of us. And at a time when football moves further away from its working-class roots by the day, it helps me remember what the game, when all is said and done, is *really* all about.

Time stands still for no man, though, and certainly no football club. My old seat in John Street now belongs to someone else, and from its pitchside vantage point they will cheer on their own, current-day heroes. I was snapped back into the present day by the sounds of KC and the Sunshine Band, as a door opened at the back of the stand and 'Give it up' blared out. Yep, the party was still going strong.

Outside the room, John Fleck took a moment of reflection of his own, looking out over an empty Bramall Lane, apart from Chris Basham kicking a ball about with his son on the lush green turf below. Fleck shook his head, almost in disbelief, and asked aloud how this had happened. At the time, the size of the achievement still sinking in, I had no real answers. There are, of course, so many, just some of which are contained in this book. The story of a season that will live long in the memory of every-one who witnessed it; how Wilder's Blades, against the odds, reclaimed their place in the Premier League. I hope you enjoy reliving it. It was a hell of a ride.

chapter one

Beginning of the end or the start of the beginning?

Summer 2018

Mayfair, London. May 2018. Months before Sheffield United's 2018/19 season culminated in promotion and the glorious scenes that went with it, the foundations were laid 140 miles south of Bramall Lane in the inauspicious surroundings of a neutral hotel in London's Mayfair district. With the future of United manager Chris Wilder seemingly hanging by a thread, Blades co-owners Kevin McCabe and Prince Abdullah agreed to put aside their vast differences. For the good of the club, something of an uneasy truce was brokered.

By this stage McCabe and Prince Abdullah disagreed on a great deal of things, their relationship soured by disagreements over how the Blades should be governed. Their partnership began in 2013, when the Prince was effectively gifted a 50 per cent share in United's football operations in exchange for financial investment, but had broken down irretrievably and in April 2018, after United's hopes of reaching the Championship play-offs were dealt a critical blow by a home defeat to Preston North End, Wilder felt he could no longer hold his tongue.

"For a club to be successful, there has to be harmony, direction and a plan," said the United manager in his post-match press conference, his first public intervention into the falling-out between McCabe and Prince Abdullah. United at that time, Wilder felt, lacked all three of those things and almost exactly two years since he walked through the door of his boyhood club, he was considering walking back out again. It was a seismic bombshell; one that reverberated all around the red-and-white half of the Steel City.

Just 12 months earlier Wilder, in his first season in charge, had led United to the League One title, with 100 points and 30 wins and scenes of celebration and connection that had not been witnessed at Bramall Lane for some time. United supporters loved Wilder because he was, as the song goes, 'one of their own' - a lad from the city who'd grown up overlooking their stadium, a supporter of the club, ex-ball boy, player and now manager. After six years thrashing about in the wilderness of League One, Wilder had put United back on the footballing map, especially when they threatened a second successive promotion before falling away. But, little by little, the dream looked like it may turn into a nightmare.

Wilder felt the strain, too. He wiped a tear from his eye after leading United on an end-of-season 'lap of appreciation' following the Preston game and wondered, time and time again, whether it would be the last time he heard fans on the Kop proudly sing his name. The thought of walking away from the club - *his club* - appeared inconceivable to many, but Wilder is a principled man who will not be ruled by sentiment. Heart would not rule head, and his message was clear and consistent. Things at the top had to change.

Eight days after the Preston game, and the tears and frustration that followed it, United closed their season with a 3-2 win at Bristol City. Chants of 'Chrissy Wilder, we want you to stay' were heard from the away end at Ashton Gate just seconds after kick-off and in the visiting dressing room after the game, skipper Billy Sharp - like Wilder, a boyhood Blade - delivered an emotional speech to his players, with an ominous caveat, thanking them for their efforts 'whatever happens'. The inference was clear, and more than one player has since admitted that they thought it was the end of Wilder's time at United, and the end of an era for the club.

Soon after departing Ashton Gate, Wilder and his family flew to California with his future still very much in the air, and his stock in the game also as high as it ever had been before that point. Wilder had tasted success in his playing career, reaching the top-flight with United, but described his career as a 'steady-away' one and admitted he could have done more with the ability he possessed. He then discovered an ability, and a passion, for coaching after getting involved with the running of a Sunday League team in Sheffield, well before he hung up his boots.

Under Wilder, and his close pal and co-manager Ian Whitehorne, The Bradway enjoyed unprecedented success in the Meadowhall Sunday League and after injury curtailed his playing days, Wilder took his next steps on the coaching ladder in the unglamorous surroundings of the Northern Counties East League, and Alfreton Town.

In just seven months at North Street Wilder won four trophies, and later took cash-strapped Halifax Town - who had no training facilities, players or even footballs when he arrived - to an against-the-odds Conference play-off final, before they went bust under the strain of vast debts.

A spell as Alan Knill's assistant manager at Bury got him back into football before Wilder was lured back into management by Conference side Oxford United, leading them back into the Football League. Oxford were then well-placed in League Two when Wilder's decision to leave for Northampton Town, firmly entrenched in relegation trouble at the time, raised a few eyebrows on the circuit. Now with Knill as his assistant, Wilder steadied the Sixfields ship and then transformed the Cobblers into league champions just one year later, winning a remarkable 99 points against a backdrop of yet more financial strife. Staff went months without wages, and Wilder's card was once declined as he filled his car with petrol.

Taking the next step was inevitable and after meeting with Charlton Athletic, and being impressed with controversial chairman Roland Duchâtelet and then-chief executive Katrien Meire, Wilder and his coaching staff were poised to be unveiled at The Valley before, well past the 11th hour, the invitation came from United. As the terrace chant goes: 'it was our sixth year in division one… then Chris Wilder came home'. While that United homecoming should have been a fairytale one for Wilder, the reality was anything but. In his own words, there was real work to be done at Bramall Lane.

The season before, Nigel Adkins' Blades had slumped to 11th in League One - their lowest league finish since 1983, when Margaret Thatcher was the country's prime minister - and, more urgently, were more disconnected from their fan base than at any other point in their long and proud history.

United had plummeted to such depths that anger on the terraces had given way to apathy and when Adkins insisted on leading his players on a now-infamous 'lap of shame' at the end of the season, only a few hundred fans could be bothered to stay behind and boo them. In a damning indictment of how far the club had fallen, the majority simply shrugged and went home.

What a difference a year made. Twelve months later United, a club reborn under Wilder, blitzed their way to the League One title and broke records galore in the process. On the pitch, Wilder had built an honest and hard-working team, playing with a swagger and vibrancy that was a joy to watch, but arguably his biggest success at Bramall Lane came away from the field.

Despite a rocky start, what he called the 'connection' between fans and club had been very much restored and after threatening an unlikely tilt at the Premier League in 2017/18, ultimately finishing 10th in their first season back in the second tier, that bond was as strong as it had ever been. Things, though, are rarely ever that straightforward at United and the fear that Wilder would walk away, suddenly seemed very real indeed.

"My words were honest, as they always have been and always will be. I was open about it," Wilder later said. "I've got a clear vision of how I want this club to go forward. I think what the players and staff had achieved allowed me to give my opinion. I've always said that I'm an employee of the club and I respect that status. But I'm the type of guy who walks in the front door and I'll walk out of the front door if it's not right. There were no threats, but it had to be right."

* * *

As the dust settled on the 2017/18 season, and uncertainty lingered menacingly over Bramall Lane, Stephen Bettis was settling nicely into his new life over 5,000 miles away in Santa Monica, on the Californian coast. Bettis had spent a year as United's chief executive as they won the League One title and enjoyed a close working relationship with Wilder, before leaving to pursue business interests in the United States. As Bettis relaxed on the terrace of his home, his tranquillity was suddenly interrupted by the ringing of his mobile phone. Wilder's name flashed up on the screen. He was heading to California.

Initially, Bettis was unperturbed, assuming Wilder was on the lookout for tickets to watch LA Galaxy or the Dodgers. Although the United manager did take in a game while he was Stateside - watching Adrian Heath's Minnesota United lose 2-0 at Los Angeles FC - he had more pressing matters to discuss with Bettis. He had flown out to America with one primary goal; to bring United's former chief executive back home with him.

Wilder had made the return of Bettis one of his key conditions in preliminary contract talks with the Bramall Lane hierarchy. After receiving the go-ahead from McCabe and Prince Abdullah, the only step left was to persuade him to swap Santa Monica for South Yorkshire and trade his new life for his old one, back by his side as United's chief executive. "I basically told him I was coming over and was going to be staying nearby, so I'd probably pop in," Wilder told the *Sheffield Star*. "And then I tied him up and kidnapped him! Well, maybe not quite. But I made things pretty clear." Wilder, Bettis added, "can be pretty persuasive" when he wants to be. But Bettis was receptive to the idea, feeling that he had unfinished business at Bramall Lane.

Bettis' role, and his initial departure to America, was later revealed to be just one of many things McCabe and Prince Abdullah did not see eye-to-eye on, when their messy and very public 'divorce' proceedings were heard before a judge in the High Court a year later. Their grievances and some of the remarkable revelations that emerged in court, including a loan for United from the bin Laden family, could fill a book of their own but there was, at least, one bit of common ground to be found between the two men and their advisors; the importance of keeping hold of their manager.

Wilder, at one point over the summer, had been as short as 1/4 with one bookmaker to leave United, with Sunderland mooted as one possible destination. Although the Black Cats were still reeling from relegation to League One, the Stadium of Light job was more appealing than it may have seemed. Stewart Donald, who had worked closely with Wilder during their time at Oxford, had recently completed his takeover of Sunderland from American billionaire Ellis Short and the club was on a much firmer financial footing. Donald, observing the uncertainty surrounding Wilder's future from a safe distance in the north-east, prepared an official approach.

"Early on, I never really thought the gaffer would leave but then, when he came out and said what he did, you had to take it seriously," admitted George Baldock, the defender Wilder had signed from MK Dons the previous summer. "I'd have been devastated if he'd have walked because he was a massive part of why I jumped on board with this club. He's a massive part of the club anyway, being a fan and an ex-player and having that connection and mutual respect with the supporters. Together with the skipper and people like that, he's the heartbeat of the club and it would have had a massive impact if he left.

"He never said he was going to leave but he didn't know what was happening at the club, and it was quite emotional after the Bristol game. It felt a little more real then and I can tell you that when we realised he was staying, as a group we got together and said: "Let's go for it now'. He deserves every plaudit he gets because of the job he's done.

"He works as hard as anyone and he's brilliant. Everyone at the club is in it together, including the coaches who aren't as well-known as Alan Knill and Matt Prestridge. I class the chef as a friend of mine. Everyone plays a part and this club wouldn't be successful without each and every one of them. But the manager demands that, and it all stems from him."

At the time, though, it felt like the whole club was holding its breath before United's co-owners temporarily suspended hostilities, and a breakthrough was eventually made. Wilder received a new contract until 2021, the clarity and direction he so desperately craved and, although he was at great pains to point out that his stance had never been one solely about money, an improved transfer budget as well. "It wasn't game-changing," Wilder later reflected, "but it was something that needed to be looked at. A small investment from each owner to give us an opportunity to move forward because I think if you stand still in football, you move back. We had to improve, and we had to make sure that we used the figure wisely.

"I didn't go on the record and say I'd leave, but we had to see what path the club wanted to take and what the owners wanted to do. Thankfully, to their credit, they got together and we improved. We have to keep improving because everyone else around us is and, if you don't, then you will suffer and struggle.

"As we've seen from a few clubs. I didn't want to undo the hard work of the first year and go backwards. But I can't lie and say it wasn't a difficult period. I was thinking: 'Is this the beginning of the end?' rather than the start of the beginning, and wondering: 'Has it run its course?'

"I'd savoured every moment at the club and loved every minute of working in the capacity I did. We had got something going in the right direction and I was anxious that we needed to clear things up. But yeah, there was a nagging thing in the back of my head that it might be the end. I'd talked it through a lot with family and close friends, and I was quite emotional during and after the game at Bristol.

"I think people had got wind of how I felt the week before against Preston, and I was thinking 'Is this the last time I'm going to have all these experiences at Bramall Lane?' I was so proud of the way the players played at Bristol, how they'd gone about it all season and what they'd done for me. We're a close-knit group of players, staff and supporters.

"But things had to change and if they didn't, that would have been the end of my time at Sheffield United. But I didn't have a gun to anyone's head and full credit to the owners, because we all wanted the club to go in the same direction. Without being arrogant or shying away from what needed to be said, it wasn't about me or anyone else. It was about the direction of the football club and if we need to discuss that openly and honestly, then we do. Thankfully the return of Stephen was a key thing for me and there were other bits and pieces that needed to happen. Thankfully they did. I was close to leaving, but I was delighted to stay. The direction the club has gone in now is a brilliant one… and hopefully, it's the start of a new beginning."

chapter two

Summer preparations

Pre-season 2018

After the flames of uncertainty surrounding his Sheffield United future had been finally extinguished earlier in the summer, Chris Wilder and his coaching staff could instead look forward to the other small task at hand - fine-tuning a squad to mount a challenge for promotion to the Premier League. But as a relaxed Wilder cracked jokes with members of the media at an impromptu press conference at Bramall Lane, while the ink dried on his new contract, a shift in United's mentality also emerged.

Taking what Wilder called 'punts' on players from lower in the football pyramid had paid dividends for United, with the likes of John Fleck and Enda Stevens impressing since arriving in South Yorkshire. Now, though, United were largely setting their sights on proven, established players at Championship level.

It was a policy, however, that presented its own problems; especially considering Wilder had been handed a budget that, although improved since the previous season's, was still dwarfed by many of their Championship rivals. The previous January, United were well-set in the race for promotion but when they were rocked by the broken leg suffered by talisman Paul Coutts, Wilder's budget forced him to take 'punts' once more, on Ryan Leonard, Ricky Holmes and Lee Evans.

It didn't prove enough to maintain United's position in a division dominated by Wolverhampton Wanderers, who spent almost £16million on Ruben Neves in pre-season, while Fulham joined Wolves in the Premier League after signing Aleksandar Mitrovic on loan from Newcastle United in January and paying him around £60,000 a week in wages.

"We looked at the market and that approach served us well with the likes of John, Enda and Mark Duffy, who'd been at

Burton Albion," Wilder said. "We tried as well with the Ryan Leonards and Ben Heneghans of this world. Ricky Holmes, as well. We didn't have a lot of money in the January transfer window but we still needed players, so we took punts on them. The growth of the team sort of overtook them a little, with no disrespect to those lads, and we had to top it up. We had a really good group of core players; the team was well-balanced and ticked a lot of boxes. But we needed to go and put a bit more quality into the group."

The previous season saw United, fresh out of League One after six years, attack the Championship with hunger, momentum and ability and they went top of the league in November. That was the night Coutts suffered his horrific injury, away at Burton Albion, and United never really recovered. They took only two points from the six games that followed, although they did remain in mathematical contention for the play-offs until the penultimate game of the season.

Players such as Fleck, Stevens and Jack O'Connell impressed throughout as they enjoyed their first consistent experience of the Championship and Wilder saw enough from his players to believe that, with the right quality additions, United could go one better the second time around.

"I think you improve from going through the process, in these fabulous games against top players and managers and teams," Wilder later reflected. "We looked at what other top clubs were doing in the league and it's like anything else in life… you're generally better for experience. It's like a rookie on a golf tour. Is he better after a season? Of course he is, because of the experiences he goes through.

"We recognised we had to hit certain targets if we were to improve on the season before, from a player point of view and a staff one as well. There were certain things we had to do better as staff, and needed the players to do better. But on the back of a year of experience in the Championship, we grew and improved."

The calibre of player Wilder was chasing may have changed, but his requirements had not. Any potential addition to United's group still had to pass Wilder's multi-point checklist, which covered their technical and tactical acumen as well as their character and temperament. His requirements, according to the manager himself, are simple; players are expected, rather than asked, to 'run around and compete'. In return, Wilder gives them the licence to express them freely in United's exciting, innovative and, at times, baffling 3-5-2 system, where the two 'outside' centre-halves operate as auxiliary wingers and create attacks as often as they stop them.

The formation had helped United sweep all before them in League One and worked well, despite initial reservations from some supporters, in the Championship as well. Even if Wilder and Alan Knill, his trusted lieutenant, did have to work hard to stay ahead of the curve.

"The game evolves and a few more teams are playing three at the back, so we will do something a little bit different," Wilder said. "There's a little routine we do on the pitch, and we didn't see it before. We seemed to be the only team doing it. But earlier in the season, I said to Alan that one team had started doing it, and he said 'another team did it the night before'! I'm not going to reveal what it was, but that's what happens. It's a really small thing, but people have picked up on it.

"We have to be bright and smart and pick up on what other teams do. And we have done. We watched a team in pre-season in depth, how they dealt with a certain situation. We have to be on the ball, and ready to change. There are some quality coaches and managers in this division, so we have to be up to speed with what everyone else is doing."

In football, though, success doesn't happen on the quiet and unfortunately for Wilder and United, the rest of the game also seemed to be up to speed with what they were doing as well. Approaches for United's prized asset, the young Welsh international David Brooks, felt almost inevitable after the youngster recovered from glandular fever and returned to the United side for the 2017/18 run-in. Premier League side AFC Bournemouth began sniffing around Brooks a month after he made his senior debut for Wales, the country of his mother Cathryn's birth, while Tottenham Hotspur also monitored the forward's progress. Brooks had exploded onto the scene earlier that season with a man-of-the-match display in the 4-2 derby-day win over Wednesday at Hillsborough - only the second league start of his career - and took the headlines again with a late winner against Leeds United at Elland Road.

Although he had signed a new long-term contract, officials at Bramall Lane privately recognised that the writing was on the wall eight months later when the youngster changed his agent and joined Harry Kane, Wilfried Zaha and former Blades striker Che Adams on the books of Unique Sports Management. And so it proved. Just 36 weeks after signing that deal at United, Brooks was unveiled as a Bournemouth player after Eddie Howe's men returned to the negotiating table with an improved offer. United had no concerns about the player becoming a disruptive influence if he was denied a move to the Premier League and Wilder tried in vain to convince the player he would be best served by staying another season at United. But Brooks expressed a desire to make the move and, given the fact the south coast club would make him a millionaire and give him a chance to play in one of the world's best leagues, he could hardly be blamed.

"I don't think anything surprises you in football, especially nowadays," Wilder said at the time of the deal. "We don't live in an ideal world. In an idealistic situation, you keep everyone from your academy. We've been in League One for six years, we're moving up, but we're not in the Premier League. We don't live in that world now when, in the 60s or 70s, you'd have nine or 10 lads from Sheffield who bleed red and white. There are too many people involved now, good and bad. There are personal situations to take into account. You have to work to the best of your ability to get the best for the club."

United wisely inserted a sell-on clause in the £11.5million deal that took Brooks into the Premier League and the player certainly took his chance, later making history by becoming the first player to win both Wales' player of the year and young player of the year awards at the same time. "We half-expected

Brooksy to move on because we'd all heard the rumours and saw him being linked with the Premier League," Duffy admitted.

"To be totally honest, was it a big blow? He didn't play that much in the first season before he got ill, and it was more a case of what he might have brought. With young players you never know what you're going to get and from his point of view, he could never miss the opportunity to go on and play at Premier League level. Looking at how he did in his first season, you can maybe say he would have been brilliant for us. But football doesn't always work out like that.

"It's been a massive thing for him; he's gone on and done unbelievably well. A lot of the lads all keep in contact with him, and he messaged me towards the end of the promotion season, congratulating me. I'm looking forward to locking horns with him again… and maybe trying to nutmeg him! But seriously, the gaffer saw that his head had been turned and no-one wants a player at a club who wants to move on.

"We got a good price, Brooksy got what he wanted, Bournemouth got a good player… it was win/win for everyone, really. He's gone and produced the goods, which we all hoped he would, and he might be sold again so you'll never know where he'll end up. Whatever happens, we all wish him the best, for sure, because he's a genuinely nice, nice lad."

As Brooks settled into his new apartment in Bournemouth, the attention of United's coaching staff instead focused on the players still at Bramall Lane, as well as those they were still hoping to bring in before the transfer window slammed shut. Injury scuppered a loan move for Chelsea's Kasey Palmer in pre-season and Knill embarked on a scouting trip to Scotland to watch a couple of games north of the border, including a remarkable 5-5 draw between Hibernian and Rangers. It seemed quite fitting, really, considering that one of the biggest conundrums ahead of the new season for Wilder and Co. was the identity of United's next goalkeeper.

Jamal Blackman, a giant of a shot-stopper on loan from Chelsea, had enjoyed a steady rather than spectacular campaign on loan at Bramall Lane the season previous and lost his place to Simon Moore at various points, because of a combination of injury, suspension and loss of form. So when Wilder and his trusted lieutenants scoured the English game for Blackman's replacement, they had one prerequisite in mind; the ability to make big, important saves at key times, and win points. Step forward Dean Henderson.

The Manchester United loanee was fresh from an impressive loan spell in League One with Shrewsbury Town, who had defied pre-season expectations of relegation - from their own manager, Wilder's friend Paul Hurst - to reach the play-off final at Wembley. They eventually lost in extra time, to Rotherham United, but Henderson excelled underneath the Wembley arch, keeping out an early Millers penalty and making several eye-catching saves before eventually being beaten. Wilder, who rated Henderson as the best goalkeeper in the English League that season, knew he had the right man.

Still, United did their due diligence on the player and Wilder was impressed that the youngster's motivations to move again on loan were orientated by football, rather than finance. Henderson also spoke at length with Darren Ward, United's goalkeeping coach, before telling Wilder, in an in-depth conversation in his office, that he thought he could genuinely help United get promoted to the Premier League.

The Red Devils' decision to allow their goalkeeper to join the first and original United, too, showed that the Blades' hard work in establishing contacts with top Premier League clubs was continuing to pay off. Blackman and Cameron Carter-Vickers, from Spurs, both played their part for United after their promotion to the Championship and, although James Wilson's temporary move from Old Trafford to Bramall Lane didn't work out, the way United handled the striker made the right impression with the Red Devils' hierarchy.

Wilder, too, was impressed by the approach taken by United's namesakes from Manchester, with no demands that Henderson play games or, as has often been the case when some top clubs loan out their young players, financial penalties due if he didn't. The goalkeeper's parent club, though, did demand detailed reports on his progress and regularly dispatched a delegate over the Pennines to visit United's Shirecliffe training base throughout the season. Henderson had previously shown a willingness to get his gloves dirty during loan spells at Stockport County and Grimsby Town and agreed to sign a new deal only if the Red Devils' hierarchy agreed to let him leave Old Trafford on loan again.

"I am a player who will step out of my comfort zone and back myself to go and play," Henderson said after being unveiled at Shirecliffe. "I want to improve and will back my ability. It is not a case of going to Manchester United and saying: 'I am better than him and him'. It is about proving I am better. I want to go out and show people that I can become the best goalkeeper in the world one day."

With the goalkeeper conundrum solved - and with most of the nation distracted by England's run to the semi-finals of the World Cup in Russia, helped by ex-Blades trio Kyle Walker, Gary Cahill and Harry Maguire - attentions then turned to other areas of United's squad to strengthen. United tentatively explored the idea of approaching rivals Wednesday for striker Sam Winnall, before being discouraged by the numbers they were quoted. Then Wilder received a call from an agent about a player. More often than not, they prove a waste of time. This one, though, was different.

chapter three

A Gold-en signing

July 2018

Although his injury record sometimes preceded him, David McGoldrick had enjoyed a stellar career at Championship level. After coming through the ranks at his boyhood club Notts County, the striker enjoyed spells at Southampton and Nottingham Forest before finally appearing to settle at Ipswich Town, spending five-and-a-half years at Portman Road and persuading Premier League side Leicester City to move for him.

It was something of a sliding doors moment for the striker; the deal broke down, McGoldrick stayed in Suffolk and the following season, the Foxes upset the footballing world by winning the Premier League. Less than four years later, after being released by new Ipswich boss Paul Hurst, McGoldrick was on the proverbial footballing scrapheap.

He remained confident that the call would come from another club, but admitted that there were occasional 'dark times' as he waited for the phone to ring. Rehabilitation on an old injury at St George's Park gave him a welcome distraction but training on his own, and fielding well-meaning, yet ill-timed, questions about his future from his family, began to take its toll.

Then eventually, the phone did ring and on the other end was Sheffield United boss Chris Wilder. "We got word from an agent that David might be available," Wilder recalled. "I spoke to Mick McCarthy and a couple of people at Ipswich about him, and we knew a bit about him ourselves.

"We thought: 'Do you know what, we're not losing anything by getting him in, are we?' So we asked him to come in for a couple of days and what I will say is, from David's point of view, what a brilliant attitude he showed. In a day and age when footballers get a lot of stick, he wasn't precious at all about us wanting to look at him for a few days. You can dress it up how you want, as a trial or whatever, but he was coming in for us to take a look at him. David was being held back by a couple of injuries and we wanted to talk to him, see what his feelings were, and look at him from a medical point of view. He wasn't precious about that, at all.

We quickly made a decision and wrapped that up. With Leon Clarke, Billy Sharp and then David, we thought it gave us good variety at the top of the pitch and good experience, too." More than one of McGoldrick's close confidants advised him that he was too good to go on trial, but the striker was keen to show what he was capable of and earn a deal at United, which he described as "a big club... a perfect fit for me".

John Fleck, who played with McGoldrick at Coventry City, drove into the car park at Shirecliffe and was baffled to see his old teammate there. McGoldrick told him he was on trial at United; Fleck didn't believe him. More than one player has since described McGoldrick as a 'class act' in training on that first day. After signing a deal with United, on the eve of their prestigious friendly with Italian giants Inter Milan at Bramall Lane, the striker added the opening goal for good measure.

Argentinian superstar Mauro Icardi then scored the equaliser at the Kop end after linking up with Italian international Antonio Candreva, before Slovenian star Samir Handanovic denied Sharp a late winner in front of 18,000 fans at Bramall Lane. "Ten days earlier I didn't have a club," McGoldrick laughed. "That just shows how crazy football can be."

The striker's United career was off and running, but any satisfaction over that particular deal for Wilder was tempered somewhat when news of his pursuit of McGoldrick's former Ipswich teammate, Martyn Waghorn, emerged in the media. The United manager's budget had been improved in the summer, but it was still necessary to squeeze every last ounce of value out of it and, as he publicly vowed that United would not break the bank to sign Waghorn, there was a suspicion behind the scenes that their interest had been deliberately leaked to spark a bidding war for the striker.

If that was the intention, it certainly worked. Derby County soon joined the race, agreed to meet both Ipswich's fee and the striker's wage demands - of almost £30,000 a week - and United missed out. It was just another reminder for the Blades of what they were competing against in the Championship.

At the same time, admiring glances at United's own players were made. A derisory bid of around £250,000 was rejected for goalkeeper Simon Moore from West Bromwich Albion - recently relegated from the Premier League and with parachute payments burning a hole in their metaphorical pockets - while United were approached by Brighton and Hove Albion, with a view to signing defender Jack O'Connell. "I don't think the club thought it was the right time to sell me and I don't think it was the price they wanted, either," O'Connell said.

"I was happy to stay anyway - I'm happy at the club. But it was hard at the time. It was in pre-season and my dream is to play in the Premier League. I had an opportunity to do that. I spoke to the gaffer and he said to see how the season went, so I stayed. And with how it all panned out, it was obviously the best decision I've ever made."

The Liverpudlian couldn't help but raise a wry smile when he was reunited at Bramall Lane with his former Brentford teammate John Egan, the Republic of Ireland defender who had been Wilder's first-choice summer target and became United's record signing when he put pen to paper. "I didn't know much about John at Brentford when he came in at Brentford... only that he'd come in to take my place!" O'Connell laughed. "When John came in, that's when I said to the manager there that I wanted to leave. There were too many centre-halves and I definitely wasn't going to play, so I ended up at United. I reminded John of that when he came in, yeah!"

Although the deal to prise Egan away from Griffin Park cost United less than £4million initially, it did contain various future clauses - including one if Egan helped United to gain promotion to the Premier League during his time in the Steel City. Achieving that ambition was the motivating factor for the player to make the move north and Egan's first interview as a Blades player began with him talking about helping United back into the top flight. The defender knew all about the Blades after a short loan spell at Bramall Lane earlier in his career, from Sunderland in 2011, and Wilder had tracked the player since those early days in English football, too. United aggressively pursued Egan after identifying him as their top close-season target, and their hard work paid off when the defender told Brentford that his heart was set on a move to Sheffield.

"At the back end of the season before, we identified what we needed to do better and which positions we needed to strengthen," Wilder said. "The top of the pitch was one and we needed someone at centre-half and goalkeeper, as well. We needed to keep more clean sheets and John ticked a lot of boxes for us. He was our main signing and we had to work very, very hard to get him in because negotiations with Brentford were quite tough at times. But I was delighted to get him. We felt John was a young player who could grow with us and have an international career, and stay with us for a number of years. And I still think that to this day."

With centre-half, goalkeeper and one striker ticked off, United's coaching staff ramped up their search for another area highlighted for strengthening - the 'No.10 ' position. It is a spot in United's system that Mark Duffy had made his own since arriving at Bramall Lane from Birmingham City, but one that nevertheless requires a great deal of both ability and intelligence to play. Given the licence by Wilder and Knill to roam anywhere on the field and get on the ball, Duffy made the role look almost effortless at times as he seamlessly stepped up into the Championship. Now, after the summer sale of David Brooks, a player to challenge him was sought.

Unfortunately for United, though, players with a similar ability level to Duffy don't come cheap and the Scouser's signing, in 2016 on a free transfer, must surely rank as one of Wilder's pound-for-pound best. The loan market instead represented United's best opportunity to bring in cover and competition for one of their most important players and another exhaustive search of the market saw United move for Liverpool youngster

Ben Woodburn, who interested both Aston Villa and Wigan before Jürgen Klopp personally intervened and advised him to move to Bramall Lane. Woodburn, at that point the youngest goalscorer in Liverpool's rich history, arrived at United to some fanfare. At the same time, though, words of caution were sounded about the player.

This was the teenager's first loan away from Anfield and, although financial penalties would be imposed on United if Woodburn didn't play senior football, the 'worst-case scenario' had been factored into the finances of the deal before it was approved. Despite the youngster's big reputation, Wilder would not let anything but on-field performances impact upon his team selection. Woodburn, though, was seen as a natural replacement for his Wales teammate Brooks and his arrival gave United supporters a further boost ahead of the season's opening day, against recently-relegated Swansea City.

"I understand supporters want to see new players," said Wilder at the time. "We brought in David McGoldrick, who's a good player by the way, on trial and I was reading: 'Wilder can't attract top players and the board have got ambition.' Then we signed John Egan and McGoldrick and it all changed. Then, when Ben Woodburn came in, it went to another level. Suddenly I was reading how we were going to win the league! I sat there thinking 'hang on.' But that's the way things are now, I suppose."

chapter four

A month of two halves

August 2018

New season, new players, new hope. But as Chris Wilder strode into the Bramall Lane press room to give his views on Sheffield United's opening-day performance against Swansea City, it was a case of the same old story after the visitors had returned to Wales with a 2-1 victory. "A loss is a loss whether at the start or end of the season and it still hurts," said Wilder. "It should hurt the players. It hurts myself, and it hurts our supporters. We don't do 'unlucky'... we have not defended properly. It's not unlucky, it's just poor defending, and not putting the ball in the back of the net. We had a good period after half-time when we were on the front foot. We have worked hard. When we have opportunities to score we have to take them. This is the Championship and you don't get seven or eight golden chances like we did in the division below."

For the United boss, the complaint was a familiar one. Wilder had bemoaned his side's profligacy often throughout the previous season, as their once-bright hopes of promotion steadily fizzled away, and this time the main culprits were John Lundstram and new boy David McGoldrick, who made his debut against the Swans. Another pulling on the Blades shirt for the first time, goalkeeper Dean Henderson, made good saves from Joel Asoro, Jay Fulton and teammate Leon Clarke's attempted clearance, and things looked rosy for United when full-back George Baldock sidefooted the hosts in front from Lundstram's cut-back.

Oliver McBurnie, who scored against United on loan at Barnsley in 2017/18, repeated the feat for the Swans' equaliser. McBurnie had been viewed as a possible summer signing before his parent club handed him a new contract, and Wilder's frustration was compounded with five minutes remaining when Yan

Dhanda swept home the visitors' winner. By Monday morning, when he met the media at Shirecliffe to preview the following day's trip to Middlesbrough, Wilder's mood had relaxed somewhat - even if he was frustrated by having to play the game at all, while the other 22 clubs in the Championship put their feet up and enjoyed a midweek break.

Sky Sports had brought the game forward by two weeks to help with their scheduling, and the only thing more evident than Wilder's bewilderment at that decision was his admiration for Boro boss Tony Pulis, who he described as a 'proper, solid football man'. In Wilder parlance, describing something as 'proper' is a real sign of respect and 'proper, solid' is a level above, reserved only for a select few in the game. His reverence for Pulis had grown throughout the years but was cemented a few weeks before the game, when the pair were at a managers' meeting and his compatriot was, in Wilder's words, "rattling into referees". "I thought: 'Go on Tony!'" he smiled.

Wilder's mood soured somewhat down by the Riverside, though, when his side went 3-0 behind within 25 minutes thanks to more indecisive defending. The game was dead and buried. Some more words from their manager at half-time provoked United a little and they improved vastly in the second half, with Woodburn impressing during a cameo off the substitutes' bench. But by then the damage, from United's point of view, had already been done.

"Early on, I thought I had to show people that I was worthy of the fee United had paid for me, and show the lads that I was good enough," admitted John Egan, United's record signing. "Looking back on the first two weeks, I think I was trying *too* hard and the first two games certainly didn't go to plan. I think they were looking for the receipt after the Boro game to get a refund for me! Thankfully the gaffer kept the faith, I grew into the system and the team and as a back three or a five or six - whatever you want to call it - we were a really good unit over the course of the season."

A local newspaper's headline after the Boro defeat described United as both 'generous' and 'fragile' - not typical traits of

Wilder teams - and with United sitting bottom of the table after two games, not too many fans were dreaming of promotion glory come April and May. A poster on S24SU.com, a popular United fans' forum, ran a poll the day after the Boro game and asked supporters about their expectations for the season. Almost 40 per cent of fans predicted a mid-table finish in 2018/19 and almost 10 per cent expected a relegation scrap. Although almost 30 per cent of fans thought United would challenge for the play-offs, less than seven per cent predicted a top-six finish. Not a single voter believed United would achieve automatic promotion.

"It was quite difficult up at Boro," McGoldrick reflected at the end of the season. "I thought I had a good game against Swansea but we had strong words in the dressing room at Boro, and went from there. We didn't look back, really. Yes, we lost games but the words the gaffer said at Boro, and the belief he showed in us, were good turning points in the season. He told us we had to buck our ideas up and that no-one was safe. Everyone had to fight for their place and we had to improve or we wouldn't have success. He told us how good we were and wanted us to show that, or else we'd be lingering in mid-table. We went from strength-to-strength after that."

After two games, though questions were being asked by some sections of United's fan base about Wilder's decision to sacrifice a creative No.10 in Mark Duffy for a midfield three of John Fleck, Lee Evans and Lundstram against Swansea and Boro. "I have no regrets about the selection," Wilder later insisted. "It's the nature of the game that there are going to be questions when we get beat, but why would I not pick the best team, the team I thought was best suited to playing the game? What it does do is open it up for other players." Duffy had been briefed by Wilder in pre-season about his planned approach but, after coming off the bench at Boro, was told to be ready for the next game, against QPR at Loftus Road that weekend.

Two defeats from two games - and doubts over their season prospects, from pundits and supporters alike - meant that United once again had their backs to the wall and had no real option than to come out fighting; a position that their manager didn't particularly mind. Two years earlier, soon after Wilder took charge at Bramall Lane, United lost three of their opening four games and fell to the bottom of League One before eventually winning the title with 100 points. "We came steaming back," Wilder remembered, pointing to that particular experience. "It's quite easy to manage when it's going well, and we've done well over the last two years. But there will be questions from the fans... we have to do better and show what we're all about."

Although it's still unclear whether those questions hurt, offended or just simply irritated him, it was clear that they had *some* effect, judging by Wilder's reaction to a battling three points at Loftus Road. United's route to victory was about as straightforward as the one on the Underground to Shepherd's Bush (a mix-up involving two stations with the same name causing one journalist a mad dash to make kick-off), but after the very impressive Eberechi Eze had put QPR ahead, goals from Billy Sharp and McGoldrick's penalty got United up and running with what was, at the time, a rare win in the capital under Wilder.

McGoldrick came off the bench to replace Sharp just after the hour mark and was impeded by Jake Bidwell to win the penalty. With regular taker Sharp off the field, there was initial confusion as to who would take the spot-kick before McGoldrick was offered the chance to open his account for the Blades from 12 yards. As any striker would, he gratefully accepted and sent Matt Ingram the wrong way in front of the travelling Blades fans packed behind that goal at Loftus Road. Sub McGoldrick was then withdrawn himself late on, and was forced to cut short his post-match chat with the assembled media as a bout of dizziness struck.

As the striker sat in the dugout with his head in his hands, trying to regain his bearings, one national journalist attempted to continue the interview, but was politely turned away. So it was left to Wilder to come out fighting and take aim at what he called "noise and nonsense" surrounding his side. "People were saying all sorts of things after two games," he bristled, words dripping with sarcasm. "We just wanted to go out there and get a result... the one nobody thought we could. We're really struggling with that character stuff, aren't we? We have over the last two years. We've not shown any bottle, any spirit or desire... we're all over the place, having fights in the changing room all the time. I don't sign players who don't want to put it in for this football club. I told them beforehand... 'If people are questioning you, you know how to shut them up'."

Wilder, though, is not a manager to let the grass grow under his feet. On deadline day, before United boarded the train to London, an approach for midfielder Evans was made by Wigan Athletic and the deal was sanctioned. The reasoning became more clear a week later when news began to filter through about a move for Oliver Norwood, then of Brighton and Hove Albion and something of a promotion expert in the Championship. In the previous two seasons, Norwood had helped the Seagulls and then Fulham into the Premier League and worked with Alan Knill, United's assistant manager, during a spell at Scunthorpe earlier in his career. With the loan window still open for business after the permanent deadline had passed, United negotiated a loan-to-buy agreement with the Premier League club and Norwood was cleared to make his United debut.

Ironically, it came in the EFL Cup against Hull City, a club who had also tried to secure his signature in the summer. "They tried quite hard, actually, but they couldn't get a deal done and Sheffield United did. I'm quite glad because I would much rather come to United than go there, if I'm honest," said Burnley-born Norwood, with typical northern bluntness. United had first enquired about Norwood's availability in the summer but, with Evans, Lundstram, Fleck, Ryan Leonard and Paul Coutts already at the club, there was little room for manoeuvre - on the midfield roster or in the budget. Then, late in the window, Wigan boss Paul Cook made a decisive move for Evans.

Evans' £1m fee covered the majority of Norwood's transfer when it was made permanent the following January, and Wilder later sold Leonard to Millwall for a seven-figure sum and brought in Martin Cranie on a free. "Ollie covered Evo and Martin covered for Lenny," Wilder later reflected. "That, pound for pound, is possibly some of the best business we've done at the club. It shows we're willing to wheel and deal. In that window we lost David Brooks, which was a big blow for us, and I wanted him to stay for another year. But from his point of view, it was a big jump and he was going into the Premier League.

"Maybe if it was a year or so later and we had a little more power, he wouldn't have gone but although the majority of the money did go back into the football club it did give us a little bit of flexibility to do business, whether that was in the first window or more importantly the second window in January. Ryan Leonard wasn't really playing and there was an interest from Millwall because they'd sold George Saville to Middlesbrough and needed a midfielder. Lee had been in and out and Ollie became available so a deal was concluded, to financial gain for us. Possibly it's one of the best bits of business we did. It epitomised the way we work and think on our feet."

As expected Norwood made his debut against Hull - led by former Blades boss Nigel Adkins - and gave the Tigers a glimpse at what they could have won with an exceptional display. His only misstep came in the penalty shootout - when he blazed his spot-kick over the bar, as United went out of the cup on penalties - but United's supporters had seen enough of the Northern Ireland international to be very encouraged indeed. It was Norwood's first appearance at Bramall Lane since the following season when Fulham, who had signed him on loan from Brighton, triumphed 5-4 in a remarkable game which ultimately propelled them to a play-off final victory over Aston Villa. Leon Clarke and young Ryan Sessegnon both scored hat-tricks and at the final whistle, several Fulham players slumped to the turf in exhaustion. Norwood was one of them.

"It was good," he grinned, with a glint in his eye. "I remember thinking: 'Thank God that's over'. I was knackered! For me, that just summed up Sheffield United under the gaffer. They just kept going and never gave it up. I think it was 5-2 at one point? If we'd have carried on for a bit longer, it might have been 7-6 or 8-7 or something. An incredible night. It's one of my most memorable games in football. It had everything. I remember speaking to Knilly afterwards and he said that's what the gaffer is like. If someone's going to beat us, then they've got to earn it. If they're better than us then that's fine. But they're going to have to be because they won't out-run us or out-work us."

Norwood's league debut then arrived against Norwich City, a vibrant and exciting team assembled by German coach Daniel Farke. United and City had enjoyed two excellent battles the previous season, winning a game apiece at the other's ground, while Wilder and Farke were portrayed in some quarters as mortal enemies. That largely emanated from Wilder's passionate post-game monologue after the game at Bramall Lane when, after being offended by a number of things including City's time-wasting antics on the field and their bus arriving late, he accused Farke's men of lacking 'respect'.

City's brazen gamesmanship inspired a humorous chant from United fans in the return leg at Carrow Road - encouraging their players to run down the clock by *playing football the Norwich way'* - and although a rivalry has been cemented between fans of the two clubs, and their touchline demeanour may some-times suggest otherwise, a lot of mutual respect exists between Wilder and Farke, too. And, indeed, United and City. "We had a drink afterwards at our place, and had one at Carrow Road, too," Wilder said, ahead of August's meeting. "I said some things from my point of view at the time that I believe were correct, and how it works here, but everyone has the right to do what they want to do. I say it as it is, and move on. There's no ill-feeling or lingering situations, anything like that. No problem between me and their manager at all."

***

On a weekend when Jade Sharp climbed Mount Kilimanjaro to raise money for charity, her husband Billy's biggest challenge was to find a way into Wilder's starting line-up after being benched for three of the first four games of the season. By his own admission, Sharp would have sulked earlier in his career, but his advancing years and the captaincy of his boyhood club had matured him. It helped, too, that he was still producing the goods on the field - despite being seemingly written off every season - and goals against QPR and Hull, a stunner after coming off the bench, saw him back in the side against Norwich. Wilder had praised Sharp as a 'perfect captain' before the game but it was a centre-half who opened the scoring, Egan heading home Norwood's driven corner with the help of the referee's goalline technology.

Then, Jordan Rhodes - the Wednesday loanee who'd been given a rough reception from the home crowd - tapped in Onel Hernández's cross, and his provocative celebration in front of the Kop did little to enhance his reputation at Bramall Lane. Wilder was forced to pick up his players at half-time as they disconsolately trudged into the dressing room level at 1-1 - "I didn't realise we were 3-1 down," he said to them - but Norwich were handed a golden chance to go in front after the restart when Jack O'Connell's clearance ricocheted off Tom Trybull and landed invitingly for Moritz Leitner, who was clearly offside in United's half. A cacophony of noise rose around the ground as Bramall Lane waited for the linesman's flag to go up, but it never came. And as Leitner, Hernández and Teemu Pukki raced unopposed towards Dean Henderson's goal, every fan in the entire stadium held their breath.

Henderson, though, stood tall, using every ounce of instinct that had been drilled into him ever since he fell in love with goalkeeping, diving around in the mud and becoming the hero. Leitner, he noticed, looked panicky and didn't appear to see his teammates either side of him. Maybe he wanted the glory himself? Either way, it didn't matter. Henderson saved the shot with his body and celebrated wildly, as Bramall Lane erupted. The goal may not have actually stood anyway - fourth official Mark Heywood would have advised referee Darren Bond that the German was offside - but Henderson wasn't about to miss out on a moment in the spotlight.

Later in the season, the goalkeeper admitted he felt that the Norwich save was the moment he *really* arrived at United. "I remember thinking: 'If he passes here I'm snookered'. Everything just seemed to go silent. I thought he was surely going to pass it, so I just waited, waited and waited. Just stood there, really," Henderson said. "Then I got close enough to make the block and it came right off the badge. 'Go on then!' Big celebration. The noise sounded as loud as a goal to me. It was obviously a big moment in the game but it's something I've done countless times in my career. To do it in that arena was special, though, because the sound was deafening. For me, it's like scoring a goal… that's what a goalkeeper dreams of. Three against one, they think it's in, and then I make the save."

In his last appearance at Bramall Lane, in the last Steel City derby, Rhodes was substituted to merciless jeers and chants mocking his expensive price tag when he signed for Wednesday. *'What a waste of money...'* And the unhappy memories continued for Wednesday's record signing when Sharp netted an injury-time winner, nodding home McGoldrick's knockdown from Chris Basham's pass.

Rhodes slunk from the field as soon as the final whistle blew - which didn't escape the attention of the Blades fans he had earlier goaded - and a new cult hero was born in the shape of Henderson, who had sprinted the length of the field moments earlier to join in the frenzied celebrations which followed Sharp's dramatic, late intervention.

"I'm a passionate boy, and I really want to do well anywhere I go," the goalkeeper said. "I become a fan of wherever I go, too. It was the same at Shrewsbury last season, and now the same at United. And I'm as confident as they come. You've got to be, at the end of the day, to play here. You've got to have something behind you and a bit of personality, and that's something I stick by. I'm only 21 years old, so if I don't have any confidence or an ego about me, then I'll have a tough time."

Henderson is generally not one for understatement, but describing himself as 'having confidence' undersold his mindset by a long, long way. Even the way the youngster walked oozed self-belief. "He looks as if he's carrying carpets under his arms," one teammate joked. Crucially, though, Henderson also has the ability and temperament to back such confidence up. "He took a bit of getting used to at the start. I've never known anyone quite like him!" smiled defender Baldock, who sat next to Henderson in the United changing room throughout the season.

"But he's a great lad. He's got his own way of self-motivating, that's for sure, but one thing I can say is that he talks the talk, and the kid can walk the walk as well. I'm sure he's going to go on to play for England and I hope he does because he works so hard and has such a good mentality. He deserves everything he gets because he's been brilliant for us."

Despite growing up at the biggest club in the world, Henderson has retained a humility that was drilled into him from a young age by his parents Dougie and Yvonne, as they grew up in the Cumbrian town of Whitehaven. During his spell on loan at United the goalkeeper struck up a heartwarming friendship with Harri Parker, the terminally-ill youngster bravely battling congenital heart disease, and later in the season Harri's mum, Jeni, shared a touching video on social media of her son teaching Henderson and Kieran Dowell how to perform the 'floss' dance.

Harri is also close to former United striker Caolan Lavery, who spent the promotion season on loan at Bury, and Jeni said: "Dean, Kieran and Caolan do so much behind the scenes with Harri. He just sees the video as three mates having a laugh, and that's exactly what it is. The lads are amazing, and he loves their visits.

"He always gives them a cuddle and tells them he loves them. In his eyes, Dean, Kieran and Caolan are his best friends, who just happen to play, or have played, for his football team. They sit chatting about school and his visits to hospital or Bluebell Wood hospice; they have a laugh at each other and play computer games. It all feels very normal for Harri, which is what we try and make every day."

Meeting striker Lavery was one of the items Harri ticked off his 'things to do before I pop it' bucket list and Jeni added: "Seeing Harri happy is all I want - his laugh is infectious and his cheeky ways are funny. These lads aren't only making Harri happy, but they are giving me and my family cherished memories to look back on when Harri gains his wings. It's like they are part of our family now."

Henderson was a relative spectator in United's last game of August, when they beat Bolton Wanderers 3-0 away from home. At the end of the 2018/19 season a whopping 57 points separated United and Bolton in the table but, as inconceivable as it later sounded, Phil Parkinson's men were joint top of the Championship at the time of United's visit, while United were still weighed down by two defeats in their first two games of the season. Ordinarily, such a scoreline may not raise too many eyebrows when it came up on the vidiprinter but this was one of the most imposing, professional and impressive performances of the entire season from Wilder's men. Duffy got United up and running with a calm finish before Kieron Freeman's cross-cum-shot found the corner, and Fleck capped a memorable day with a third following an intricate passing move.

It didn't prove enough to earn Fleck a long-overdue place in the Scotland squad, but the result did at least banish the memory of Wilder's first game in charge of United, at the same stadium. That day, in 2016, United were beaten 1-0 but, given the passage of time since and the success that followed, one journalist naively thought the pain of that defeat may have subsided. He was swiftly reminded that it hadn't. Not one bit. "It wasn't a good memory at all. Why would it be when you get beat?" Wilder hit back. "I don't like getting beat, 100 per cent. I didn't enjoy it one bit. We're always evolving with every experience, from when I started to now. I'm a miles better manager now than when I started, by the way. We have to try not to make mistakes and try to improve."

Answering the questions
by Ian Rands

Just 48 hours after the end of a World Cup that had taken the country on a rollercoaster of emotions, it was back to a dose of grounded normality with United's first competitive pre-season game. For some, though, that sense of 'business as usual' had hit home two weeks earlier, when United followed the template of the past and cashed in on a star player. This one, though, felt different. David Brooks was possibly the most promising and exciting talent seen at Bramall Lane in years. Whether you viewed his sale as good value for an undoubtedly talented player - but one who had struggled to recover his form after a debilitating case of glandular fever - or undervaluing a player who showed glimpses of being a potentially world-class player, it still felt somewhat inevitable. And disappointing.

The hope was that a recuperated Brooks might provide the spark we had so badly needed when the previous campaign had ended in a whimper, after Paul Coutts suffered a broken leg and none of the January signings, Ricky Holmes, Ryan Leonard and Lee Evans, managed to fill his boots. Three wins from the final 12 games of 2017/18 only told part of the story; United had thrown away winning positions in three of the five draws and two of the five defeats. We had become increasingly fallible at the back, and our failure to convert pressure and possession into goals saw us drop away from the top six.

Those bemoaning the boardroom, though, were pacified somewhat by the arrivals of Dean Henderson and John Egan. Henderson was evidently rated at Manchester United and an England U21 international, while Egan was aerially dominant, athletic and arguably better than what we had. Key moves in eliminating the errors at the back. The only concern, with Egan's club-record fee, was how much was left to strengthen up front and the attacking role that Brooks had vacated?

Despite 19 goals from Leon Clarke the previous season, signing a forward was considered a priority by most fans and management alike. Yet it is fair to say that taking released Ipswich frontman David McGoldrick on trial had done little to enamour those wanting to see a bigger name, a player less injury-prone and with a better goal frequency.

Talk of multi-million-pound deals for Martyn Waghorn and Sam Gallagher probably didn't help McGoldrick's cause but he soon proved his worth in pre-season, including a goal against the mighty Inter Milan. Then, it was time for the real thing. Swansea at home, a tea-time kick-off, live on Sky Sports, a 2-1 defeat after taking the lead. One bad result on the opening day was never going to define our season and at the time I felt that in the long run, it may not be such a bad thing.

If we had held on to the one-goal advantage, it would have masked a number of deficiencies that you could guarantee would now be addressed... although that is probably doing Wilder and his staff a gross injustice. They are not daft. But as fans, we might have been blinded by the win. The biggest concern, though, was how laboured we looked in the final third, which had carried over from the previous campaign, through pre-season and into the new league term. The first half was stale fare from two sides finding their feet and neither goal-keeper was threatened. As frustrating as it was to see United dilly-dally out wide before putting over a poor cross, we were hardly flooding the box with options either. It was difficult to see where a goal was going to come from.

On balance Swansea probably deserved the win, despite the Blades' superior possession and greater number of shots. Statistics are fine, but they didn't tell the full story of a disappointing start, and with Swansea fresh out of the Premier League, with a new manager and many of their better players having left, imminently departing or refusing to play, there wouldn't be a better time to face them. It was a great opportunity to put a marker down for the rest of the division, live on Sky. Then came possibly the worst 25 minutes of Wilder's reign, at the Riverside. United did actually create the three best chances of the game in an improved second-half showing - although they were dead and buried by then - and the continuing profligacy only added to the frustration. The lethargy (of body and mind) in that first half was alarming, and fans were genuinely concerned. As supporters, we had been spoilt by Wilder's reign so far and when that first half went as badly as it did, on the back of some harsh words after the Swansea defeat, that concern was probably well-merited.

Pride had been severely dented and, while paying fans are

entitled to voice their opinion, the ironic cheers for Henderson when he caught an aimless ball late in the first half, the half-time boos and a repetitive chant of "We're f****** s***" suggested both a lack of recognition of what this team had achieved in two seasons, and an unsubstantiated lack of faith in a manager who didn't shy away from addressing failings in his team. Still, social media was awash with overreaction. Some fans suggested that Wilder had given up or that the club should refund fans. And even for the most positive Blade, there were worrying signs. The hangover from the end of last season had lingered.

Our team spirit had rarely been questioned under Wilder but it was noticeable against Swansea how heads dropped when they equalised, while at Boro fans saw finger-pointing and heated debate among players, all with slumped shoulders, as the game went away from the Blades. We needed leadership on the pitch. Someone to lift the players, to dictate play, to organise and cajole. Off it, among the supporters, calmness and level heads were in short supply, certainly when Evans' loan departure was announced with no imminent replacement. But Wilder has always weighed up possibilities and acted decisively; players who aren't working out as hoped are moved on quickly and improvements made. Yet some fans were not prepared to wait and see what that improvement would be, instead bemoaning a (short-term) weakening of the squad.

At QPR, boosted by the return of Sharp and Mark Duffy, we looked instantly more like a 'Wilder side' and we started with a degree of energy that had been lacking to that point. And although no-one realised it at the time, the signs for the season ahead were there. Sharp's first goal of many; the vital contribution of McGoldrick; Henderson with the joy of a child on Christmas morning as he joined in the singing with the away following, post-match.

He and McGoldrick visibly endearing themselves to Blades fans, early in their careers at the club. Then the signing of Ollie Norwood was announced; a man with clear Championship pedigree which genuinely excited the fans. The upgrade on Evans had been completed; the mutterings were once again quelled.

After the recriminations and frustrations of the previous encounter at the Lane, the visit of Norwich - like Mel B's dresses - now held a little more spice than it used to. The Canaries' time-wasting the season before was unlike anything I have seen in years and while this game didn't quite reach those levels, it wasn't far off at times. The fact that referee Darren Bond added only three minutes on, as the clock reached 90, astounded many in the ground. It was enough time, though, for United to finally make Norwich pay. From the off Norwood was busy, wanting the ball, dictating play, and his link up with John Fleck was reminiscent of the Coutts/Fleck partnership, with each taking responsibility in turn and driving United forward.

Norwood's set pieces were a joy all game and even when Wednesday loanee Jordan Rhodes scored, taking the kind of chance he doesn't miss unless he is wearing a blue and white shirt, I still felt optimistic, telling friends at half-time: "We will win this 2-1". Both sides had opportunities after half-time and if you look back at the season for turning points, the second 45 minutes against Norwich is one. United needed to back up the win at QPR with another, to gain a footing in the table and build confidence. But it was a match that could have gone away from us.

At one-all, and with three minutes of injury time going down quicker than Alex Tettey with 'cramp', even I was doubting my half-time optimism. Then Chris Basham played a Norwood-esque ball into McGoldrick's path and Sharp forced home the cross. Delirium. Wilder was down one touchline; Henderson ran the length of the other to join in celebrations. A deserved win and, while there was still work to be done, both defensively and on delivering a full 90-minute performance, there was suddenly much to feel optimistic about. You could sense the enthusiasm in the fanbase again at Bolton away, on that Bank Holiday weekend, when all was well in the world again.

A friend said at the time that he was glad we didn't go on to score four or five, so as not to draw attention to how good we can be as early as we did the season before. A variety of emotions, then, for Blades over the opening weeks of the season. Cracks had shown and were quickly repaired. Wilder had faced a level of questioning and scrutiny he hadn't come up against so far in his time in charge. And he answered with three wins in three, taking his side up to seventh. Still early days and tougher tests to come, starting with Aston Villa's visit to the Lane. Now that game could really demonstrate where we might finish come May, and a win would certainly start to draw some attention back to S2.

The Ice' man cometh
by George Baldock

As I sit here at the end of the season, looking back to the first game of the season and my goal against Swansea, it almost feels like a few years ago rather than a few months! Over the course of the season, I could probably have had a few more too. But being honest, I'm not too bothered who scores the goals as long as they get scored and we win games.

I remember against Swansea we had a great start and going 1-0 up with less than half an hour to go, so to lose the game was so, so disappointing. And then we got the beating at Boro. But from there, we picked up and went on a good run, going from strength to strength all season. It was important for us to learn as the season went on and after the Villa game later in the season, the way we saw games out was brilliant.

It sounds stupid looking back at a game we lost 3-0, but at Boro, we had a few chances and it could easily have been 3-3 on another day. There was a strong message from the gaffer at half-time along the lines of: 'Liven yourself up! What are you playing at?' And in the second period, Ben Woodburn came off the bench and did well and we had a few chances. After the game, he said: 'Well done for the second half but don't let the first half repeat itself'. We came back firing like we always do; that's something we always do, this team. We come back from setbacks really well, so it really put us on a platform for the rest of the season.

The Boro game was also my last for more than a month because I picked up an injury in the first half, and knew it was quite a bad one. But because we were two or three goals down at the time, I knew I couldn't come off. It's just not in my make up, so I had to go on. Looking back now, I shouldn't have played on and may have potentially made it worse. But I had to. I just felt that coming off at 3-0 down would be a bit cowardly; might look as if I was taking the easy way out. It might have looked like I was throwing it in, and I didn't want to do that. So I got it strapped up and carried on. I'm not saying I'm a big hard man or anything, but I'd have felt embarrassed if I came off after a bad display. Who knows, the damage might have already been done? You never know. But as long as we got to our end goal, that's all that matters to me.

After the game, I had all the scans and they revealed it wasn't so good, so I had to have some time off. Kieron Freeman came in and did brilliantly, which is another strength of this group, because of good recruitment from the gaffer getting two players in every position to do a job for the team. We've always been there for each other when the other has come in and done well; either through injury or lack of form or tiredness. Kieron played a massive part that season. It helped having such a good player pushing me and likewise, when he's had the shirt, I like to think I pushed him too. It's the same everywhere around the squad - look how well Chris Basham did with Martin Cranie behind him, and Ollie Norwood knowing that Paul Coutts and John Lundstram were pushing him.

Mark Duffy since Kieran Dowell came in, Billy with Scotty Hogan. There are examples all over the team - Dean Henderson will be the first to tell you how hard Simon Moore pushed him in training, all season - and for me, that played a huge part in our success. I've played at every level in the Football League and also in the Conference and abroad, so I guess you could say I've done it the hard way to get to the Premier League. But to get promoted with Sheffield United is an unbelievable feeling. A few lads in this dressing room have also played down in the Conference, as well as the gaffer of course, and that gives us all

an insight into how hard you need to work to become a professional footballer first and foremost, and then to be successful.
We know we don't have a God-given right to play at a high
level and win games of football; you get that desire and hunger
instilled into you from early in your career.

At that level, you know how much points can affect people's
lives because three points at the weekend can help people to
feed their families, at a level where the wages aren't as good.
It's imperative that you work hard to win games because it's
about more than just three points. I also had a spell in Iceland
as a young player which gave me some more experience, on
and off the pitch. I was at MK Dons at the time and was a little
too enthusiastic and eager, flying into tackles and trying to win
stupid balls I was never going to win. So I picked up a lot of
injuries and my season was really stop-start, so Karl Robinson
asked if I would consider an opportunity to go and play abroad
over the summer. I jumped at the chance. As a young lad I
thought I could do with some growing up, and what better way
to do that than moving away from my family, playing football at
the same time? I came back and went into the Conference with
Tamworth and it was a really good period for me, to toughen
up and become a man really.

Not all the loans worked out, though. I went to Northampton
when I was maybe a little too young, playing central midfield,
and the way we were playing... let's just say the manager wasn't
really suited to my game. I remember one game we played on
Sky Sports, and you know the graphic they put up on screen
that shows the pitch in thirds to show where the ball had been?
Three per cent of it was in midfield. Three. And I was playing
centre midfield, just watching the ball fly over my head and then
come back again. It was a real eye-opener, into what football is
about and different managers and styles. I went to Oxford and
came across the gaffer's side there, and it really kick-started my
career. I really did a lot of growing up and established myself in
the Football League.

As I say, I came up against the gaffer a few times at Oxford
and I always knew he played good football, and I played against

his United side in the season they won the League One title with 100 points. From afar I knew I'd love to be a part of it, and then I got a call from my agent saying there was an interest from them. And from then on, there was only one place for me. I said that there was a possibility of helping this club into the Premier League - although I didn't realise it'd be so soon! - and then I was banging on my agent's door, asking if it was happening yet and telling him to make it happen.

In the end, I sacrificed something in my contract at MK to make it happen because I was honestly absolutely desperate to get it done. It was the best decision of my life. I knew I had to play for this manager and this football club, so the stuff in my contract wasn't worth it. I saw the United fans at MK Dons in the promotion season - when they brought about 7,000, all in fancy dress - and that was ridiculous. I knew I had to be part of it. Nothing was going to get in the way of me playing for this football club. The fans did set the bar quite high at Stadium MK that day - I'd never seen anything like it before - but the Sunday we had at Stoke after we'd won promotion to the Premier League... I couldn't believe the scenes. It took us about an hour and a half to get from John Street into the ground once we got back to Bramall Lane. It was absolute mayhem, crowd-surfing off the bus. Definitely memories to last a lifetime!

The boys had just won League One when I signed and it was already a tight-knit group, but I was quite fortunate that I already knew a few of them from previous clubs, mutual friends or just playing against them. I'll never forget on my second day of training when we played an 11v11 game, two 3-5-2 formations. Off you go. I was up against Enda Stevens, who like me had played full-back for a lot of our careers, and we were looking at each other all the time and thinking: 'What are we supposed to be doing here?'

But that quickly got smoothed out. Fortunately! It was a good way of throwing us in at the deep end, to see if we'd sink or swim. In my first season, we had a go but were disappointed in the way it ended, finishing 10th because we knew what we could have achieved. But it wasn't to be and everyone in the squad benefited from that year of Championship experience, the manager and staff as well as the players.

We developed into a really good side, a much better side than we were last year. The points total we ended up with and the number of clean sheets we kept reflect that, too. It was a good experience for everyone, and we kicked on massively. The season before we lost games when we should have drawn and drew games when we should have won them, but the promotion season was different. When we weren't at our best we either took points from games or nicked them, apart from maybe Forest away and Bristol City when we weren't great and got punished. Times like Rotherham away, we got something out of the game. Leeds away we weren't sparkling and won the game when a draw might have been fair. Against Brentford, at home with 10 men, we ground out the win when we weren't at our free-flowing best.

That proved pivotal and made a big difference from the season before. It's always the sign of a good team, when you're not on top form but can come through. We kept clean sheets and beat some really good teams, which I think showed how good we were. Now, I just can't wait to see what the Premier League holds. My brother, Sam, had a little taste of it with Brighton but didn't play too much. He just told me that my life will change if I'm involved in the top flight because the spotlight is completely different, and so much more heightened. But he also told me to enjoy it and embrace it.

He's also delighted for United as well as he's overjoyed for me on a personal level - genuinely, too - because he told me that he believed we were the best side in the Championship to watch that season. I obviously live in Sheffield and it's impossible not to see how much it means to people. After the Ipswich game we went out and a few grown men were getting emotional, thanking us for our efforts because of how much heartache they've had in the past. Now, they're buzzing to have got one over on their neighbours. Honestly, I love being part of a city that loves its football so much. And, from our point of view at least, long may it continue.

chapter five

Heroes and Villa-ins

September 2018

As he sat back on a comfortable sofa in the bottom building of Sheffield United's Shirecliffe academy after a typically-brutal morning on the training pitches above, Enda Stevens winced at the memory of his side's below-par start to the 2018/19 season. "It didn't start off too well with two defeats, did it?" Stevens asked rhetorically. "But I just had a feeling. I spend every day with these lads and see them up close, so I know exactly how good they can be. That was the frustration against Swansea and Boro... we weren't showing what we were capable of. The season before, we couldn't win more than three games on the bounce. Our biggest hurdle was overcoming that.

"Still, I thought we could do something special. I've never known a group and a team with more character than this one, especially with the demands of a club as big as this. The fans want to see us picking up results and they've got used to that with the gaffer and Alan Knill in charge, so they've got every right to moan if we're not playing well and winning. We have to carry that pressure. Every game is a pressure game, but we don't just show up for the big games and down tools when there are not many people in the ground. We show up for every game. I think we fear not winning. We fear not being success-ful. Every single lad at the club cares about the other lads, the club and the manager and the staff and the fans. And their own careers. Because of that, we put it all on the line when we walk out onto the pitch."

United had bounced back well from their disappointing start and after three league victories in a row, were now flying. That was more than could be said for Chris Basham's beloved drone, though, which he'd brought especially to film United's team photo day at Bramall Lane in early September. After changing into United's full home kit for the group photograph Basham raced to his car to fetch his new toy - but after excitedly marching to the centre circle with it, experienced some difficulty getting it airborne. Stevens and Ben Woodburn wandered over to offer assistance and moral support, before a crestfallen Basham eventually accepted defeat, muttering something about firmware 'updates' as he slunk back to the dressing room. Only later was it pointed out to the defender that Bramall Lane is close to Sheffield city centre, and so is probably in a no-fly zone.

In years gone by, team photo day used to be a relatively straightforward task but has since snowballed into an event that needs almost military levels of planning; not least from boss Chris Wilder, who often can't resist making sure everyone is lined up correctly when the time comes to face the cameras. As well as the traditional squad photo, United's staff had their own picture together before a representative of myriad club sponsors took their seat next to Wilder on the front row.

Each player then had an individual headshot before posing with a blank cardboard shield, which would later be digitally superimposed with their 'stats' from the FIFA 19 computer game. In between, there were obligations for other sponsors, the club's in-house media team and then eventually the press, who had gathered to preview that weekend's home clash against Aston Villa.

Goalkeeper Dean Henderson, always good value for journalists, was put up for interview and, after breaking off to take his place for the official group photo, gave an impassioned - and completely unprompted - insight into his opinions on some of his fellow youngsters at Manchester United. Henderson, it transpired, agreed to sign a new two-year deal at Old Trafford only if the hierarchy there agreed to let him leave on loan, first to Shrewsbury and then to Bramall Lane. "All the under-23s football is a myth," he added. "Most people just prance around thinking they're this or that. They get good money and they don't know what's hit them when they come out on loan, so they never bloody play. I've been on the bench at Manchester United a few times and travelled with the first team, which was great.

"But after a while, you start to wonder what you're doing. I was basically just standing around, collecting balls and watching other people play. I wanted to be involved, not a ball boy." On the *original* United, Henderson added: "We had a tough start but every team has got to gel and it takes a bit of time. We stick together through the good and bad times and we'll go a long way together here. The amount of ability in the team is there for all to see. Villa are going to be strong in the division, but it's all about us. If we perform as we did at Bolton, then we'll be fine."

How those words proved prophetic as, just 48 hours later, Wilder's Blades hammered Villa 4-1 in one of the best displays of attacking football seen at Bramall Lane for some years. It was certainly an unhappy homecoming for Villa boss Steve Bruce, who began his career in management with United some years earlier and worked with Wilder during their time together in South Yorkshire. Later, when Bruce was in charge of Villa's arch-rivals Birmingham City, he allowed Wilder's Oxford to use their Wast Hills training facilities and the United manager spoke effusively before the game about his respect for both Bruce and Villa, whom he described as probably the biggest club in the division.

His side, though, simply tore Villa apart. Jack O'Connell headed the opening goal in just the sixth minute - "It was such a good ball from Ollie Norwood that I couldn't really miss," the defender later said - and Norwood hit the post with a deflected effort before O'Connell's big pal Mark Duffy made it two, driving from the halfway line and smashing the ball home. Norwood then found the bottom corner, via a helping hand from hapless Villa goalkeeper Ørjan Nyland, with a cheeky free-kick when the whole of Bramall Lane - and Nyland in particular - expected him to cross, and it was four in the second half when Norwood dispossessed Anwar El Ghazi too easily and found Kieron Freeman, whose cross was lashed home by skipper Billy Sharp.

David McGoldrick was denied what would have been a deserved fifth by a smart stop by Nyland, and the former European champions restored a touch of pride by pulling one back thanks to El Ghazi's calm finish into the bottom corner. Nyland then denied McGoldrick again from substitute John Lundstram's pass before the United midfielder gave the home crowd arguably their biggest cheer of the afternoon, with a perfectly-executed challenge on pantomime villain Jack Grealish which got enough of the ball, but also sent Villa's star man flying in the air and then crashing to the turf.

John Fleck made a mockery of his continued exclusion from his international squad by completely nullifying Scotland midfielder John McGinn and Wilder's own personal highlight came when he sent on new boy Conor Washington for his United debut and watched him enthusiastically chase a long ball down the line late on, with the game in the bag. After signing a short-term deal with United, Washington spoke at length about how he had given up on a career as a professional footballer and worked as a postman. His break eventually came, but the hunger remained and his determination, with the game comfortably won, delighted his manager. "I absolutely loved that from Conor," Wilder admitted afterwards.

The Blades boss, though, was less pleased by the comments of stadium announcer Gary Sinclair on the stroke of half-time, when United were 3-0 up. Sinclair, a long-term fixture on the public address system at Bramall Lane, informed the delighted home crowd that "unfortunately there are only two minutes of stoppage time" at the end of the first half. Wilder revealed later that on behalf of United he had apologised to Bruce and to Villa for the remark, and spoke to Sinclair in his office after the game. "We are a humble club and I'm a humble manager," Wilder added. "It won't happen again and it is not acceptable, but we move on. It was a bit of over-enthusiasm. We realise we have a hell of a long way to come. It's our second season in this division and we have had one really good result, but that is all it is.

"There are a couple of clubs in the Championship who talk

the talk and sometimes don't walk the walk. I just want us to be humble and work hard, and carry on the attitude we've had for the last two years. There is no way I will allow that to get out of hand." Sinclair defended his comments by insisting he "would never say anything to embarrass Chris or the club." He added: "I didn't say it out of arrogance, but sheer joy at witnessing the best 45 minutes of football in years. I didn't want the half to end, simple as that. No offence was ever intended."

That episode couldn't take the shine off a simply stunning afternoon for Wilder's side, however, and the manager re-members fans in the Copthorne hotel bar next to the ground congratulating him on, in their words, the best display they had *ever* seen from a United side. "It was an incredible perfor-mance," Wilder reflected at the end of the season. "To take apart a team like Villa, in the manner that we did... it was one of those days you treasure as a manager, when everything comes together.

"It wasn't against the bottom team, this was Villa - with Grealish and Jonathan Kodjia and McGinn and a lot of play-ers who've had really good careers. The way we went about it made it a special afternoon for the club, I think. We were ag-gressive and positive, we played at a tempo and scored some great goals. We recovered well from a poor start and got our season up and running. It really cemented the belief for us, and I think that's when we said we had a real chance of being a force in this division."

Journalist Alan Biggs remembers United legend Brian Deane drawing comparisons with Brazil after the game and later wrote in his column: "Make no mistake, this display was absolutely exceptional. How good? In my view, as fine an exhibition as United have produced since the Currie-Woodward era. THAT good." It was high praise indeed from a veteran of the lo-cal media who has followed United's fortunes, good and bad, for decades. And rather than the era of Tony Currie and Alan Woodward, the result also helped Wilder to banish some more recent nightmare memories; of United's home clash with Villa, the season before.

In that game, Wilder's Blades were well on top of their illustrious opponents throughout but found 'keeper Sam Johnstone unbeatable, before Robert Snodgrass scored a superb winner in the dying minutes to give Villa all three points. It was, the United manager told the press on more than one occasion, a perfect snapshot of the quality in the Championship and how big players, in big moments, stand up and be counted. But it was his team this time who stood tall, with goalscorer Duffy admitting it was the kind of day he dreamed about when he was playing in the Conference for sides such as Vauxhall Motors and Prescot Cables.

"Never in a million years did I think I'd ever be in the Championship, scoring against teams like Villa," Duffy chuckled. "We played free-flowing football, some of the best we've played since I've been at the club, and were quite solid at the back even though they scored late on. If anything it got a bit too easy for us and we slacked off a bit, took our foot off the gas. That was something we tried to learn from. But it was a brilliant day when you look back at the season. A real good day."

Like his manager, Duffy also believed that the manner of United's demolition of Villa, more than just the result, gave them an extra shot of belief that they could compete at the top end of the Championship. But still, off the pitch, the gulf between United and clubs such as Villa was even more vast than the difference had been on it, on that glorious September day. Villa paid striker Tammy Abraham *more* than he earned at Chelsea to ensure he signed on loan at Villa Park for the season - about £55,000 a week, plus bonuses for goals, wins and ultimately promotion - while United, in a different market altogether, were forced to be far cuter in their approach. Although it didn't mean they were any less successful.

After sanctioning moves away from Bramall Lane for Lee Evans and Ryan Leonard, the final piece of Wilder's summer squad-shaping puzzle was put in place when Martin Cranie, the reliable defender formerly of Huddersfield Town and Middlesbrough, signed a short-term deal at Bramall Lane. Cranie had helped the Terriers into the Premier League via the play-offs in

2017 but was without a club after leaving Boro at the end of the season previous. A spell training with United's Championship rivals West Brom came to nothing before he received the call from Wilder - which his wife Keri always suspected would arrive.

"We came to Bramall Lane with Middlesbrough, it finished 2-1 and I remember thinking, 'How are they doing this with the system?' We were being totally peppered," Cranie said. "It was amazing stuff to watch, the centre-backs charging up the wing. I didn't know if this was their plan or just off the cuff. Obviously, since arriving I know how much has gone into this style. Teams cannot cope with the overload down each side. The gaffer has got it just right.

"In the summer I was getting phone calls and hearing the odd whisper, but I said to my agent: 'Just ring me when something is concrete'. There were a couple of other Championship clubs interested. I was umming and aahing whether to go there but then the manager rang me. This was perfect for me. Funnily enough, my missus did say at the start of the summer: 'I think you'll end up at Sheffield United'. I have no clue how. I had never heard anything. But the manager told me when I signed that he had tried to get me before, in the previous January window. Obviously that didn't materialise but I got here in the end. And if you want any transfer news, just ask my missus!"

Although it may have gone unnoticed amid the euphoria of the result, there was more good news for United against Villa when Paul Coutts cleared another mini-hurdle in his comeback from a broken leg by being named on the bench against Bruce's side. Coutts, Wilder said, had "absolutely done my nut in for two or three weeks before to get him back on the teamsheet, so in the end I relented". But the bigger milestone for the Scot came a few days later, during the international break, at the slightly less glamorous surroundings of Sheffield FC's Coach and Horses ground; exactly 292 days after his leg was shattered at Burton Albion and United's season began to unravel.

After a long and painful journey back to fitness, Coutts felt stronger than ever - literally, it turned out, as he invited journalists to run their hand over his leg to feel the build-up of calcium reinforcing the area of the break. And his long-awaited return came when Wilder took a strong Blades squad to Dronfield to face the world's first club, in a testimonial for their longest-serving player Matt Roney. Roney, a Blades fan, was approaching 500 games for Club after making his debut 13 years earlier, and Wilder said: "Sheffield has got great rivalry between the two professional clubs, but it shouldn't be forgotten what else is going on. I've known Matt for a long time, he's a great bloke and for him to play 500 games for the world's oldest club is a remarkable achievement.

"Because we are in the centre of the city, because our ground is right at the heart, we expand into all areas of it. It's important that we are part of the community, that we represent and help where we can." An 11-2 scoreline, in favour of a Blades side at full strength apart from their international players, suggested that their generosity did not quite extend to the pitch once the first whistle had been blown. McGoldrick helped himself to four second-half goals, while Cranie and fellow new-boy Marvin Johnson enjoyed their first appearances for the club in front of a full house. But on a night the Coach and Horses paid tribute to Roney, and raised vital cash for his chosen charity Macmillan, Coutts was undoubtedly the star attraction.

His next challenge was to break into the team. Norwood had established a good partnership with Fleck since arriving on a loan-to-buy deal in the summer from Brighton and Hove Albion, and Coutts couldn't retain his place on the bench as United lost their first game back after the break, although the 1-0 scoreline at Bristol City didn't quite tell the full story of the game. McGoldrick, in particular, missed a number of chances on a profligate afternoon for United, covering his face with his shirt in frustration. United looked for a reaction in midweek, at home to Birmingham City, but one was not forthcoming. An impressive Blues side were one of the few all season to dominate United on their own turf and were perhaps unfortunate not to return to the Second City with more than a point from the goalless draw to show for their efforts.

   Given both City's well-publicised brush with the English Football League's profit and sustainability rules, and Wilder's own past experiences of clubs' money issues, it was inevitable that the United manager would be asked about matters of finance rather than football in the build-up to the game. Wilder was in charge of Halifax Town when they were liquidated under heavy debts, and worked against a backdrop of financial insecurity at Northampton Town when staff went for months without being paid, so was understandably unsympathetic towards clubs who gamble with their futures. "Like a lot of people, I can't quite get my head around it when teams put themselves in this position," Wilder said. "But, time and time again, you see them doing it. It's a big talking point in this division and it doesn't look like going away.

   "Something needs to happen to get to grips with it. What's the point of putting rules in, in whatever sport you play, if no notice is going to be taken of them? If the rules are in place, they should be implemented. No question about it. No messing. That's how it should be."

   Wilder was similarly forthcoming in his assessment of the game against Garry Monk's Blues, shouldering the responsibility for his side's below-par display after making five changes and seeing the visitors twice hit the woodwork. The United manager wasn't overly impressed by the pink Adidas boots on the feet of Norwood against Birmingham, either, and the Northern Ireland man was noticeably back in black for the weekend clash with Preston at Bramall Lane.

   That switch of footwear - and the changes in midweek - appeared to do the trick when United went 2-0 ahead, Basham scoring and dedicating his goal to his son, Luke, on his fourth birthday. But the visitors hit back to level at 2-2 when the impressive Callum Robinson and then Daniel Johnson netted in the space of two minutes and on a day of huge traffic delays all over the city, caused by the arrival of Sheffield Hallam University students, the frustration of United fans looked to have been compounded. A number of fans who turned around and went home after being stuck in traffic for hours probably didn't regret their decision when Johnson netted the equaliser, but McGold-rick proved to be United's hero when he calmly slotted home Stevens' cut-back in the 87th minute to send Bramall Lane bonkers. United escaped with all three points but knew they had been in a real contest. Wilder used the problems Preston had caused his side as a reference point throughout the season and was also aware that United's next fixture would test his side once again, both on and off the pitch.

Millwall away.

Those two words instantly conjure up so many connotations for anyone with even a passing knowledge of football but, as it turned out, the prospect of a trip to The Den in its current guise didn't actually have Wilder waking up in the night in cold sweats - primarily because he remembers how it used to be. Millwall's former ground, on Cold Blow Lane in New Cross, is less than a quarter of a mile away from their current one and, as a 19-year-old playing there for United, Wilder was sent off for a rash tackle on Jimmy Carter.

Carter was Millwall's local hero, rather than the old US President, but the reaction was no less severe and Wilder remembers trudging back towards the dressing room and having "cups of tea, cups of coffee and cups of something else" chucked at him. "I went in for the tackle, he didn't, and it looked a bit messy," Wilder added. "I might have done more than a three-match ban if that challenge had gone in now! The game has changed a little bit since then.

"Afterwards we had to stay in the changing area on police advice. Apparently, there was a madman on the loose, running around all over the place. So we did what we were told and waited for everything to calm down! I don't mean this in a disrespectful way but, being honest, it's not quite the same as it was.

Even so, you still see the floodlights when you come out of South Bermondsey station and all that. It's still a tough place to go and we want Bramall Lane to be the same. Of course, there are boundaries people shouldn't cross. But we want the opposition and opposition managers to get a little bit of stick, to be made to feel uncomfortable. And that starts with us as a team."

Millwall continued to be an unhappy hunting ground for Wilder, even long after he "walked the plank" to the dressing rooms at the old Den after his run-in with Carter. In his first season in charge of United, a last-minute defeat - after O'Connell had inexplicably handled the ball in his own area - sent United bottom of League One.

The story of how Wilder bought £ 100 of beer for his players on the coach home has since become the stuff of legend, and the history books show that it proved an inspired move. Millwall won the play-offs that year to follow United into the Championship and in 2017/18, after a 3-1 defeat to the Lions and with the substitutes nervously waiting in the tunnel, Wilder could be heard giving his players both barrels in the away dressing room at The Den.

This time around - and despite Sharp's header opening the scoring, moments after the striker had missed a penalty - it threatened to be a case of the same old story for Wilder's Blades when goals from Jake Cooper and Lee Gregory, a Sheffield-born Blades fan and former academy player, turned the game on its head. Then McGoldrick was summoned from the bench to equalise calmly from the penalty spot before turning in Duffy's ball across the box from close range for another late, late winner, sending the United fans in the top tier behind that goal into raptures.

After the final whistle had sounded, those Blades supporters further rubbed salt in the wounds by mimicking the famous 'Millwall roar' and McGoldrick said: "It was funny. We got a corner and just before it was taken I looked up and saw the clock, and thought: 'I got one around this time against Preston'.

"I just had a sense I was going to get another chance to do it again! It was important to get that goal against Preston, when Enda went on one of his runs and cut it back, and Millwall was one of the best performances of the season, for me. We found ourselves 2-1 down suddenly, got a penalty and scored, and then Duffy and Kieron Freeman combined for a tap in for me. The overloads we work on every day in training came off for us, and we were delighted because everyone knows that's a tough place to go and get a win.

"I might have looked calm and laid-back at that moment, but I can tell you I wasn't inside! It was a good game and a bit of a statement for us, too. It showed we have character, which was vital. We knew we couldn't play tippy-tappy football throughout the whole season. We had to be a tough, ruthless bunch as well and we did that. It just showed how much we care, and how tough we are. Personally, and collectively."

Playground football
by Phil Rose

Limbs. All over the shop. That's become a thing, hasn't it? Along with 'scenes', often 'in the away end'. Chris Wilder and Alan Knill have invented a new way of playing, with overlapping centre-backs, and they've also forced me to look at new ways of celebrating goals. In 2018/19, I sacked off 'limbs' and 'scenes'. I was basically rocking the 'head shaking disbelief' look. 'How did they do that?' I'd actually debuted that in 2017/18, when the ball was rolled perfectly into David Brooks' stride at Elland Road and he stroked it home. But, the first time I can remember bringing the 'nodding noggin' out in the promotion season, was at home to Aston Villa right at the beginning of September.

We were played five, won three, lost two at that stage. It looked as if we might be getting it back together after losing the first two of the season. But, you know, the Championship. Big, proper clubs, bang at it, week in and, indeed, week out. Villa at home. Oooohhhh! Nervous. We killed them. My head nearly fell off with all the shaking. I had to go to the next game, away at Bristol City, in a neck brace and drink the ale through a straw!

I know far more about the different hop profiles in West Coast-style pale ales, made by modern British breweries, than I do about football tactics. But, as best we can, let's deal with 'the system'. The Wilder acolytes will tell you that no-one has ever seen anything like it before. No. I'm not having that. Indeed, I've even played in 'the system'. Carterknowle Junior School, 1969. Think about it. United actually play school playground football. The ball is over there. Everyone get over there.

The shorthand is overlapping centre-backs. The sofa strategists know they need to sound a bit more sophisticated, like Pep Guardiola or Jürgen Klopp. So, they'll pitch it as 'overloading in key areas'. But, we're a no airs, no graces club. No harm in calling it playground football. It emphasises the fun. It connects with the young 'uns at Carterknowle. What mesmerised me at that Villa game were the angles. You get Enda Stevens out left. Jack O'Connell and Oliver Norwood playground him. They trust each other. They trust their skills, little half-turn flicks to get two foot of space. And they know their obtuse from their acutes. Trigonometry in the classroom. Playground football at the tuck-shop break. Love it.

Have you noticed Darren Ward on the touchline alongside Wilder and Knill? Nominally he's the goalkeeping coach. But he also plays a key role in attacking and defensive coordination at set pieces. Darren is most noticeable when we're putting a sub on. Showing the charts to the sub. Waving and pointing to the players already out there. You, yes you. Pick him up, yes him. I recently asked Darren on Twitter whether I could have his clipboard as a souvenir. He shattered my dream by explaining that he just uses a piece of paper and a pencil.

Anyway, in the absence of the real thing, here's how I imagine the coaching notes for United's first against Villa. When crossing the ball, put it where someone on your team might head it. Not too low. Not too high. Not in front of where he might head it. Or behind. When you're up for a set piece. Get in a position where you know the crosser will put the ball. Jump in the air. Try to get the top of your head higher than it would be if you hadn't jumped. Don't mess about blocking or wrestling a defender. Ball. Jump. Head.

Ladies and Gentlemen. I give you Norwood and O'Connell. One. Nil. Six earth minutes. Norwood really announced himself at that Villa game. Signed less than three weeks before it, the Villa game was only his third league start. He crossed for that

Plan A O'Connell header. And he bagged the third goal with a cheeky, around-the-wall free kick that caught the 'keeper in a hammock (well, napping at least). And, man, those angles. For me, though, being a football supporter is not just about results. There. I've said it. Surely this club, of all clubs, proves that being a fan is also about the connection.

There has understandably been a lot said about Wilder and his connection to the club and us fans. Everything seems to have fallen into place. An owner Blade, a manager Blade and a captain Blade. (Billy Sharp, not him with the swords and the hat). But, it's worth remembering, we're Blade Overloaded. Take Derek Geary. Yes, the Blade Derek Geary. Del; 94 appearances between 2004 and 2010 . Del now coaches United's Academy U18 and the Futures U19 sides. Look, I'm not a grass. But, Del's half-time team talks to his players have to be heard to be believed.

He clearly prefers the swearing and profanity method of player motivation. If you've had a stinker on the left-wing... cover your ears, young man. Thankfully, during the game, he's much more about encouragement and explanation. Although how the players understand his accent as he barks instructions is beyond me. Anyway, I want to explain the role Del played in a lump-in-the-throat moment I had this season. Of all the times and places to become over-emotional: Shirecliffe, half eight, on a miserable September night. I didn't expect that. United Futures were at home, under lights and on the plastic, against Hallam U19s.

United were cruising 2-0 at half-time but Del grabbed a coffee and sat back in his chair as his charges gathered on the pitch to hear what was needed in the second 45. Instead, a non-cape-wearing hero, in United tracksuit, with clipboard, notes, the lot, gathered the team around and calmly delivered his debrief on the first half and his plans for the second. Step forward Harrison Neal, a box-to-box midfielder in United's academy system. In 2018/19, he played 19 times at Under 18 level but here, in plain sight, was this wonderful club, deliberately giving one of their promising youngsters extra responsibility.

You, yes you; 17 years old, with the boots on. Step out of

your comfort zone. Stay off FIFA on the Xbox (Do they still make those?) for a night. And THINK about the real game and how your mates are playing. Stand up. Be counted. That says everything about the values of our academy. Del set 'em up in the first half; 2-0. Harrison set 'em up for the second. Four goals; 6-0 on the whistle. What a club. What a connection. United closed September out with an away game at Millwall. Unfortunately, I can't tell you much about it. But, I can explain a simple truth. This is Sheffield United - this is a drinker's club. Sure, we're welcoming and diverse. If you're a Blade, I'll fight to my dying breath to preserve your right to support the club in the way you choose. But where I'm from, beer plays a big part. Meet your mates down the pub. Get your round in. Get at it. And man, CELEBRATE.

You've seen the footage. John Fleck wants a Corona. Richard Stearman finishes his pint and puts the empty glass on his bonce. Wilder with a Peroni on the go. A drinker's club. I write an irreverent beer and football blog. I sometimes get asked if I know any good pubs for (insert name) away? Sends shivers through my liver, that question. It depends what you're after, pal. I could recommend a cavernous chain pub with the lunch-time kick-off on the big screens, and Carling at two-and-a-half English. And upset the fellas who need a small, squirreled-away, one-room, craft beer bar with nothing south of 6.2 per cent abv on. Or vice versa. Minefield.

But, as it happens, down my drinking wormhole, Millwall away is the best possible beer and football day out. Because of The Bermondsey Mile, a stumble of breweries and bars between Tower Bridge and South Bermondsey, in the railway arches (and just off). Look, we're not playing at this. If Knill and Co. can do the scouting reports and the planning, so can we. The full Marcelo Bielsa-style dossier had 16 different breweries to attack. Wasn't it Mike Tyson who said: "everyone has a plan until they get punched in the mouth?" At the very first bar (Southwark Brewery), the bar staff couldn't find the key that opened the shutters.

Our first blow. But we're Sheffield United. We'll come at you.

Relentless. Wave after wave. When we debriefed afterwards and looked at the stats, we knew we could have done better. We had started with an xBT - expected Brewery Ticks - of 16. Our final total was 11, a Brewery Completion Rate of 69 per cent. Not perfect, but that will get you over the line more times than not. Anyway, I had little idea of what was happening on that day.

But, I've looked it up. We won 3-2 at Millwall.

Dreaming of the big time
by Mark Duffy

Being released from Liverpool as a kid broke my heart. I don't mind admitting that, at all. I fell out of love with football completely; I didn't want to play anymore. I didn't want that rejection again in my life. I got back into football only because my mates wanted me to have a kickabout - they knew I could play a bit, so they asked me to come and help them out. That then led to me climbing the ladder, through Vauxhall Motors, Prescot Cables and Southport.

Playing down the leagues was tough but you've got to keep believing in yourself and hope things go your way. I did always have that belief in my ability, though. It was just about getting the opportunity, and sometimes I made steps up that didn't work. My time at Birmingham City didn't work out, for example. It's sometimes about finding the right place and the right team. I did that here and everything clicked into place. We've gone from strength to strength.

When I finished at Liverpool I used to have sleepless nights, wondering where my life would go and in what direction. I went to college and looked at taking an apprenticeship at the local council. That's where I saw my life going; my uncle did something similar so I could see myself following in his footsteps. What I never did imagine myself doing was scoring against Aston Villa at a packed Bramall Lane, as a Championship footballer. Days like that are what I used to dream about when I was playing in the Conference and everything just seemed to click. That was the day that gave us real belief that we could compete at the top end of the Championship. I've had people speaking to me about my journey up the ladder quite a lot, and not even just since promotion - but over the last year or two.

It is a big kick in the teeth when you get released or don't get a contract but you've got to keep the faith, continue to work hard and try to improve yourself. Sometimes it's good to go out and play 'proper' mens' football lower down the leagues, take yourself out of your comfort zone to a level where there's a lot at stake. Sometimes players try that and just get lost; it swallows them up.

But when you see players go down the leagues and then get a chance to come back up, more often than not they grasp it because they know what it's like down there. It's a lot tougher than in the Championship, put it that way! The physical side of things, when you're getting booted up in the air all the time... pitches aren't great, facilities aren't great, travelling on match-days... in the Championship everything's done for you, in a sense.

You've got it easy. You have to appreciate where you've come from, and I like to think I've done that. It makes it so much more special for me, too, to achieve at this football club. At United there's a huge connection, between players, staff and fans; everyone saw the celebrations in bars with the fans at the end of the season. We're just one big group; if someone walked in who didn't know football, they wouldn't be able to tell who were fans and who were players. Everyone had a good time and I had people from all over messaging me saying: 'What a day that seemed!'

These are just great times to be a Blade. It's been well-documented that there have been some tough periods in the last few years, so it's important to enjoy the good ones when they come around, too. And no-one can say we haven't done that! We all appreciate it and know that success like this might never happen again because you never know what's on the cards in football, and a lot of us have really got here the hard way too. So we're determined to enjoy it.

What does that non-league background teach you? I think it instilled a real hard-working mentality into me and made me a better person. It keeps you grounded... If I was a manager, I'd want those values in my players, so it's no coincidence that the gaffer has assembled a group with that mentality and had success because of it. If there's one thing you can say about this group, it's that they go out there and work hard. Each and every player goes out and gives their all and if it's not good enough, we shake the hand of the opposition and say 'Fair play, you deserved it today'. Because the chances are they will have.

The gaffer's formula sounds so simple - 'go and get players who'll run around and put a shift in'. Managers all say the right things but if everyone did that, everyone would be promoted wouldn't they? It's not as simple as it sounds. Sprinkle a bit of ability on a group who put everything in, and it's a perfect formula really. As a Liverpool fan, I'd hate nothing more than to go to Anfield, watch Liverpool get beat and not put a right shift in. I'd have a moan as a fan so as a player, I can understand when the fans have a moan at us. But I like to think they know that we put everything on the line.

We might not win every game, but afterwards we can look each other in the eye and say: 'Do you know what, we weren't great today, technically or whatever, but we ran about and left everything out there'. And I think the fans buy into that. In our first season in the Championship since winning promotion, we had the play-offs in our hands for much of the season but we let it slip. We missed Paul Coutts after he broke his leg at Burton, because he was such a big part of how we played. We took two points from the six games after that and it had such a big effect on us.

But during the summer, after a few weeks thinking about it and after the disappointment had settled a bit, I thought it was a good first year back in the Championship and it let everyone know that we were at the level we needed to be. We weren't going to be hanging around the bottom end of the table and I thought that with a few additions, we could potentially kick on. I remember we played the friendly against Inter Milan at Bramall

Lane and thinking: 'We've got a real good squad here'. Not just a good starting 11. That strength in depth is a massive thing.

It's almost become a bit of a cliché in itself that everyone talks about, but you can't win anything with a strong 11 only. It's a squad game, whether that's the lads who aren't playing pushing lads every day in training, or then coming in when injuries or suspensions hit. There's been no gap in quality or levels here. Anyone can drop out of the team and someone else just as good or effective can come in, and importantly take to it like a duck to water.

I had a bit of time on the other side of it myself, at the start of the season. The gaffer spoke to me in pre-season and said that it was a tough first couple of games, against Swansea who'd just come down and Middlesbrough away, and we didn't know what we were going to get. So we changed the system and went a bit more structured in midfield - I wouldn't say 'defensive' - and I dropped out. Boro away was a tough, physical game but I came off the bench with about 20 minutes to go and did well. The gaffer then told me I'd be back in for the next game so it goes back to being ready to grab the chance when it comes; making it as tough as possible for the gaffer to drop you.

I got a few messages throughout the season from people saying it was a shame that I couldn't last more than 60 minutes, and I felt like they were questioning what I do from Monday to Friday. So I put out a message on Twitter to clear things up, to make sure the people who were questioning me and my professionalism knew that I work as hard as any other player and that the reasons for coming off might be tactical, or I might just not be playing well.

I'm a person who's hugely motivated by proving a point, though, and to show people who doubt me that they're wrong. I feel the motivation to go and prove that I can play at the level I'm playing, every single week; my aim, in every game, is to go out and be the best player on the pitch. And I'm not ashamed of that. I say I love a challenge, but it was only when I watched Liverpool's Champions League semi-final against Barcelona that I realised United were going to be playing against some of those players. Mo Salah, Sadio Mane, Virgil van Dijk... it's mad. With respect, when the gaffer first came in we were playing at places like Rochdale and Southend, and now the club is looking at Man City and United, Liverpool... the list goes on. It'll obviously be tough. But other clubs have done well up there, so it's not impossible. The main strength of the group, for me, is the togetherness and I think that can take you a long way.

United's fans are so passionate about the club and the team so they'll always have a fondness for us, I think. I know Tony Currie quite well, he speaks to me a lot (and tells me to 'Bloody shoot more'!) and he and his side from the early 1970s are still legends now. I've experienced a little bit of that already, with a goal I scored against our neighbours.

When the derbies come around and you see goals from Michael Brown and Michael Tonge against Wednesday, mine will be in there with it. When I retire, hopefully in many, many years to come, it'll be great to look back on the success we've had in my time at the club. It's been unbelievable, and it's been a pleasure to be a part of it.

chapter six

A welcome return

October 2018

On October 3, 2018, at Blackburn Rovers' Ewood Park, Sheffield United faced another stiff test of their emerging promotion credentials; a dark and dank Wednesday evening over the Pennines, on a ground where the hosts had not tasted defeat for 17 games, stretching back more than a year. They passed with flying colours, a brace from Billy Sharp and a clinical, professional performance sealing a 2-0 win and sending United joint top of the early Championship table. Among all that, though, the highlight of the game, from a United perspective, was a substitution in the 74th minute.

That, more than anything, was a measure of Paul Coutts' importance to the United cause, as the midfielder made his long-awaited absence after almost a year out of the game through injury. Eleven months earlier, Coutts had broken his leg in a game against Burton Albion and when he took his first steps onto the field at Ewood Park, the cheer was as loud - if not louder - than the ones which greeted Sharp's goals. "To see that boy back out there on the pitch," Wilder said, "was magic for me."

"That's what made it special," he added. "Football can be a clinical game at times but we're not a cold-hearted club, and I'd never want us to be. Watching our fans give him that reaction, knowing how hard he has worked… I can't deny it was very emotional. We brought him on because he's ready and we felt he could bring something we needed. He's put so much into coming back, so credit to the lad himself - as well as the medical staff and his teammates for helping him, and his family for supporting him."

Coutts described his treatment from supporters, before and

after his injury, as "different class" after privately fearing he would be forgotten about while he was sidelined. "Couttsy was a legend here, a massive part in the club's success over the last few years, and he was unfortunate to pick up that injury," fellow midfielder Oliver Norwood said.

"He deserves an enormous amount of credit, coming back from that because it's such a horrific injury. We're all friends and there was banter between us but it can be hard sometimes, when you are friends yet all competing for the same spot. But we were all men about it, grown up about it. Everyone in the squad had the right attitude and we knew we'd all benefit from promotion.

"But I've been in that position when you're not playing in every single game, and it's hard when you have that taken away from you. But the reaction of all the players who weren't in the starting 11 or the 18 on a match-day was phenomenal. I'm not saying this to patronise people, but it had a massive effect on the lads who were playing because you felt that you don't want to let them down. They worked so hard and you could see that it killed them, to not play. But the positivity they brought to the dressing room was fantastic and they deserve a huge amount of credit."

After they went clear at the top of the table, after their 1-0 victory over Hull City at Bramall Lane the following weekend, a headline in the *Sheffield Star* described "modest United" as the "real deal" and, by this point, belief was coursing through the squad. It wasn't simply the results that suggested United were better equipped to maintain their promotion push, though, but the manner in which they were achieved - with verve and a swagger, but a quiet humility as well. There was, too, a healthy dose of schadenfreude in the victory, courtesy of David McGoldrick's penalty, with former United boss Nigel Adkins in the away dugout.

No United fan will need remembering about Adkins' sole season in charge at Bramall Lane, which saw the club slump to their lowest league placing since the early 1980s, but the man himself appeared rather bemused after the game when a journalist put it to him, rather politely in fact, that his time at United hadn't gone *quite* to plan. Under Wilder, though, the Blades were only looking up, and Adkins was at least gracious enough to tip them for a sustained promotion challenge.

"Sheffield United have suffered over the past few years, but they are on the up now and it's only a matter of time before they are back in the Premier League," said United's former boss, who also predicted that Middlesbrough and Leeds United would join United in the top flight at the end of that season. "United are now well equipped. They have an excellent manager, an excellent group of players and are going to be able to deal with injuries. They have got real passionate support who will get behind them."

Adkins would not be the last opposition manager to tip United for promotion and with each passing week, and each positive result, their credentials were becoming increasingly difficult to ignore. The league table, after all, doesn't lie, no matter how often you hear a player or manager say they aren't looking at it. Everyone does. It just doesn't always tell the full story.

Paul Parker, the former Blade now employed as a pundit, described United as 'regimented and not interesting' on the eve of their game against Frank Lampard's Derby County (who can now revert to their previous name after Lampard returned to Chelsea). Parker's view understandably attracted much derision from Blades fans on social media and was then made to look even more ridiculous during the game at Pride Park when Chris Basham, *a centre-half* in United's 'regimented and not interesting' system, scored at the back post. From open play.

The only disappointment for the Blades was that they were already 1-0 down by that point, Derby's Craig Bryson finishing off a good move straight from kick-off with just 19 seconds on the clock. Basham gave United a lifeline when he finished confidently after superb work from John Fleck, before Jack Marriott risked the wrath of his family, many of whom support United, by scoring the winner with 13 minutes remaining.

Wilder had skilfully avoided comparisons with former Chelsea and England star Lampard in the build-up - before jokingly 'confessing' under duress that he'd have rather enjoyed the playing career and lifestyle enjoyed by his rival - but was in no mood to hide his true feelings after the game. He didn't so much dissect United's performance at Pride Park, as smash it apart.

"I can do that to the players… because I'm the manager of the football club and they are employees of the football club," Wilder said. "And, on top of that, they earn a damn good wage. There is no bigger advocate of this group than me. I don't bash them up for the sake of it. But what I will do, and will always do, is tell it like it is.

"I won't dress it up because we've lost. I'm not bothered about psychological stuff. They won, and we've lost. End of. People were telling me afterwards 'what a great game' and 'you must be proud to be taking part in it at the top end.' It's nonsense. I hate all this 'isn't it great to be involved at the top end of the league' and all that rubbish. I hate it. Football is only great if you win."

With United riding high, and Lampard still getting to grips with life at Pride Park, Derby's victory was seen in some quarters as something of an upset - an idea that Wilder, as he shared a drink with the former Champions League winner in his office afterwards, struggled to comprehend.

Earlier in the season, Derby had blown United out of the water financially to sign striker Martyn Waghorn and had, in Mason Mount, a player that had recently been called up to the full England squad; United's group, by comparison, had been assembled on a shoestring by Championship standards. "Whether we should have been there, among these powerful clubs or not, I don't know. Maybe we weren't expected to be," Wilder admitted.

"But the target was to get in a position around Christmas, where results and performances were consistent. That was our mentality. I've been a manager for a long time and I want my team to play well… that goes without saying.

"But I hate sitting in the other manager's office and having people tell me how well we played. Then, we're back on the bus with nothing to show for it. At the same time, I don't want everyone jumping through hoops and saying everything's brilliant if we just played okay. We have to play well, and win."

United certainly played well in their following midweek game but were denied the win right at the death against Stoke, who fielded around £70million worth of players in their starting line-up and left a Champions League and five-time Premier League winner on the bench alongside a former Barcelona player. But Darren Fletcher and Bojan could only watch on as a nomadic £150,000 striker in Leon Clarke put United ahead, before that was cancelled out by a clever free-kick from Joe Allen in the last minute. The introduction of giant striker Peter Crouch changed the course of the game after a dominant United performance and when Welsh international Allen stood over a free-kick, in a good crossing position, the whole of Bramall Lane expected Crouch to be the target.

Instead, Allen shifted direction to beat Dean Henderson at his near post and, after dominating the recently-relegated Potters for the entire game, United were left with just a point to show for their efforts. It was a bitter pill to swallow for Wilder but in the immediate aftermath, he was in more reflective mood.

Although he insisted that Stoke had 'dodged a bullet' by nicking a point late on, Wilder thought the result needed to be put into perspective and told his devastated players afterwards that it was more important to consider the bigger picture. It certainly looked healthy, from a United perspective. Wilder's men were on course to overtake Middlesbrough and go top of the Championship until Allen's late intervention, and the manager raised a few eyebrows afterwards when he told the media that his first priority for the season was reaching the safety mark of 50 points.

"Throughout the season there were a lot of clubs who were expected to do better than us, in terms of where we've come from, the players we had and the money that we spent," Wilder reflected at the end of the season. "So if we have a chance to deflect, I'll try to take it! But that was, from my point of view, right up there in terms of performances, especially considering the calibre of player we were up against.

"My agent is also the agent of Ashley Williams, who's admitted since that they couldn't cope with Sheffield United that night. I was aggrieved by the manner of their equaliser - and the free-kick shouldn't have been given either, for me - but pound for pound, that was right up there. We handled their front men [Benik Afobe and Saido Berahino] really well and took the game to them. From start to finish, apart from a mad few seconds, we dominated a really powerful football club in the division."

The disappointment of not going top of the table didn't linger, though. United did return to the summit that weekend, courtesy of a 4-2 victory over Wigan Athletic at Bramall Lane and a hat-trick for skipper Sharp. Incredibly for a striker of his calibre, it was Sharp's first treble for exactly 10 years, two months and 11 days, when he scored three times against QPR in his second spell at United.

This one was pretty similar actually," Sharp said. "I could feel a bit of momentum with goals at the time and like any striker, I go into a season wanting to score as many as I can. To score two hat-tricks for United in a season, and bring up a hat-trick of hat-tricks for this club in my career, is unbelievable really. A lot of fans say to me: 'You're living our dreams' and I actually am. It's incredible."

When he walked into Bramall Lane in 2016, one of Wilder's first acts as United manager was to find a screwdriver and take down the great number of motivational signs that had been installed, at considerable expense, by his predecessor Adkins. Wilder was similarly decisive when it came to the identity of his United captain, calling Sharp while he was away on holiday and informing him that he was to be the skipper of his boyhood club. The news, Sharp remembers, took a while to sink in, but it proved to be an inspired decision. The armband has matured Sharp as a person and as a player and before he walked away with the matchball to give to his sons, he admitted that he would have previously sulked after being left out of the United team.

"But I'm the captain of the club now and I've got to set an example," he added. "So the main thing for me is supporting the team. If I'm not scoring goals, I want to be doing other things for the team and for the club. We've got great togetherness in the changing room. The staff work hard on it but, as a group, it comes naturally to us. They're an easy group to captain. We're all decent people and we're all ready to work hard for each other. It's not about individuals. People talk about 'us' not 'me'. I used to just target 20 goals every season which, looking back, was a bit selfish. I know I've got to work hard and, if I'm not scoring goals, do other things that help the team and the club. Luckily I'm scoring goals at the minute, but the most important thing is to do well as a team and a club. We believe we should be at the top of the table, and there's no reason that we can't stay there for the rest of the season."

Talksport Singles
by Jonathan Bradley

Three months is a long time in football. It's a long time in any walk of life, but with October it usually signifies the end of the settling-in period; awfully similar to that 'honeymoon period' in any new relationship. Luckily for United, we were becoming seasoned Championship competitors, in only our second season since promotion, and things were looking incredibly positive. An impressive start to the campaign meant we travelled to Blackburn who, rather similarly to us a year previously, were riding high on the crest of the promotion wave after going up from the third tier.

They hadn't lost at home in what seemed like forever. If we were to come away with a victory it certainly would be a statement of our intent. As always, it wasn't just the football that made it a memorable evening. "Who you support, mate?" quipped a young supporter to me in what could be only described as the busiest McDonald's in the whole north-west. "United," I told him. "Get yourself ****** off then!" he responded. Charming as this was, it wasn't the most amusing interaction with the locals we had and, as we approached the away end, our anticipation to get in and enjoy some of the terrible lagers only grew as two of the locals were competing as to who could do the best horse impression. What?

Ewood Park welcomed us as we exchanged nodding glances, handshakes and pleasantries with various acquaintances. We were sure of a tough test. It was something we pulled the bones out of while listening to Talksport, absolutely bamboozled at the prospect that they were running a dating website called 'Talksport Singles'. Just imagine the blokes on there: 'Ken, 64, from Rochdale who likes beer, Brexit and boobs' came to mind. Our imaginations were running wild but ahead of us, the reality soon became apparent of how tough this game would be.

Blackburn, much like their manager Tony Mowbray, lacked any real charm but did a reasonable job at stopping us. The highlights of the first half included a firework being tossed into the away end which I'm sure has taken a few years off of my life expectancy. United though looked good value despite the home side's resilience. The second half seemed to be following a similar pattern to the first until a clever shift in formation by Wilder resulted in Billy Sharp - who else? - putting us ahead. The celebrations in the away end were pretty special, something which would be hard to top. In typical style, though, Wilder hadn't finished yet.

When Paul Coutts was introduced from the bench shortly after, grown men were shedding tears of joy. Myself included. When a player breaks his leg, it's very rare that he ever returns to the same level and the impact that Coutts' injury had on our first season back in the Championship was unparalleled. We never really recovered. Despite the odd wonder-strike, Lee Evans was otherwise bang average and never managed to run a game and dictate play in the same way Coutts masterfully did. What will always stick with me about *that* night at Burton, when Coutts got injured, was the real sense of horror among the fans. Those initial fears sunk in more and more as the season rolled on and if it wasn't for the signing of the impeccable Oliver Norwood, the Coutts hangover might have stretched on even longer.

Despite Norwood's impressive form, and his outstanding contribution throughout the season, this was Coutts' moment and no-one could take it away from him. Although in retrospect it's difficult to say he had a major contribution towards promotion to the top-flight on the field, sometimes in football the more subtle moments stick with you. This was one of those moments. As Wilder pushed Coutts towards the fans later that night, the look on his face will stick with me forever. What a horrendous year he must have had. Going from playing the best football of your career - for a team whose supporters, teammates and management all adore you - to lying in a hospital bed, after you've had your leg snapped.

This wasn't just a football moment, but a massive moment in the life of a modern Blades legend. Couttsy, what a man. I was lucky enough to be in the Copthorne Hotel with the players after promotion was confirmed, and witness Coutts in true, full flight - doing 'Skittle bombs' - yes, they still sell them - with my mate Mark, moments before throwing up in one of the bins. What a legend. Anyway, back to the football.

Another highlight came when Enda Stevens whipped in a ball of immense quality for Sharp to grab his second. The term 'limbs' is often overused these days, but I cannot think of a better adjective to describe what followed. This was even topped when the players and Wilder came over at the end. Dean Henderson basked in the glory of getting one over Blackburn - he had previous with their fans after the 'Jelly Babies' incident the season before - and Coutts just grinned at the away end with a look of sheer joy. We'd done it; beaten a team who hadn't lost at home in a very long time. We couldn't, could we?

A few suggestions of potential suitors from our latest favourite online dating platform were muted in the car, but our attention soon turned instead to Hull at home the following weekend. A rather dull afternoon ended in United beating a bang average Hull side, with a penalty from David McGoldrick. Still not injured, the man known as 'Didzy' was proving himself to be a pretty steady addition, considering all the hyperbole that followed his much-understated signing. His fifth of the season placed another number in the W column and set us up nicely for

our trip to the Midlands to meet "Mr Bleakley's" Derby County.
A late Saturday kick-off is always a real drinkers' treat and
handed the United faithful a great chance for throat lubrica-
tion throughout the afternoon. Upon arrival in Derby, my good
friend Alan put his son in a taxi with our friends as we took the
cheaper option by walking across the city. In passing, anyone
having a crisis of confidence about living in Sheffield should take
a walk across Derby city centre.

When we made our way to the ground, the atmosphere in
the away end was jovial, to say the least. The mood took a turn,
though, as we finished the last of our beers to find out we were
1-0 down within the first minute. Despite that, United put together a very accomplished 45 minutes of football, working the
ball well and pushing for an equaliser.

One eventually came, just before half-time with the afore-
mentioned 'limbs' making a further appearance as Chris Basham smashed home a vintage "Wilderball" goal for the Blades.
At half-time we enjoyed a beer - my friend, Carly, holding three
pints in her hands and one in her cleavage, a feat both remarkable and impressive in equal measure - and felt confident of
going on to win the game, and going top of the league. Sadly
the highlights of the afternoon ended at half-time as a late Jack
Marriott strike put an end to our hopes.

A seemingly familiar fate faced us the following Tuesday as
we faced the underachieving Stoke City at Bramall Lane. Leon
Clarke started in front of Billy - a move many of us perceived to
be an error of judgement on Wilder's behalf - but how wrong
we were. He had the experienced, and expensive, Ashley Williams on toast and was rewarded with a goal. Sadly we ended
up being short-changed as a late Joe Allen free-kick saw questions asked of both Stevens and Henderson.

It all seemed a little too familiar. Players in goal and at left-
back had been criticised after United had dropped points
against the likes of Bristol City and Aston Villa. Fortunately for
us, any questions were emphatically answered in abundance,
come May. The month ended with a superb win over Wigan
at the Lane, which included a hat-trick for our very own Billy

goat (or should that be G.O.A.T?) Despite a 4-0 win, the performance wasn't scintillating but it certainly was very efficient. Sharp's contribution again proved invaluable, adding yet more weight to the argument that he should be considered as one of our greatest ever players. A few years ago, in my lifetime that honour belonged to Phil Jagielka. Now, without question, it belongs to Billy.

As for the dating game, United's relationship with the Championship was certainly heating up. We had moved in and now, after well over a year, were getting comfortable. And in a good way! Billy was scoring for fun, we were resilient and even after some disappointing results, we were responding. And if any suitors fancied Chris, 51, from Sheffield he was very much off the market. He was in a long term relationship with Sheffield United - and was very happy with how it was going!

Third time lucky
by Oliver Norwood

It's been a long road for me to play in the Premier League finally, and it really began when I was seven years old and signed for Manchester United. I was lucky enough to stay there until I was 21 and learned so, so much, not just on the field. I learned about values and principles in life, how to carry and conduct myself and behave, in and out of football. I learned a lot on the pitch too, because United had arguably their most successful recent years at the same time as I was in the academy.

I trained and worked alongside players like Paul Scholes, Ryan Giggs, Gary Neville, Wayne Rooney, Rio Ferdinand, Cristiano Ronaldo... seeing how they went about things and worked at their game, 'away from the lights' as my gaffer now, Chris Wilder, likes to say!

It was a real eye-opener, to see how these stars worked on the cold, wet December and January mornings when no-one was watching. They set incredible standards every single day and it was something I learned a lot from. Ole Gunnar Solskjær was my reserve team manager before I left and I still speak to him and a few others, but we've all grown up; I've got my own little boy now. But they were special times. The amount of players Manchester United produced from their academy, not just for themselves but for elsewhere, is remarkably high and I think it's because they produce good human beings as well as good footballers, with life values and manners. Life skills.

We learned them from, for me, the greatest manager of all time in Sir Alex Ferguson and that filtered right the way down to the under-sevens. I'm sometimes asked in that respect if there are any similarities between Sir Alex and the gaffer here, and I think there are. The biggest one, definitely, is that they are both winners. They do whatever it takes to win, and I think that's ingrained in you. You can't just turn it on and off like a tap. And those life values are so important whether you've learned them at Old Trafford or in non-league, where a few of our players have played.

That's the thing about footballers. Almost everyone, at some stage, has suffered setbacks - hasn't quite made the grade at a certain level and had to go away and rebuild. I did that to a certain extent but some have done it far more than I have. The prime example is Mark Duffy, who's a fantastic role model for any young boy who gets knocked back and thinks it's all over for them. The way the gaffer has moulded us all together has been fantastic, and I enjoyed my first season at Bramall Lane so much. I really hope to be a part of it for many years to come, because the manager we have is special.

Why? The way he goes about his work. He questions us, puts demands on us in a way that he knows will get a reaction from us, and the best thing for me is that he tells us how it is. There's a lot of smoke blown up people's backsides because that's the industry we're in; it's a bu*****t world, with agents and boot companies and managers and chief executives - at other clubs, rather than this one - all getting involved. I'm not frightened to say that but this manager wouldn't ever get involved in any of that, and I think we're quite fortunate at this moment in time to have him in place because I think he'll manage at the top, top level.

I mean that. And we just hope it's with us! It must be a dream for him to lead his boyhood club in the Premier League.

He's been so good for me, as well. I remember saying to him, just before we won promotion: 'You rescued me'. And it's true. Not many people probably realise what happened at Brighton towards the end of my time there. I moved there after the fun and games of the 2016 European Championships with Northern Ireland, when we reached the last 16, and it was a difficult period for me in my life.

My wife Abigail was pregnant and was really ill, so she wasn't able to get down to Brighton a lot of the time. We were living apart and it did affect my football because, of course, you're concentrating on the wellbeing of your wife and baby. We're only human beings at the end of the day and although we got promoted to the Premier League that season and I played quite a few games, it was a bit of a blur to be honest. My head wasn't fully there and, when I went back in pre-season, I was basically told I could go out on loan.

I went to Fulham and luckily, I fell back in love with football again. It was so enjoyable; my wife was healthy and had given birth to my son, and a massive weight was lifted off my shoulders. We got promoted in the play-off final at Wembley, which was an incredible day. And then it was back to Brighton. They told me I was surplus to requirements and could go, but the way clubs sometimes treat players is incredible.

They said I could leave, but then turned down bids when they came in and started asking for silly things. I don't think clubs realise sometimes that they're messing with people's lives. I had plenty of arguments, saying: 'You don't want me here, so let me go'.

I was training on my own, running up and down the side of the pitch while the first team lads were training, and there were days when I didn't want to go in and face it. But I ground it out. I know people may read this and think: 'Well, financially you were fine' and yeah, I earned the most money of my career to date at Brighton. But for me, football has never been about money. I play football because I love playing football and to have that taken away from me... it was hard. It's all I've ever known since I was six years old. So it was difficult to keep going at times and I'm quite lucky that I had the support of my wife in the summer. Without her, I'd have been close to tearing my hair out at times.

But my family and my little boy got me through the hard periods, and I realised I had to do it for them. It wasn't just about me anymore. So I feel that United came in for me just at the right time, and that's what I mean by the gaffer rescuing me. I think it's another masterstroke from the manager.

He seems to have assembled a squad of players who've suffered setbacks, hasn't he? It's a special group, and not just because we got promoted. It's a special dressing room, and Billy Sharp's in charge of it. He sets the standards in there but at the same time, we're genuinely all friends. We spend a lot of time in each other's company outside of football and so when things perhaps aren't going your way on the pitch, you look around and know that your mates will go the extra yard for you, and you will for them.

I looked next to me in midfield and know that John Fleck had my back, and I had his. Behind me, John Egan and Jack O'Connell, with Chris Basham and Dean Henderson as well. In front of me, Duffy and Billy and David McGoldrick. Even lads like Paul Coutts, Martin Cranie and Richard Stearman throughout the season. I could single out any player who was a part of the group in that promotion season and think: 'Yeah, I'd take him to the trenches with me'. That's a big thing in football. Because it's not always like that.

I said to my agent when I signed that we'd have a good shot at the play-offs, but I never dreamed we'd go up automatically. It just goes to show that when you have a manager like ours, and the players we have, how far a bit of hard work and talent can take you. The way we play suits me so much and it helped me hit the ground running.

But the thing about our system here is that no one player could do what he does without the rest of the lads. I think every single player in the promotion season was outstanding; I was surprised that we didn't have more players in the team of the season, especially defensively. Those lads were fantastic.

I did find it funny, though, listening to so-called experts and hearing them say how we shouldn't have been up there. It baffled me. I think what they meant is that they didn't want us to be up there. I think they wanted Leeds and Marcelo Bielsa, because of his reputation in the game. But unfortunately for them, they didn't have what we have in our dressing room.

I did wonder if we might get some credit when the job was done but we enjoy going under the radar anyway, proving people wrong. I think that again goes back to the lads' mentality and where they've come from. To bounce back from the adversity some of these lads have experienced takes a lot of character and a lot of pride, and I think that's come out on the pitch at points when things have got tough.

We looked after each other because we've had a lot bigger setbacks in our careers than losing a goal. At the same time, though, it's not just about mentality. We're not just lads who are brain-dead and can't play football. We have some fine, fine players in the dressing room. Enda Stevens, for me, has been incredible, as has Didzy. Billy has done what he's always done - he's been questioned before: 'Can he play at that level?' Of course he can. The gaffer's recruitment for me has been smart because every single player has a point to prove and wants to progress in their careers.

It's been special so far, and the Premier League season will be special too. The Blades in the top flight. Who'd have thought it after we were written off all season? After my third promotion there in three years, I'm hoping I can actually get a chance in the Premier League this time! I've been asked what the secret to getting promoted is and I think it helps when you get the chance to play in a good team! But seriously, for me, it's about dressing room spirit. People might raise eyebrows when I say I'm looking forward to playing at Burnley, but I'm a Burnley lad so it'll be nice to play there... it'll be nice to prove a point at Brighton, too.

I think there's a drive in me, that I wouldn't be denied that opportunity to play in the Premier League. I think that, before I went to my grave, however old I'm going to be, it was something I wanted to tick off my list. I've been rejected the last two times, and with Manchester United, too, but I've finally got there in the end. That determination is just something built in us. It's definitely in me.

I've never been given anything, I've had to work for everything I've got and I think it all goes down to those values that you learn, wherever you learn them. We're lucky to be footballers and are in a privileged position but we're not given that position. There's a lot of stuff that goes on through the week, a lot that people don't see. You have to try to see through all that and enjoy the good times as and when they come.

chapter seven

Derby-day disappointment

November 2018

During the summer of 2018, after the red-and-white half of the Steel City breathed a collective sigh of relief over the future of manager Chris Wilder, the dust settled on what had largely been a successful first season back in the Championship for Sheffield United. There had been success and disappointment along the way, but steadily the country's collective attention seemed to turn to Russia, to cheer England - and a number of ex-Blades - in the World Cup finals. Gareth Southgate's men had barely touched down on Russian soil when the release of the 2018/19 fixture list smashed through the close-season tranquillity, with all the subtlety of a Jack O'Connell header.

Supporters left starved of club football since the beginning of May could now decide how and where their Saturday afternoons would be spent for the duration of the forthcoming season. Trips near and far, to newly-promoted Rotherham United and recently-relegated Swansea City, added extra intrigue, but for the majority there was only one club who caught the eye as they scanned the fixture list - United's fiercest rivals, Wednesday.

The previous season's clashes with their neighbours from the north west of the city had done little to dampen the anticipation, either. The first derby became known as the *'Bouncing Day Massacre'* when United, shorn of several key players, scored four goals at Hillsborough for the first time in their history.

The 4-2 scoreline told only half the story of a pulsating game, though, as United went 2-0 ahead early on, before Wednesday dragged themselves back level in the second half. Hillsborough was literally rocking soon after Lucas Joao's equaliser as thousands of home fans bounced up and down in jubilation. Then came Mark Duffy.

The Liverpudlian, fresh off the substitutes' bench, scored a superb individual goal just 106 seconds after Joao's equaliser to turn the game in United's favour one more, before former Owls striker Leon Clarke scored his second of the game late on to strike the dagger further into Wednesday hearts. Wednesday never really recovered from that defeat, finishing 15th in the table - five places and 12 points behind the neighbours they thought they had left behind - and by the time of the return leg at Bramall Lane, things *really* had gone full-circle.

Wednesday defended for their lives to earn a point and their players celebrated by throwing shirts into the crowd at the end while one Owls fan remembers fellow supporters dancing on tables in a pub at full-time; overjoyed at not being humiliated again by their biggest rivals.

The fixture computer scheduled the first 2018/19 instalment of the Sheffield derby for November, although the date was later switched to a Friday evening at the behest of Sky Sports. By the time it rolled around, United were going into the game on the back of a 1-0 defeat at Nottingham Forest and were again enjoying the better of their rivals, sitting 10 points and 14 places higher in the table. Wilder - hinting heavily at both the millions spent by Wednesday on players, and the names still on their roster - scoffed, though, at suggestions that the Blades should have been seen as favourites.

"Underdogs or favourites? Everybody will have their own opinion on that," he said before the game. "Sometimes you have to look a bit deeper. But we have gone about it our own way. I'm not interested in what has gone off over there. But they have some tremendously powerful footballers who they've spent big fees and wages on. That doesn't take the pressure off us though. Because we still want it."

Under the ownership of Thai businessman Dejphon Chansiri, Wednesday lavished huge sums of money on players in an attempt to win promotion to the Premier League for the first time since the turn of the millennium. But doing so proved beyond them - losing in the play-off final in 2016 and the semi-finals a year later - and their heavy spending, on both fees and wages, fell foul of the English Football League's profit and sustainability rules.

Wednesday were subsequently hit with a transfer embargo in the summer of 2018 but at the same time, kept almost all their top earners, including Gary Hooper, Barry Bannan and Steven Fletcher. Despite the embargo, Wednesday's squad remained packed with quality players at Championship level and Chansiri had chosen to place his expensively-assembled roster in the hands of Jos Luhukay, a Dutch manager who was relatively unknown before he was unveiled at Wednesday. Luhukay had enjoyed spells at clubs including Borussia Mönchengladbach and Hertha BSC in the past and his pre-match comments, about having experienced bigger derbies in the Bundesliga, didn't go unnoticed by Wilder.

"It is the biggest for me, for my pals and my family," Wilder replied when the subject was broached in his own pre-game press briefing. "This is the derby for us. It's what we've been brought up with. I know what it means to people like Len Badger and also, on the other side, for lads like Mel Sterland. It gets a grip of you. It's fierce. I'm not from Liverpool or Manchester so this is the big one, the biggest by far, for me."

Wednesday made the short trip into the centre of Sheffield on the back of four straight defeats while United's preparation was hardly ideal, either, as their loss at the City Ground saw them knocked off the top of the Championship table. But they received one boost in that game when David McGoldrick avoided the yellow card which would have ruled him out of the derby, and another on the eve of it when Chris Basham committed his future to Bramall Lane by signing a new contract.

"There's nowhere else I'd want to go and play," Basham said at the time. "This club is definitely on the up and I really want to be a part of it for the next two-and-a-half years. I've been here a long time, my family love the city and with them settled I'm able to focus on my game and playing consistently well. Hopefully we can enjoy a double celebration on Friday night."

Derby games between United and Wednesday would be good material for an in-depth psychological study; not just to analyse the vast difference in mentality that often exists between supporters of both clubs, who otherwise have so much in common. Wednesday fans have always tended to see themselves as superior to United, whose fan base is generally viewed as more humble; yet it is the red and white half of the city who have the superior record in derby games, which have often been a great leveller for whichever side has found themselves on top at any particular moment in time. The most famous instance was Boxing Day in 1979 when United, top of the old Division Three, lost 4-0 at Hillsborough and fell out of the promotion race altogether.

Blades fans of a certain vintage will remember the 1951 derby at Bramall Lane more fondly - United winning 7-3 - but there was to be no such "goal-fest" this time as again, the Owls nullified United and escaped back to Hillsborough with a point. Wilder, who had begun one of Sheffield's biggest days of the year by giving his time to a community event at Bramall Lane, was understandably frustrated at the goalless draw but had no cause for complaint about his side's dominant performance.

The post-game stats showed that United had enjoyed a remarkable 75 per cent of possession, with 19 shots on goal, and would likely have registered a comfortable victory had McGoldrick converted a first-half penalty, which was instead well saved by young Owls goalkeeper Cameron Dawson.

Duffy, who won the penalty after being fouled by Morgan Fox, remembers Wednesday fans "celebrating like they'd won the league" after the game, before Wilder revealed that Dawson is actually a distant relative. Family tree - and the result - aside, Wilder was delighted by his side's display. "It showed how far we've come, even though I know people don't always want to hear that," he added.

"We pegged back a team that got to the play-off final a few years back, then the play-off semi-final, but they resorted to booting it anywhere. We totally dominated a team with big names, big players, big wages and big numbers, a powerful football club. I know which dressing room I'd rather be in after the final whistle. I'd rather be in ours and I told the lads that, too."

One local newspaper report accurately described Luhukay as 'relieved' after the game and, in the other dressing room at Bramall Lane, Wilder jokingly told McGoldrick that, as a boyhood United fan, his penalty miss had ruined his weekend. "I really put it on him," smiled the Blades boss. But privately, Wilder and his coaching staff were impressed by the striker's reaction to the disappointment.

"I remember it well," grimaced McGoldrick at the end of the season. "It's weird, because I felt like I had a good game with my whole play. To be honest, it haunted me for weeks after but I got messages from some of the staff telling me not to worry about it and that I'd been fantastic. Little things like that really meant a lot.

"Missing a penalty at any point isn't great, but to miss one in a derby... so, so much worse. It wasn't a nice time but it's part of football. I could have let it affect me, but I tried to bounce back as quickly as I could. It's funny though, isn't it? If he dives the other way I'm the hero but he went the right way, he's the hero and I'm the villain. The margins are fine but you accept that when you step up to take it. The fans were fantastic with me but it did haunt me.

"I couldn't sleep for a while after that and I didn't want to go on any social media. I'd go on Instagram, there'd be pictures of the game and I just wanted to block them out. It hurt me and no doubt hurt a lot of fans. But there have been more good moments than bad for me in a United shirt and the positives have far outweighed the negatives so far."

McGoldrick's previous experience of football in the Steel City came earlier in his career, when he had a loan spell at Wednesday under Gary Megson. "Crazy times," he remembered, shaking his head. "On a Tuesday we'd go to the park and into the woods, and just run. We didn't see a football. I wondered what I'd got myself into. I wasn't his type of player and he wasn't my type of manager but it was an experience. It was a short spell and all my good memories of Sheffield have come with United. I made it over to the right side of the city eventually."

United's performance against Wednesday had placated Wilder a little, after he had publicly questioned his players following their defeat to Forest at the City Ground. Poor defending from Kieron Freeman allowed João Carvalho, a summer signing from Benfica, the opportunity to cross for striker Grabban to glance home past Dean Henderson.

Carvalho and Grabban cost a combined £19million when they arrived in Nottingham and players of that calibre, Wilder reminded his players, could, and would, hurt United given half a chance. United, the manager felt, had to be at the very top of their game, or damn near close, to get positive results in the Championship.

"When we're not at our best, do we just become an average team?" Wilder asked aloud after the Forest defeat. "I honestly can't remember the last time we won or drew a game when we weren't at full tilt. Maybe I should take that as a compliment of sorts because we're still in the picture, so it shows we are getting the absolute maximum from the players. It's certainly something we're going to have to get better at if we want to maintain a challenge and I guess we'll find out. I don't think, during my time here, I've ever said that we've been absolutely battered but won."

Was that his genuine belief, an emotional response in the heat of the moment or an attempted psychological ploy? "No, I stand by my thought that we had to play close to our maximum to get results, whether that was attacking or defensively," Wilder said at the end of the season. "We couldn't afford to carry anyone. We were a little bit more resolute as time went on and our game management was better. We had periods when we didn't play free-flowing football for various reasons, whether that was changes or injuries or suspensions or a bit of tiredness creeping in.

"Maybe the pressure played a part too, as the stakes became a lot higher after Christmas. We were a bit more pragmatic and resolute in certain parts of the game, which we had to be, but we still had to be at our best to win games. Earning close to two points a game after Christmas summed that up. We weren't at our best at Forest but were still good enough to get something out of the game, which was quite bittersweet. But we had to be close to our maximum - either offensively or defensively, if not both - to win games of football."

Privately, as another international break gave the majority of his squad a breather from the Championship's relentless schedule, Wilder felt that the eight games his squad then faced before the turn of the year would be a good indication of their automatic promotion credentials and began to stress to them the importance of accumulating points.

For the first time since joining from Brighton in the summer Oliver Norwood remained at Shirecliffe for an international break - the Northern Ireland midfielder was banned for his country's Nations League clash with Austria so was granted permission from boss Michael O'Neill to miss the friendly against the Republic of Ireland - but there was finally a breakthrough in John Fleck's pursuit of a full Scotland cap, when he was drafted into a decimated senior squad to face Albania and Israel after Aston Villa's John McGinn became the *11th player* to withdraw with injury.

Fleck, though, bizarrely missed Scotland's trip to Albania because the Scottish FA felt his late call-up didn't leave them enough time to make travel arrangements - the flight to Tirana actually left Edinburgh at two o'clock in the afternoon, the day after Fleck was notified of his call-up - and he was left on the bench at Hampden Park as James Forrest's hat-trick beat Israel 3-2. It was nevertheless a seminal moment for Fleck, who had inexplicably been overlooked by the Scotland hierarchy for a number of years. And his former Rangers teammate Lee McCulloch admitted he hoped it was the first call-up of many, after insisting Fleck has the potential to become one of Scotland's most important players.

"I get asked about Scotland quite a lot and why I wasn't being called up," Fleck revealed. "There are a lot of good players

in that position; McGinn, Barry Bannan, Callum McGregor…
we're similar heights and similar sorts of players. So it was just
one of those things, and those boys were all playing well. I've
always had the same mindset - just keep playing consistently
well and you'll end up getting there. It doesn't need to happen straightaway. Whatever happens will happen, whether it's
tomorrow or next year.

"As long as I keep working hard for United, that's the most
important thing for me. I couldn't really answer the questions
about why I wasn't being called up, I could only work on my
side of things. I had no problem with it because I knew that the
boys being picked were good players as well. I just wanted to try
to improve as a player and knew I'd eventually get recognised if
I kept doing that consistently well for United."

A break from the Championship's relentless fixture schedule
also saw thoughts drift towards the January transfer window,
which United's staff had identified as crucial to their hopes of
sustaining their promotion challenge. A year earlier, when a
threadbare squad was crying out for an injection of quality in
January, budget restrictions forced United to go down the route
of quantity instead and take speculative gambles on players
such as Lee Evans, Ryan Leonard and Ricky Holmes.

James Wilson also joined on loan from Manchester United
but was a flop of a signing compared with, for instance, Aleksandar Mitrovic, who joined Fulham on a temporary deal from
Newcastle United. Mitrovic scored 12 times in 20 games - including a brace against United at Craven Cottage - and helped
Fulham into the Premier League, via a play-off final victory over
Aston Villa at Wembley.

While Fulham's players - including Oliver Norwood - celebrated, Wilder instead launched a detailed investigation into
the previous campaign to discover how, and why, his side had
fallen away and finished 10th after topping the table at various
points earlier in the season. The review was in-depth, analysing
United's technical and tactical approach, and all theories were
disproved apart from one; depth, both in ability and numbers. It
was a problem Wilder first sought to address in the summer of

2018, trading players to improve the squad's overall quality, and would look to continue in January - with some funds from David Brooks' big summer move to Bournemouth still at his disposal.

Before then, though, there was still work to be done on the field and when United returned to action after the international break, they made the short trip to the New York Stadium, the home of their neighbours Rotherham United. The Millers have generally shared a good relationship with United over the years - probably aided by a mutual dislike of Wednesday - and both Wilder and his assistant, Alan Knill, represented them, as a player and manager respectively, long before they traded their previous Millmoor home for the impressive New York Stadium a stone's throw away.

Knill was Rotherham's manager during one of their worst periods of financial struggle in the 2000s, and remembers rattling a bucket for spare change before an away game at Southend when the reality of the club's troubles hit home and administration loomed large. United, for their part, helped out by holding similar collections before home games, and then loaned two of their brightest young stars to Knill's Millers in 2006. United paid the full wages of Stephen Quinn and Jonathan Forte as a gesture of goodwill to their neighbours and, just a year later, Quinn was playing regularly for United in the Premier League.

Wilder also retains a genuine affection for the Millers after moving there when his first spell as a player at United came to an end and predicted an absorbing clash with Paul Warne's side - although his comments were also interpreted as a thinly-veiled dig across the city at Wednesday, after their park-the-bus approach at Bramall Lane just before the international break. "It will be a different game to the last one... they'll come for us," said Wilder, before pointedly drawing similarities between his side and Warne's. "Very hard-working, working-class football clubs, not arrogant, don't get above their station and have to work extremely hard for everything that goes their way," was his summation.

Jack O'Connell has less fond memories of Rotherham after a loan spell under Steve Evans earlier in his career - Evans' decision to berate the defender after his debut has unsurprisingly stuck in the defender's mind ever since - and there were more painful lessons to come at the New York Stadium for the Blades. United had their noses bloodied by a dominant Millers side, who were still indebted to Jamie Proctor's injury-time equaliser to earn them even a point from a game they fully deserved to win. United looked set for a comfortable afternoon when Duffy gave them an early lead with a composed finish before the tricky Jon Taylor, who caused Freeman problems all afternoon, netted the equaliser via a wicked deflection.

Basham restored United's advantage when Freeman flicked Billy Sharp's cross into his face on the goalline, but Henderson made a number of fine stops to deny Semi Ajayi and Clark Robertson, among others, before he was finally beaten again. The New York Stadium erupted as Proctor found the back of the net in injury time but from United's point of view, the equaliser was a comedy of errors. Substitute Marvin Johnson lost the ball too easily on the halfway line, Enda Stevens missed his tackle on the Millers' right wing and when the cross came in, Norwood took the ball right off Basham's toe as the defender shaped to hoof it clear. Proctor gleefully accepted the gift.

Wilder's displeasure at his side's performance was clear for all to see, and then hear thanks to the paper-thin walls of the New York Stadium. The manager locked his players in the away dressing room for almost an hour after the full-time whistle and when he did finally emerge, to dissect a result that left United fifth in the table and five points behind leaders Norwich City, it was clear that not all his anger and frustration had been left behind. "There is no point me mugging myself off and saying we were unlucky and should have won," he said. "Rotherham were miles better than us."

The only player to emerge with any real credit was his goalkeeper, who Wilder described as "outstanding". Henderson is something of a pantomime villain with Millers fans, who remember his decision, during his time at Shrewsbury, to describe himself as 'The Greatest' in a Twitter post. That tweet was pinned on the Millers' dressing room wall before they faced the

Shrews and when a mistake from Henderson had gifted Richard Wood the winning goal, Warne's players weren't shy about reminding Henderson of his pre-match message. Later that season, Shrewsbury met the Millers again in the play-off final at Wembley and Henderson was outstanding, saving a penalty and making several eye-catching saves before being eventually beaten - again by Wood - deep into injury-time.

Henderson told the Millers fans that he had "loved the banter" during the game against United and then further highlighted his confidence levels, not just in his own ability, when he described the Blades as 'the best team in the division' during his post-match interview. "When we played Wednesday in the derby a couple of weeks ago, we terrorised them," he said. "No one can get near us when we play like that. It could have been 6-0, seriously. Then we come to Rotherham, who have just been promoted from League One, and we don't turn up. Which is frustrating. It's an honest changing room and we know what we've got to improve on. We've got to learn how to see games out and, as good as we are, we're not doing that."

Although his own verdict on his side's performance was damning, both publicly and privately, Wilder was disappointed to see his side's attitude and character questioned after defeat at Rotherham and believes they issued the perfect response in midweek, with a hard-fought 3-2 win at Brentford's Griffin Park. After Wilder had resisted the temptation to make the wholesale changes he had threatened at the weekend - only Conor Washington and John Lundstram came in, for Duffy and Sharp - United were 2-1 ahead after 15 minutes after Ezri Konsa's own goal and a stunner from Norwood followed Neal Maupay's opener for the hosts. John Fleck's own goal from Romaine Sawyers' cross dragged the Bees back on level terms, before substitute Leon Clarke came off the bench to win the game with a composed finish.

United, Wilder said, were an "angry team" at Griffin Park after they were questioned at the New York Stadium and the manager described their display as a "proper Sheffield United performance". Norwood, who captained the Blades for the first time after Sharp dropped to the bench, later singled out the moment he received the armband as one of his highlights of the season. "I didn't expect it at all, to be honest, especially because I'd only been at the club for a few months by that point," he said. "The gaffer obviously trusted me enough to give me the honour of leading the lads out, and it genuinely is an honour because it's such a good group. It's special to be the captain at any club but especially this one, because of the history behind it."

Of the Rotherham game, Norwood said: "We were crap as a team. We couldn't pass the ball to each other... we were so bad. Credit to Rotherham for the way they played, but we were so crap. The last goal still haunts me. Marv got it and lost it, Enda missed the tackle, I took the ball off Bash's toe with the last kick of the game and set the lad up. It was comical but we got torn to pieces by the gaffer afterwards. It was another moment when you look around and see the character you have in the dressing room. We went to Brentford and were really good. It was night and day from Rotherham, so that was perhaps another turning point for us."

More than just a game
by Chris Reilly

The first thing I do, like many of my fellow Blades fans, when the fixture list comes out, is look for when we are playing 'them lot' from the other side of the city in S6. It's fair to say, I think, that the balance of power in Sheffield had changed since United's return to the Championship, after Chris Wilder galvanised our club again, right from its very core. We had an identity back and some passion, too. And in the previous season, not only did we silence a lot of critics... we, and Mark Duffy in particular, managed to stop some bouncing, as well!

I always get knots in my stomach before a derby game. (To be fair, I get knots before any game, but more on that later). The nearer the game draws, the less I sleep and the less I can eat. All the banter intensifies on social media, and memories of past derbies are replayed over and over. Michael Brown's screamer against *them* at the Lane, beating them on April Fool's Day at Hillsborough. Laurent D'Jaffo scoring, but still never smiling. Remember that old cliché: 'Form goes out of the window'? I believe that to be true, but the game was as one-sided a 'contest' as you'll ever see. The stats don't lie, do they? In the first half, when Duffy won the penalty, I did what I normally do and say 'I can't watch this', turning around to face the fans.

For about two seconds, before I cave in and turn around again. David McGoldrick - a signing who surprised a lot of us, but turned out to be a shrewd acquisition, to say the least - stepped up, after what seemed to be an eternity, but Cameron Dawson was the hero. It wasn't to be, and so another 0-0 at the Lane against 'them lot'. Despite the disappointment, though, there was generally a sense, I felt, that United could do something special this season. Going into the Rotherham game I felt we were finally being taken seriously on a national level, by the media and other football fans alike. When the Millers levelled I remember thinking: 'Here we go again' - maybe that's the pessimist in me - but even I thought we could hang on when we retook the lead, before the equaliser eventually came.

It felt like a massive punch, square in the chest and the draw felt like a defeat. A really bitter pill to swallow. We'd taken two points from two matches and twice lost the lead. Was anything wrong with our character? Victory down at Brentford was a perfect way to answer those doubts, and the promotion season is going to be remembered for so many years to come, for so many different reasons. What we achieved was remarkable but the way it was achieved, especially the form after Christmas, was unbelievable.

I've been to three play-off finals with United and we've lost them all, without even scoring a goal, and there is nothing worse than that feeling, looking around at your fellow Blades all suffering the same pain before preparing for the longest journey home since... well, the last play-off defeat! How refreshing, then, to watch the Villa/Derby play-off final knowing we didn't have to go through all that. Unlike the conclusion of Game of Thrones, our season had a stunning ending! On a personal note, though, it didn't have the best of starts for me because I had a wobble with my mental health.

I've struggled with it since I was diagnosed with severe depression at 16, and then severe anxiety as well. Over the last few years, I feel that mental health has become less of a taboo subject and more accepted and understood by a lot more people. But in the second half of 2018, it really took its toll on me, and I began self-harming again. The support I received, from United fans on social media, was nothing short of incredible and really touched me. A lot of people shared stories of how they, too, were going through hardships and I received support from not only fans, but also players on occasions. It just goes to show how we are 100 per cent United and a team who are at one with their fans. We're in this together, through both ups and downs on the pitch and in our personal lives, too.

My great-uncle Keith first took me to watch the Blades when I was a kid, after also taking my mum and uncle when they were young, and as soon as I walked down the steps to my seat - hearing all the fans singing, a sea of red and white on three sides of the ground - I was hooked. I was sat with complete strangers but in that moment of ecstasy or agony, it feels as if they're your family. You share the good and the bad times together and although these people may not even know, or ever will know, they play a key part in how United help me with my mental health. For someone who can be sat in a room full of family and friends, yet still feel completely and painfully alone, that can be more important than I can even describe.

At its worse, you aren't living; just existing. The best way to explain it is that I'm just watching someone else take over me, like I'm on autopilot. At the start of the season, I actually didn't even renew my season ticket, which isn't like me at all. I just couldn't bear to leave the house. I was on a self-destruct path and pushing people away, but as well as my family I also realised I belonged to a bigger family as well. Of Blades. I deleted all my social media once but then one day, I had 85 private messages from various people, asking if I was okay and seeing if

I could meet them because they were concerned.

Some were people I've never actually met, some were others I have sat with at United games. But it didn't matter. I was absolutely overwhelmed by how many people just wanted to make sure I was okay. I'd become a shadow of the person I once was, but it kickstarted something in me. I realised I was far from the only person who was going through this, and tried to dig deep - take my life back into my own hands. The thing about this football club is that it will be there for you, no matter what. Relationships begin and end, friends come and go but the one constant in my life has been United. It's more than just a place I can go to every other Saturday when we're at home.

I watch games from years ago on YouTube and all the memories come flooding back - in a good way - and the wider community of Blades has made a massive difference to me. The support I received was amazing and I will never, ever forget it. People who don't follow sport, or football in particular, probably will never quite understand it; what it's like to be sitting with grown men either side of you, complete strangers, and be crying your eyes out because you've lost at home to Wigan and have been relegated from the Premier League. Or to share with them the pride and jubilation of this United side under Wilder.

Football has so many parallels with mental health. So many ups and downs, going through something with thousands of strangers at the same time. But I've never been prouder of a team of players than I have in the promotion season and no matter how many more days I live - weeks, months, years, decades - I know I'll still have one thing. United. And as cheesy as that sounds, how bloody lucky am I? To every player, staff member and Chris himself, thank you for giving us our club back. We're not going to Wembley, and I couldn't be any happier.

Allez, Allez, Allez!
by John Egan

It seems like an eternity ago now that I had my first spell at Sheffield United, although luckily my second has been a lot longer and a lot more successful! I had a month here when the Blades were in League One, and played one game at Walsall. We lost - I'm reliably informed that Walsall were a bit of a bogey team in League One for United - but it gave me a good chance to see how big the club is. It's a fantastic club, and one I am honoured to have played for and been successful with.

I'm not sure how many people know of my family's background, but I come from a really sporting family. My mother won a League of Ireland medal with Cork Rangers and my father, also called John, was a hugely respected Gaelic footballer back home, winning six all-Ireland medals.

His team in the 1970s and 1980s went down in history as one of the best ever, and they even put a statue of him up in his hometown! To be brought up with a legend of a father was great and everywhere we went, we used to get stopped in the street. I am hugely proud to be his son. I saw a few articles about our promotion that called me 'the son of John Egan' and I love that. I'll always be 'son of' and I'm okay with that.

It was Easter weekend in 2012 when he passed away and I'll never forget it. Seven years on, we were going into the Easter weekend hoping to get over the disappointment of dropping points at home to Millwall, and the next thing we know Leeds lose both their games over Easter! It's things like that that make me think someone's looking down on me from up there.

For Leeds to lose two games like that had my mind frazzled, to be honest with you. I thought: 'He's definitely looking down on me!' Coincidence or not, I believe it. It's weird how it pans out. After that weekend we were one game away from the Premier League and now we're there. I was lucky to have him as a father, and he'll always be my father.

I suppose with that sporting background, I had to do something sporty! But it was never forced on me. I just played every sport going because Cork, where I grew up, is a really sporting county. I think deep down he wanted me to be a golfer because he loved his golf! I played football, Gaelic football, hurling, basketball, rugby... everything really. When you grow up playing that many sports, you get a winning mentality because you don't play to lose. I then got a chance to come to England and pursue my football career and although it was a tough decision, it was one I couldn't wait to take.

I came in the summer from Brentford because I genuinely believed United could get promoted and in one of my first interviews, I said I'd come here to play in the Premier League. I think a few of the media lads were looking at me when I said that as if to say: 'Calm down!' I knew what United were about and backed myself to add a bit to that. I really enjoyed my time at Brentford - although it was a special feeling to go back to Griffin Park and come home with the three points - but I had a really good feeling about United having played against them twice when they came up from League One. The gaffer strengthened the squad in the summer and I remember looking at the league and thinking: 'Yeah, we've got as good a chance as anyone'.

We just got better and better as players and from the turn of the year, we were in unbelievable form. We definitely believed we'd have a good chance of the top six but expectation changed when we were around the top two, and we knew we had to grab it while it was there. Other teams may have settled for the play-offs but, as soon as there was a sniff of that top two, there was nobody in this world who was going to take it away from us.

I really enjoyed getting to grips with our system, too, although it was a bit of an eye-opener at first. Everyone just seemed to desert from their positions! But we play it to a tee. The two boys either side of me bomb on but we always make sure there's a bit of cover, and then sometimes we just sat in and soaked it up when we needed to. We were a mix of everything in the promotion season; a proper football side who could do everything. Attack together, defend together. It was really enjoyable.

It might look like chaos from the stands... and from the pitch, it definitely looks like chaos! It's organised, though. One of the gaffer's big sayings is: 'Go out the front door, rather than the back one'. For him, there's no point in just sitting back and taking your medicine. Go out and have a go. As players we've really bought into that; it doesn't matter who's in front of us, really. We'll go and have a crack at them. I've really got to know Ollie Norwood this season, because there's often just me and him while everyone else goes off and does his thing! There have been times when I've been standing on my own, against two strikers, and I'm thinking 'Jesus, if this breaks down I'll be in trouble here'. But it's a position and a challenge I really enjoy.

I'd rather us win three or four nil every game, don't get me wrong! But when you've got to keep the ball out, I take pride in that. There's a good saying isn't there? 'Attackers win games but defenders win championships'. I said it to the lads once for a bit of craic, but I think that sums it up. If our strikers are scoring then we've got to keep the ball out of our net, or we won't win. And I always thought that if we kept a clean sheet, we'd have an opportunity to win because, with players like Billy Sharp and others on the pitch, there was always a good chance that we would score.

It was a very big decision for me to leave Brentford because, as I say, I loved my time there. I had two seasons there and played a lot in the Championship, I had a great relationship with the manager and supporters. But sometimes you get an opportunity in football that's too good to turn down and when United came in for me, and the manager showed he wanted me, it became an easy decision.

I felt really excited to move here. I knew the manager had taken the club a very long way in two years and obviously, he's taken it on a lot further now. The two wins over my old team Brentford were particularly sweet, especially the home game when we really had our backs to the wall against the best footballing side in the league, with 10 men. It really set us up for the Leeds game, which we really needed to win. The Chris Basham goal and the scenes afterwards were good, because their players had been tweeting about fans getting down for the warm-up with it being the biggest game of their lives. And then no-one turned up for the warm-up. I almost felt sorry for them. Not really!

Looking back at the season, two of the biggest disappointments were Aston Villa away and Millwall at home, and we drew both games! It's mad, and shows how far we'd come that we were so down, despite not actually losing. To me, it showed that the winning mentality of everyone in the changing room was so, so strong. After Villa, we kept seven clean sheets on the bounce, winning six and drawing one of those games. That showed how much we wanted it.

Lads like Richard Stearman epitomised it for me. If I'm playing he's the first one to come up to me before the game to wish me well, and it's unique really to have someone in your position who gives you full, genuine backing and *really* wants you to do well. The feeling's genuinely mutual, too. We pushed each other in training and, when he had to come in against Nottingham Forest, because I was suspended for my handball against Millwall, I had no doubts whatsoever that he'd have a blinder and we'd have a good chance of winning the game.

I remember going up to him afterwards and telling him he was unbelievable that day. It was a feeling of pure happiness, and we have a lot of respect for each other. It's a squad game in the Championship and we knew we'd need everyone. On that run of clean sheets, how many back threes and fives did we use? I played, Enda Stevens played, Stears, Martin Cranie, Jack O'Connell, Bash, Marvin Johnson, Kieran Dowell... without those lads we wouldn't have achieved what we achieved. They say you're only as good as your squad and that's spot on.

I've got so much respect for David McGoldrick as well; he's a top player and a top man. A really good guy. He fully deserved the player of the year award, after coming on a free transfer! When Billy was injured towards the end of the season, Didzy really stepped up but he'd been incredible before that too. He went away with us with the Republic of Ireland and showed everyone how good he is.

He was brilliant all season; both out on the pitch and in the changing room. We had a great time partying after promotion because we put so much into the season and needed to let our hair down. It was great that we were allowed to do that, as well. As you've probably seen from the videos there was nothing bad in it; it was all fun and good craic. Everyone knows the line.

I didn't expect my *'Allez, Allez, Allez!'* song to blow up quite as much as it did, though. I came up with it a while before and couldn't keep it to myself! I just wanted to sing it for the lads, I didn't think I'd be getting signed by Jay Z for his record label. But it was great fun and everyone seemed to enjoy it. I saw Letterkenny IT win the Trench Cup earlier in the season and they put a video of their version up on Twitter. I thought: 'That looks class, it looks like they're having a good time!' So I was just bobbing along with it thinking of my own words: 'We've got Billy Sharp, he's a legend at the Lane...'

It all rolled off my tongue and in 10 minutes it was done. It was mad how it came to me and when I sang it to myself, all the lads were asking me what I was singing. I said: 'I can't tell you, I can't tell you' and I told them to wait until we went up. The last line's about being on a journey to the Premier League so I knew I had to wait until we were up. When it was all confirmed, I knew I had to sing it then!

It's good to have a bit of banter with your teammates after being in the trenches with them for the nine months before, and to be able to share that experience with good people is fantastic. A real once-in-a-lifetime feeling. We've gone down in history at this club as the class of 2019 and, hopefully, we'll all be back at Bramall Lane in 30 years, singing *'Allez, Allez, Allez!'* for the fans when we're old and grey!

chapter eight

An early Christmas gift
December 2018

On Pep Guardiola's desk at Manchester City's training ground, surrounded with dossiers on the opposition and other paraphernalia that goes with managing one of the best teams in world football, sits a well-worn book, its pages thumbed incessantly over the space of a decade or so. *'Lo Suficientemente Loco'* reads the title and its subject is *'El Loco'* himself, Marcelo Bielsa. Guardiola, like other top coaches including Diego Simeone and Mauricio Pochettino, has hailed the Argentinian and his methods as a formative influence on his own coaching career and went a step further when he hailed the former Chile, Marseille and Lazio boss as the best coach in the world.

There is little doubt that Bielsa was seen as something of a coup when he was persuaded to pack his bags and fly 7,000 miles to join Leeds United, a once-great club now floundering in English football's second tier. Leeds had finished 13th in the Championship the season before - three places below Chris Wilder's Sheffield United, who had also done the double over their rivals from up the M1 - and Bielsa was their 14th managerial change in seven years, with Neil Redfearn taking charge on four separate occasions. The former Argentinian national coach was identified as the man to change their fortunes and, after an intense 11-hour meeting at a Buenos Aires hotel, Leeds got their man.

Bielsa's attention to detail is now a thing of legend - eventually exploding into a national and international story - and when Leeds officials first made contact with him, Bielsa burned the midnight oil to trawl through tapes of their games. By the time they met face-to-face, he'd watched every minute of Leeds' previous season and as Phil Hay, the former chief football writer at the *Yorkshire Evening Post* recalls, the club's hierarchy asked Bielsa what he knew about the Championship. He responded by running them through the formations employed by *every* other club in the second tier. In the course of Bielsa's research, though, one approach stood out; the 3-5-2 system employed by Wilder at United, with overlapping centre-halves and attacking wing-backs and a No.10 who operates with a free role and licence to cause havoc.

"As I am not very familiar with English football I take many precautions before making an opinion. But if I was in a bar having a coffee with friends I would say that the Sheffield United head coach is someone with new ideas and I have seen very few people with these," Bielsa said, before December's clash between United and Leeds at Bramall Lane that *The Yorkshire Post* billed as a 'clash of the heavyweights'. "Head coaches look at colleagues to learn from them, and we want to learn new things. Not what everyone else is doing. The ideas of our next opponent deserve to be studied. I saw things in Sheffield United that I wanted to develop and I couldn't do it."

Football is just one facet of the rivalry between these two great Yorkshire cities, which emerged long before Bielsa laid down roots in Leeds. One Sheffield Wednesday fanzine is named *'War of the Monster Trucks'* - in 'homage' to *Yorkshire Television's* decision to air the 1986 TV special instead of the post-match celebrations that followed the Owls' 1991 League Cup final victory over Manchester United - and supporters of both clubs have long suspected a leaning, if not an all-out bias, towards events in West Yorkshire rather than the south.

Wilder was still a United player in 1989/90, when a thrilling promotion race saw both Leeds and the Blades promoted to the top flight. "Calendar or Look North were all 'Leeds this and Leeds that' before adding: 'Oh, by the way, Sheffield United went up as well," Wilder said. "That's how it is. Leeds always seems to be regarded as the centre of Yorkshire and Sheffield always seems to be regarded as being in Leeds' shadow." Largely thanks to a well-orchestrated public relations drive, aimed at winning hearts and minds, Leeds has managed to establish itself as a powerhouse of the north, while Sheffield has threatened to be left behind.

Not in everyone's eyes, though. "I'm proud to be from Sheffield," said Billy Sharp, the United skipper and former Leeds striker. "I'm proud to be a Unitedite, but I'm proud of the whole place as well. I read something Pete McKee wrote on Twitter, about being in a restaurant in London and noticing all the cutlery was made in Sheffield. Steel is a huge part of our history here and I think that hard-working, down-to-earth background has shaped our personalities. There's an honesty about Sheffield and I think that's one of the things that makes it so attractive. Lots of my old teammates have moved here and never left. There's a friendliness about Sheffield and its identity is unique."

Sharp was thankful to Leeds for giving him the chance to return 'home' to Bramall Lane, for a third spell, in 2015 but also has personal gratitude to the city. In 2011 - when his newborn son, Luey, passed away from gastroschisis at just two days old - Sharp and his wife Jade were supported by Martin House, a hospice for children with life-limiting conditions based in Wetherby. "They were absolutely brilliant for us at the time," Sharp added.

"They're like Bluebell Wood here in Sheffield and also do wonderful, really important work. Sheffield and Leeds are completely different places, with different vibes. When you're in Sheffield, you know you're in Sheffield. In other big cities, you could be anywhere in the world. I don't think Sheffield gets the credit it deserves. Where I live, I'm 10 minutes from the city centre and 10 minutes from the countryside. You don't get that anywhere else. People here know what we've got going for us and I'll always shout about it."

United also had the chance to strike a blow for the city in the early exchanges of what was shaping up to be an intriguing battle for promotion with Leeds, and were buoyed by having done so twice the season before. Particularly in the game at Elland Road, which United won 2-1, Wilder and his staff suspected that Leeds had something of a soft centre and looked to exploit it, before young David Brooks scored a late winner. Un-

der Bielsa, though, Leeds were a much more formidable proposition and a clip of their game against Wigan early in his tenure,
which went viral, highlighted why. Wigan's Josh Windass was
sent clear one-on-one against defender Liam Cooper when a
corner was cleared. But before Windass could even gather his
thoughts, half-a-dozen Leeds players had sprinted back to snuff
out any danger.

While there was no danger of Wilder following Bielsa's lead
and sitting on an upside-down bucket in his technical area -
"the only bucket our manager would be interested in would
be the other way round, with ice and some beers in it," one
member of United's staff joked - it was clear that the respect
Bielsa had for the United manager was reciprocated. "You look
at our division and you can see why people watch it," Wilder
said. "You go from an Argentinian great to a lad who has been
a physio at Rotherham [Paul Warne] to a lad who has won God
knows how many Premier League titles [Frank Lampard]. But
they're all bringing great things to the table. We don't take this
division for granted. It's a fantastic division and this game is one
we are really looking forward to."

After the talking stopped, the main event largely lived up to
the hype; even if it was eventually settled by a moment of madness. Young goalkeepers Henderson and Bailey Peacock-Farrell
were at their best to keep out Aapo Halme and Mateusz Klich
and David McGoldrick and Sharp respectively, but the decisive
moment came late on when Pablo Hernandez tapped home
into an empty net, after Henderson had badly underhit a pass
straight to the feet of Leeds' Jack Clarke. United couldn't get
back into the game - Conor Washington coming closest when
he hit the bar with a late overhead effort - but it was both noticeable and commendable that Henderson did not attempt to
hide after his error, instead facing all four sides of Bramall Lane
and holding his hands up, before walking off the pitch with his
head high.

The goalkeeper felt his earlier save, from Leeds sub Halme's
deflected effort, was one of his best of the season but admits
that, because of his error, it is destined to be forgotten about.

"It's so important, especially as a goalkeeper, to find that level of consistency," Henderson said. "I'd say I conceded two goals all season from mistakes, which isn't bad from 46 games. But from the outside, all I see on Twitter is: 'Remember the mistakes against Leeds and Villa?' That's why you've got to be so mentally tough because the bad stuff always sticks in people's minds. David Seaman once said that no matter how many saves you make, if you let one through your hands everyone will come for you, because football fans are fickle. To be fair, our fans were excellent all season, which is why I loved it throughout. I built up a good rapport with them and hopefully, they were impressed with my performances."

Henderson returned to the home dressing room and apologised to his teammates for the error. "I told them I didn't mean to do it and every single one said 'Deano, you've been brilliant. Don't worry about it.' That's when I thought 'these are real boys, these have got my back'. That's what you need at times like that, the boys to give you a boost. There was only one time in the season that I didn't get that, away at Villa, but I didn't help myself to be honest. Luckily we had our Christmas do in London on the night of the Leeds game so I'd forgotten about it within about two hours, and got it out of my system. At the end of the day, and I don't mean this to sound wrong, but I was the best player on the pitch that day. I saved so many shots yet the mistake is all that's remembered. That's the life of a goalkeeper, though."

Not for the last time in the season, Henderson bounced back from the disappointment against Leeds to keep a clean sheet in United's next game, away at Reading. Henderson remembers Darren Ward, United's goalkeeping coach, telling him not to worry "about last week" and the goalkeeper asking "Why, what happened?" The error against Leeds, the goalkeeper said, was irrelevant and on a bitterly cold evening at a sparsely-populated Madejski Stadium, United scored twice in the last seven minutes to take three points - a lively end to an otherwise-tepid game that someone at Sky Sports, in their wisdom, thought would be a good pick for live broadcast.

Although Washington and McGoldrick both had earlier efforts ruled out for offside in the first half, some harsh half-time words were required to get United going; albeit from an unfamiliar source. Alan Knill, United's No.2 and something of a 'gentle giant', read the riot act in the away dressing room at the Madejski after Wilder simply shot his players a look of displeasure. His charges also had some heated words with each other during the break and the desired result was eventually achieved, laying to rest a mini-hoodoo of only three wins from 18 televised Championship games since United's promotion from League One.

A more pressing concern, though, was United's record against the rest of the Championship's top-six teams, which stood at an unhealthy one win and four defeats after they lost 2-1 at home to West Bromwich Albion on December 14. With the January transfer window looming large, the lack of squad depth at Bramall Lane was highlighted when Leon Clarke was ruled out with injury and Tyler Smith, a young striker recently recalled from a loan spell in the National League with Barrow, was named on the bench against the recently-relegated Baggies - who had four full England internationals in their starting 11.

Harvey Barnes, who will surely join that select band to have played international football in the future, ran the show for Albion and after McGoldrick had put United ahead with a smart finish, goals from Gareth Barry and Kieran Gibbs - with 823 Premier League appearances between them - sucked the belief out of United. "For the first half an hour or so, we dominated a really good side and should have been possibly two or three up. We caused them a lot of problems," Wilder said afterwards. "We made some really poor decisions and just allowed them a foothold in the game by giving the ball away really cheaply.

"In the second half, they were the dominant team. They were physically stronger. We had our moments but we still made some really poor decisions with the ball. I always thought we'd do well to get something out of the game. You've got to kill the game off. We move the ball about really well, but we haven't got that decisive, cutting edge. I'm just disappointed in the performance of the players. The mentality of the group was flat.

"When it comes to top-end Championship football we have an inability to be clinical at big moments. It is hurting us this year. We should have been out of sight against Stoke and Sheffield Wednesday, and should have got something from a tight game against Leeds. We have to keep working and keep going. But this is a story that has been happening for quite a while. Maybe we have hit a bit of a ceiling. The only way they improve it is by actions, not words.

"I know how to get to the next level, the coaching staff know how to get to the next level. Have we got the players to do that? It's a difficult question to answer because I do not want to kill my players. They have done fantastically well. Whether the changing room needs a lift or just to strengthen the squad, we need a little bit more in certain areas. We are an attractive proposition to players. Hopefully we can keep this position going into January to make us even more attractive."

Whether it was a coded message about his January plans, a psychological challenge to his players or just raw, unfiltered honesty - or even a mixture of all three - Wilder didn't mix his words, before gathering his players for an impromptu chat at their Shirecliffe training base. The question he asked them was a simple one: do we want to be contenders or pretenders? Wilder remembers his query raising a few chuckles - Enda Stevens said it made him think of the old TV show Gladiators - but the message was deadly serious. Reading were one example highlighted by Wilder. In 2017, they were a penalty kick away from winning the play-off final but, 18 months later, were battling relegation; showing that the opportunity to reach the Premier League, for any club, would not be on offer indefinitely.

United went into Christmas on the back of a point from the long trip to Ipswich Town's Portman Road - Sharp's 12th goal of the season equalising against the relegation-threatened hosts - before a real Boxing Day cracker saw them take all three against Derby County, in one of the most memorable games of the campaign at an absolutely rocking Bramall Lane. After a breathless start against Frank Lampard's men Scott Carson, the former England goalkeeper, denied Sharp with a superb save from Enda Stevens' cross before, at the other end, Baldock was forced to clear off his own goalline after Harry Wilson had rounded Henderson.

Sharp eventually found the breakthrough when he headed Jack O'Connell's centre past the despairing Carson - celebrating with a round-stomach gesture aimed at the Derby fans who had previously chanted about his weight - but the game's flashpoint came in the second half, when on-loan Chelsea defender Fikayo Tomori made a complete mess of his attempted header back to his goalkeeper and then absolutely flattened McGoldrick inside the penalty area. McGoldrick was about to tap the ball into an empty net and a clearer penalty and red card - even under the new laws of denying a goalscoring opportunity - hadn't been seen all season to that point.

The only person inside Bramall Lane who seemed to think otherwise was referee Geoff Eltringham, who inexplicably waved away the appeals. That decision raised the volume inside the ground by a few notches, but it exploded moments later when Wilson stuck a stunning free-kick into the top corner of Henderson's goal, to level the scores.

Suddenly, the game erupted. United's manager went toe-to-toe with Lampard on the touchline, as chants of 'Wilder, knock him out' rained down from the stands, and a melee involving players from both sides took place in United's goalmouth. "Their players came steaming in and tried to kick off, so we kicked off," defender John Egan recalled.

"Something switched in our heads, I think, and we just became more aggressive and angry and simply blew them away. I remember a few of their lads complaining to the referee, saying: 'We just want to play football'. They were getting bullied. A few lads started on me in the goalmouth and Didzy ran from the halfway line to back me up, so fair play to him. Not that I needed him! But seriously, that day we really switched and it was a bit of a turning point for us. Little did we know at the time how important that little scramble would turn out to be."

While United's supporters continued to taunt Lampard - one chant comparing him, rather unfavourably, with former England teammate Steven Gerrard - the Blades players set about Derby with similar levels of frenzy on the pitch, and the noise inside Bramall Lane intensified again when United went back in front. John Fleck's diving header sent McGoldrick clear of the hapless Tomori again and this time, the Chelsea loanee couldn't even get close enough to foul him before McGoldrick lobbed Carson once more and watched the ball nestle neatly in the net at the Kop end.

United grabbed a third when Egan headed the ball across goal for Clarke to finish via a deflection - the defender taking a whack to the face in the celebration for good measure - and Wilder's popular decision to let his players have Christmas Day morning and afternoon with their families, before training in the evening, had been more than vindicated.

After the game, the United manager later described his touchline spat with Lampard as "nothing, just two passionate people and two passionate teams who wanted to win" and added: "I've got no problems with him whatsoever. That's the way football is at times. It happens. On the penalty, I've seen two angles so far and, if someone is about to head the ball into an open goal and then falls over, you have to ask yourself why.

"Players in those situations don't do that. The crowd really ramped it up and got right behind the lads. We don't want Bramall Lane to be an easy place to come. And out there, it certainly wasn't. It was a proper Sheffield United performance and a proper Sheffield United atmosphere.

"There's been a lot of noise and nonsense about how we are going to fall away. But we deserved that win, we deserve to be where we are and hopefully, it goes some way towards showing that talk up for what it is. I heard all the stuff about how we couldn't beat another club who were up there with us, even though we are where we are. Derby are a damn good side and, well, we've just done that. They have some really good players and their goal was exceptional. We've been speaking in the dressing room and we'd have needed a wall 12 feet high to keep it out. But we answered the question. The key now is to keep driving it forward." Wilder's men did just that in their final commitment of 2018, although they didn't have it all their own way against Blackburn Rovers on an afternoon that wasn't quite as comfortable as the 3-0 scoreline suggested. On another indifferent day for officials, Premier League referee Anthony Taylor sent off Chris Basham for two bookings - the second for handball after an extremely harsh first, for a tackle on Harrison Reed which was barely even a foul. Again, United's supporters seized on what they perceived as poor decision-making from the official and, after Charlie Mulgrew and Stevens had hit the post for either side, Bramall Lane was rocking once more.

Referee Taylor's decision to show Rovers' Richie Smallwood a straight red - for a shocker of a challenge on Sharp, which also poleaxed his teammate Elliott Bennett in the follow-through - was much more straightforward. And moments later, with just 17 minutes of normal time remaining, Sharp opened the scoring with a composed and patient left-footed finish, after former United target Darragh Lenihan had failed to deal with McGoldrick's header. Sharp then added a second, a well-struck volley from Stevens' excellent pass, to move joint top, level with old pal Rickie Lambert, in the list of English football goalscorers since the turn of the millennium before McGoldrick added a third, chesting home John Fleck's cross from close range.

Sharp admitted afterwards, when he faced the media, that he would have played every moment of his career at United if he could. "I'd have loved to have done that," he said. "I had to go away a couple of times to benefit myself but I feel as if I've come back at exactly the right time. I feel as fit and as strong as ever and I feel I can keep going for some time yet. I've equalled what Rickie did, so hopefully, he doesn't come out of retirement. He was a goal machine, wasn't he? Luckily he's probably enjoyed too many beers to come back now! But seriously, although it's obviously great for me personally, I really just want to achieve something for Sheffield United. I need to make sure I now score even more goals and keep doing my job for my team."

Out of this world
by Andrew Senior

December 20, 2018. Zhezkazgan, Kazakhstan. At 0502 GMT
the Soyuz MS-09 space capsule touched down on the snow-
covered steppe. The crew on board were returning from 197
days on board the International Space Station. Spacewalks,
satellite launches, a daring operation to patch up a hole in the
capsule's orbital module and hundreds of scientific experiments
conducted that would gift a greater understanding of the uni-
verse to future generations.

It all paled though, at the sight of the enormous parachute
ballooning gracefully above the capsule, as it completed its final
descent. It was red and white. They were Blades. There could
be no other explanation, and these brave astronauts had been
facing the prospect of trying to follow Sheffield United's crucial
Christmas and new-year fixtures while orbiting the planet at
17,500 miles per hour. As I said in my email to NASA, their decision to return to earth was an inspiration to Blades supporters
everywhere.

It was a shame then that the first result following touchdown
was a one-all draw with bottom-of-the-table Ipswich. In fact, on
paper alone, December was a month of mixed results, including two home defeats by fellow promotion-chasers, Leeds and
West Brom. But a more probing analysis reveals the grit and
determination that would eventually lead us to the stratospheric
heights of second place and automatic promotion. December
1, 2018. Sheffield, England. Approximately 1319 GMT. At that
point, Leeds had not won at Bramall Lane since April 26, 1992.
That distant victory was as big as it gets, securing the top title in
English football for our Yorkshire rivals. Since then, there's been
chafing with Leeds during other significant races for glory.

Both teams won promotion to the top flight in the 1989/90
season, with Leeds beating us to top spot on goal difference.
And our next promotion from the Championship in 2006 came
as Leeds faded (Aah, those two words; read them again if you

like), losing their winning ways for much of March and April of that year. Come 2018/19, the same Race for Space was again being fought. Space in the English Premier League. As the table stood at kick off on December 1 – and indeed for much of the game - we were fourth and Leeds were second, separated by two tightly-stretched points. It was a simple equation. We would usurp Leeds with a victory. Unsurprisingly, both managers were desperate for the win.

Chris Wilder and 'Loco' Marcelo Bielsa come from two very different footballing backgrounds, the latter experiencing international football while the former tasted non-league. During Wilder's time at Northampton Town (2014-16), Bielsa managed Atletico Madrid, Marseille and Lazio. But as equals at the top of the Championship, both have proved highly creative, innovative and competitive. And both have voiced mutual appreciation throughout the season. Wilder has spoken of Bielsa's stature and his massive influence on the Championship, describing him as "a breath of fresh air to the division" and, when praising Bielsa's sportsmanship during the bizarre and chaotic last game between Leeds and Villa, "a true football man". Wilder even spoke with admiration about Bielsa's handling of the Spygate 'scandal'.

For his part, Bielsa considered United as the team from whom he had learned the most during the 2018/19 season, praising our new style of play and the clear evolution of our players. The game was an energetic encounter, ultimately decided, not on "a bit of magic or taking a chance", to borrow Wilder's words, but on a mistake. We were dominant. Leeds were on the back foot. But we missed some big chances and when Deano failed to deal adequately with John Egan's overhit backpass in the 82nd minute, Leeds pounced. Even so, after the game, Bielsa recognised that his team had faced a "serious opponent", and had been forced to defend often and played too much long ball. In his pre-match comments at the return fixture in March, he conceded that Leeds probably hadn't deserved the victory.

Come the end of the season – and it might have been the drink talking – Wilder's inner Blade was unleashed. "A lot of muppets from Leeds talking about precious honours…they got beat seven times since Christmas," he said. "We've been beaten once." That's part of the joy of watching Wilder in charge at United: the respect he commands as manager held in perfect balance with a genuine supporter mentality. The rivalry will, without a doubt, continue way beyond the 2018/19 season. But for now, Yorkshire is ours.

Back to December. December 14, to be specific. There's nothing like a wintertime Friday night fixture. Bright lights and Bovril at Beautiful Downtown Bramall Lane. This time we were separated from our opponents, West Brom, by just a single point. Initially the game looked as if it would be a big statement in our promotion push. As against Leeds, we started strongly, "flying down the flanks" according to the Baggies' Gareth Barry. They struggled to cope and we took an early lead in the 12th minute through a quick counterattacking manoeuvre. But equalising just before half-time - against the run of play - gave West Brom the momentum as the second half started. They grew into the game, became the stronger team and we threw it away. A hugely disappointing outcome.

Wilder was characteristically candid and by contrast, Darren Moore said: "It's always difficult to come to Bramall Lane with the passionate support they've got [presumably he had in mind here the crew of the Soyuz MS-09] but we got to grips with the game… I knew it was going to be a hard task tonight but each and every single one of them rose to the challenge." It was a difficult moment and another twist at the top of the table. The result took West Brom above us, into third place, and condemned us to a third home league game without a win ahead of the draw with Ipswich.

But this squad of players were never to be written off. Wilder knew it and fielded an unchanged side for a third successive match when we played Derby, despite the results in our previous two games. And we knew it. Nearly 29,000 of us gathered on Boxing Day to witness the most significant result of December, and possibly of the season - arguably the start of our promotion run. Yet another strong start, coming close to scoring several times in the opening 10 minutes. Another equaliser came against the run of play, when Harry Wilson cancelled out Billy Sharp's opener, by another team separated from us by a single point.

But this time our response was to dig in, stay positive and pick up the pace, while Derby fell away. It became an end-to-end exchange with tempers flaring (eight yellow cards were shown and there'd already been a fight in Henderson's goal following the equaliser). In the 64th minute, the ever-composed David McGoldrick was on hand to lob in beautifully from John Fleck's diving midfield header and restore our lead. On the Kop, there was a collective observation that the Derby fans were no longer bouncing. Twenty minutes later yet another head, this time belonging to Leon Clarke, rose to direct the ball in at the far post and secure victory. On the Kop, pandemonium.

"There's been a lot of noise and nonsense talked about us," said an animated Wilder after the game, "but I keep telling the players to go out and show everybody what we're all about and I think we did that this afternoon. We jumped all over them in the second half. The energy levels and performance levels were up there and the support they received was amazing." [Again, the crew of the Soyuz MS-09 come immediately to mind.] Our final game of the month against Blackburn was brushed aside by EFL on Quest with 30 seconds of highlights, maybe because the match delivered the expected result and there was more excitement to be found in a seven-goal thriller between Norwich and Derby. But it was a rewarding game to watch live, wallowing in the pits before turning to deliver a thrilling crescendo that demolished the opposition.

Wilder rightly described the first half as a "grind for us". It was frustrating and lacking and Blackburn were arguably the better side. When Chris Basham was dismissed for a second yellow card - which, as with the first, seemed harsh - it looked as if we would be hanging on for 0-0 and a precious point. For 20 minutes we did. Then Blackburn themselves had a man sent off (not harsh at all - a two-footed tackle on Sharp), and our fight to stay in the game paid dividends. In the space of nine pulsating minutes, Blackburn were well and truly grounded, with goals from Sharp (lift-off), Sharp again (escape velocity) and McGoldrick (enter orbit). Another three points in the proverbial.

December was a month of spills and thrills but the driving desire to succeed exhibited throughout would continue for the rest of the season: imperfect at times but never at the expense of our growing momentum. With that most beautiful of gifts, hindsight, we can look back on December 2018 and enjoy the pleasing counterpoints that were to come.

February saw us win away at the Hawthorns, March the same at Elland Road. April brought a comfortable win against Ipswich, all but sealing the promotion deal. After a 12-year absence from top-flight football, surely the entire planet was following our progress? How that would not be the case is unfathomable to me. But NASA never responded to my email. And on closer examination the parachute might actually have been orange and white.

My fairytale turnaround
by David McGoldrick

Not many people know this but after growing up in Nottingham, I'm actually a Notts County fan rather than supporting Forest. I came through County's academy so I've got a small idea how Billy Sharp feels about playing for his hometown club, although he's achieved far more at his club than I did at mine. To take your own club from League One into the Premier League in the space of three seasons is fairytale stuff, and it's an experience both the gaffer and Billy have tasted. That didn't make beating Derby on Boxing Day any less sweet, though. They did us at their place earlier in the season and we knew it would be tough, but I thought we played well to take the lead before Harry Wilson scored a 'worldie' of a free-kick to equalise for them.

In previous seasons we might have gone under but we went back and scored a second and then a third to kill the game off. It was a key time in the season and we were having trouble back then with beating teams in and around us in the top six, and I think that was the first time we beat one of them. Looking back it could have been a pivotal moment in the season and the atmosphere was ridiculous, to be honest. I remember when I scored our second, lobbing it home from John Fleck's header, the place was absolutely rocking. It's still one of the best atmospheres I've seen at the Lane and there's no better feeling in football.

It feels incredible to be a Premier League player finally, after spending the majority of my career playing in the Championship. I almost made the move to the top-flight before, though, when I was at Ipswich Town and Leicester City tried to sign me. Two days before deadline day I got the call to say a bid had been made for me out of nowhere. I think £3million got knocked back and then it went to £5million; that got knocked back and it went up to £7million. Mick McCarthy thought the deal would get done and then I think Leicester changed their mind, or the owners couldn't agree some final figures. So it fell through, and they went for someone else.

It was a disappointment because I wanted to play in the Premier League, it was close to my home in Nottingham and one of my good mates in football, Wes Morgan, was there at the time. But it wasn't meant to be, I settled down and signed a new deal at Ipswich. But I can't lie, it was difficult to take. I couldn't sleep and I was snappy with my family. The next week I was watching Leicester on Match of the Day and the year after, they won the Premier League! You always look back and think: 'What if'. We'd agreed the contract I'd sign, with the Premier League wages, and the whole thing was hard to digest. I wasn't eating or sleeping properly for about a week.

Something like that can change your whole life, and not just because of the money. Moving home and becoming a Premier League player should mean that, wherever you move after that, you should at least get a move to a top Championship side. All's well that ends well, though, and I ended up at a top Championship side eventually in Sheffield United. Even then, it wasn't straightforward. I'd got a bit of a reputation for being 'injury-prone' that wasn't really based on anything and there was a perception that it was because I was commuting to Ipswich every day from Nottingham. That wasn't true.

I had a place down there anyway, and the type of injuries I picked up didn't come from driving. I damaged a medial ligament in a tackle and then a player, from Sheffield Wednesday actually, studded me in my groin so I had to have surgery the next day. Nothing at all to do with commuting! I understand it, though. It's football and people look for excuses. But it's easy to get a reputation in football when people always have things to say. You have to be a strong man to knock them away and not let it affect you.

When Mick's time at Ipswich came to an end he said he'd leave it for the next manager to decide on my future, and Paul Hurst told me I wasn't for him. He's since said that I wasn't on his list but I've got the texts from him saying I was free to find another club. So everything was on the line for me really. It was quite late when Paul told me he was releasing me so straight-away I was looking for other clubs, hoping something would come up. I was doing a bit of rehab at St George's Park at the time on one of my injuries, which kept me focused, and I went away on holiday to Dubai with the family. The kids love it there and want to go every year, so I have to save up for the rest of the year!

But that's when I started to get a bit worried, when you see people on social media going back to pre-season training and I still didn't have a club. On holiday, I was constantly looking at my phone, thinking: 'What's happening?' But I always knew a call would come, and it was more a case of when rather than if. It was a perfect fit when a big club like United came calling. I knew all about the traditions of the club and the football they played, and I knew the manager would suit me down to the ground. It's safe to say it worked out quite well!

I also knew a few lads already, like Kieron Freeman. All season I drove Kez in from Nottingham, because he's lazy and hasn't got a driving licence yet, so I'm his chauffeur and have to look after him! I actually played at Bramall Lane the season before when he hurt his knee, and I remember speaking to him when he was on the floor and seeing his knee where it shouldn't have been. A lot of people were squeamish and couldn't look.

Before the call came from United, telling me to bring my boots on Monday morning, I'd been trying to keep fit on my own, but it's quite hard when you get tired and there's no-one there to push you on. My experience told me what I had to do. I spoke to a few people about going to United and they said that with what I'd done in the past, I didn't have to go on trial and to wait. But I knew I had to back myself. I said: 'No, I'll go in and show them that they should sign me'. I wanted to prove that I am a good striker so, from day one, I just tried to be myself. And the rest is history, really!

It's funny to look back on now but there were some dark times during the summer. It's not all about turning up at 3pm on a Saturday as a footballer and it's not all amazing. There are some dark times. But everyone has a mortgage, kids and bills to pay for and everyone has a story. I had to go and get a contract and I'm delighted it worked out. To be fair, I think United knew all about my ability but it was just a case of proving my fitness. The gaffer said to me that all he wanted me to do is run around and compete, put myself about and when I get the ball, do my thing.

He said the football would take care of itself if I put the work in. He took a liking to me and I managed to get a deal. It was a bit of a crazy week when I did sign. I played two friendlies, then signed in midweek, pitched up against Inter Milan that night, and scored! It was a whirlwind week I won't forget. I look back and wonder what the worrying was about. I was scoring against Inter and 10 days before, I didn't have a club!

That's football though, it's a game of ups and downs. It's perhaps easy to say now but I believed we could do something special as soon as I came in, and saw the amount of talent we had. I didn't shout about it at the time, but I honestly believed. I know the league really well and I knew we had a good chance to have a push. Did I think we'd be battling for the top-two? I honestly thought we'd be around there, with the staff and players we had and the signings the gaffer had made. The football we play is so different from any other team and so many can't cope with it. It was a crazy season but a pleasure to be a part of it.

Early on in training, for a few weeks, it was almost like 'wow, what's happening here? Where's everyone gone? Where's my centre-half going?' But I got to grips with it pretty quickly and I really enjoy it, with this set of lads. At some clubs, there are little cliques here and there in the corner of the dressing room, but everyone is friends here. Some really good players, too. Players who maybe should have done more in their careers, but the manager is getting the best out of them now.

We know we could compete in games through hard work and desire but you need some talent too, and we've shown that this season. My story is an interesting one, I guess, but everyone here has one. A few of the boys have played non-league, or been released by this club or that club. It fosters a siege mentality and we're a perfect group, really. People may have written me off when they saw that I'd signed, and I understand that.

The club was looking at some multi-million-pound signings at the time and every fan wants to see that. Then they see a guy coming in on trial and think: 'Where's the ambition?' I knew I had a point to prove. I had to score goals and perform. I stuck with it and the fans have taken to me, and I've definitely taken to them.

I fully understood some frustration in signing me but at the same time, I never got one bit of stick. As soon as I played they were cheering for me so I knew I had to perform to keep them cheering for me. It's down to me and me alone to prove people wrong; not just at this club but all around England.

Playing such a big part in the season in terms of games, and staying injury-free; without a doubt, it's been the highlight of my career. To top that off with a promotion, with this set of lads that I hang around with every day... it couldn't have gone any better. It's credit to the staff and physios here, the conditioning work you do every day as a player. Everyone always moans

Danny Hall

Jeni Parker

▲ Dean Henderson impressed on loan from Manchester United - and forged a bond with young fan Harri Parker

David Steer

Josh Corker

▲ Henderson joined in the celebrations after a late, vital victory over promotion rivals Norwich

▲ United worked as hard as ever in pre-season in Portugal - but were allowed to let their hair down

Sportimage

▲ Jack O'Connell's header got United underway in their 4-1 demolition of Aston Villa at Bramall Lane

Nick Davis

▲ Is there any finer sight than the Lane, in the sunshine? United found the pot of goal at the end of the season

▲ A strong United team faced Sheffield FC in the international break, in Matt Roney's testimonial   *Richard Markham*

▲ The Blades recovered well from going behind early on at Derby, but lost 2-1   *Emma Keeling*

▲ United fans saluted their players after a battling 1-0 home win over Middlesbrough   *Corbin Shaw*

▲ A dejected Billy Sharp could only watch from the bench as United capitulate away at Aston Villa

▲ Sharp's 'Mankind' celebration made the headlines - with George Baldock a willing participant

▲ Young Louie Sparks, aged 10, was United's mascot away at Ipswich and posed for a picture with Chris Wilder, his trusted lieutenant Alan Knill, goalkeeping coach Darren Ward, analyst Mikey Allen and coach Nicky Travis

▲ The two derbies against Wednesday finished goalless, but Bramall Lane was packed for the home leg

▲ Basham's arriving! One of the iconic photos of the promotion season, after Basham's winner at Leeds

▲ The press pack gathered to hear Wilder's thoughts ahead of the Steel City Derby against Wednesday

▲ United's class of 2019, featuring some interesting facials from striker Gary Madine *Bayliss Travel*

▲ John Fleck, United's Scottish hero, finally received a long-overdue call-up to the national squad *Ian Manewell*

▲ United's Kop in fine voice, with skipper Sharp's flag in the background *Mark Percival*

▲ Allez, Allez, Allez! John Egan debuted his
new song at United's player of the year awards

▼ Henderson, Sharp and Ollie Norwood were all
smiles before being introduced to the crowd

All photos by Glenn Ashley Photography

▲ Sharp showed his appreciation for assistant manager Knill, while Mark Duffy embraced teammate Fleck

▲ Limbs! The aftermath of United's first goal, in a crucial away victory at Hull City

▲ Young Luca Russell watched his heroes all-but secure promotion against Ipswich Town

▲ An explosion of joy, beer and Kean Bryan's hair greeted official confirmation that United had been promoted

▲ An emotional Wilder saluted United's travelling fans on the final day at Stoke, in trademark fashion

▲ United's players had to crowd surf off the team coach after returning to Bramall Lane from Stoke

▲ Duffy - a popular man amongst Blades fans!

▲ Gary Brunt, right, flew back from Cyprus to watch the Ipswich game with his son, Shaun

▲ Richard Stearman made the most of the celebrations

▲ Wilder took in all the scenes at Bramall
Lane from the front of United's team coach

▲ Thousands of Blades fans gathered in the
stadium car park to welcome home their heroes

▲ The party continued in The Clubhouse pub on London Road

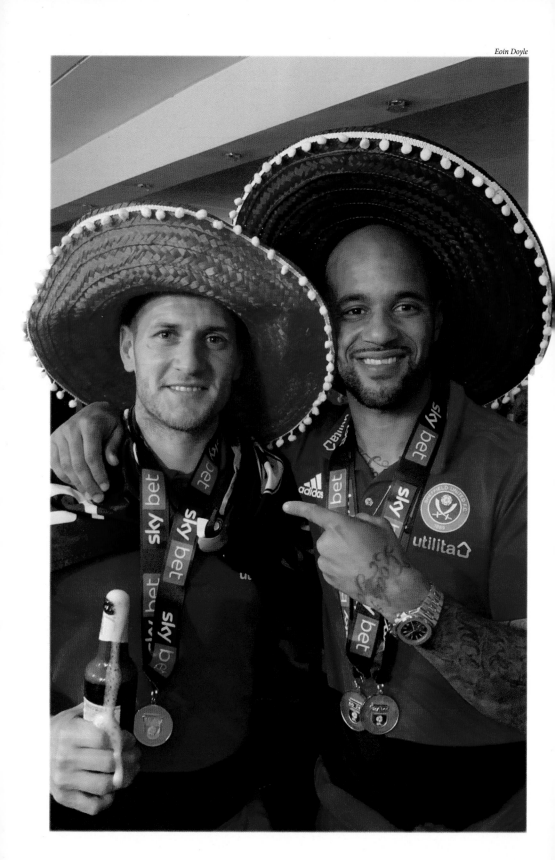

Eoin Doyle

Richard Markham

◄ Sharp and David McGoldrick scored 39 goals between them - not bad for supposed 'journeymen'

▲ Boyhood Blades fans Sharp and Wilder drank in every moment of the celebrations

Sportimage

▲ Chris the Redeemer? Wilder soaked up the acclaim outside the Town Hall - as well he should!

Eoin Doyle

▲ Sharp was handed the trophy by legend and director
Tony Currie in the Bramall Lane home dressing room

Eoin Doyle

▲ Wilder was named the LMA's manager of the
year at the end of the season, receiving the award
from Sir Alex Ferguson and Gareth Southgate

Billy Sharp

▲ United celebrated their promotion with a trip to Las Vegas, before the hard work in the Premier League began

about going into the gym and doing all that, but I've reaped the rewards this season. I just hope we can all carry it on in the Premier League, which should suit our technical players.

I think it'll suit me as well. You have to have that confidence; you can't go into games being scared and we have to do what we're good at, which I think we'll do. Whatever happens, it's been special and fans will look back in years to come and hold this group close to their hearts. I hope that's the case with me, because it's been a privilege to play for this club and be so successful.

chapter nine

The 'magic' of the FA Cup

January 2019

Planning for one of the most important transfer windows in Sheffield United's recent history had begun in earnest even before the last one, at the beginning of the 2018/19 season, had slammed tightly shut. United's first move in the market was agreed before the market officially reopened for business and its origins stretched back even further, to their clash with Nottingham Forest the season previous. By late September 2018, United had taken to life in the Championship incredibly well after promotion from League One and they travelled to the City Ground on the back of six victories in their last seven games, including a memorable and historic one over city rivals Wednesday at Hillsborough.

But despite going ahead early on through John Lundstram's shot, United surrendered their lead when Jason Cummings fired home before Kieran Dowell, a young forward on loan from Everton, hit Forest's winner. Despite United's defeat, Dowell's all-round display - capped by his impressive volley after the ball had landed fortuitously in his path - made an impression on Chris Wilder and his coaching staff, and a mental note was made. When United lost David Brooks to AFC Bournemouth in the summer, Wilder approached Everton with a view to taking Dowell on loan but he was knocked back; Marco Silva, the newly-appointed boss at Goodison Park, wanted to take a good look at the youngster in pre-season.

The landscape on Merseyside then shifted a little when Silva signed Brazilian international duo Bernard and Richarlison, sanctioning a deal for the latter which might rise to £50million, and United returned with another loan proposal. By that point, Dowell had made just two senior appearances for the Toffees that season, both in the EFL Cup, so a temporary transfer was agreed. The work that went into Dowell's signing was indicative of the painstaking attention to detail United pay to potential signings.

Wilder, assistant Alan Knill and head of recruitment Paul Mitchell ran the rule over both Dowell's attitude and ability by making a top-secret trip to Edinburgh to watch him in action for England's U21s against Scotland. They then sought character references from contacts in the game, including Mark Warburton, the former Forest manager, and England U21 boss Aidy Boothroyd. A number of United's second-tier rivals also sought Dowell's signature in January - Aston Villa reportedly had a £6m bid rejected - but the player was swayed towards United by the memories of their display at the City Ground the season previous, and by watching their performances on Sky Sports during the first half of 2018/19.

The Liverpudlian felt United and Wolves, who romped to the league title in 2017/18, played the best football in the division during his time at Forest and, as a boyhood Everton fan, was naturally drawn towards a club with a fierce inner-city rivalry. Dowell did his homework on United as well, canvassing the opinions of Phil Jagielka and Dominic Calvert-Lewin, who both swapped the red and white of United for Everton blue. "Both Jags and Dom are top lads," Dowell said. "So, when I heard them talking about United the way they do, I knew it was somewhere that would be good for me."

Dowell, possibly one of the oldest-looking 21-year-olds on the football circuit, also shows a maturity beyond his tender years when he crosses the white line of a football pitch and it was that experience of a previous loan that persuaded Wilder and Co. to make the move for him, after the loan of another young prospect from Merseyside, Ben Woodburn, proved less than successful. Woodburn featured only eight times for the Blades after arriving to some fanfare in the summer and returned quietly to Liverpool in January.

But, despite suggestions to the contrary, Wilder had no complaints about the attitude of the youngster, citing Mark Duffy's form as a contributing factor to Woodburn's lack of game time.

"It was his first loan, as well, and these things happen," Wilder said. "I've got to say that Jürgen Klopp was absolutely spot on about it. We were doing really well and Ben found it a struggle to get in the side. Jürgen understands and wasn't critical of Sheffield United at all. There was a lot of nonsense talked about it being a poor signing for us, or a poor choice from Ben to come to us… it just didn't work out as we'd have liked. But a lot of factors go into that.

"Ben had done really well early in his career and was being compared with Mason Mount and Harry Wilson, with people forgetting that Wilson had spells at Crewe and Hull and Mount spent time on loan in Holland, playing football. Ben was a bit younger, too. There was nothing wrong with his attitude and he played some little cameos, but the form of Duff and David McGoldrick kept him out. We played three midfielders at times as well. It'll be a great learning experience for him and one that no doubt he'll learn from."

There was particular irony in the fact that Duffy, a huge Liverpool fan, kept one of the Kop's brightest young prospects out of the United side but he, too, believed that the teenager would benefit from the experience of his time at the Lane and become a better player for it. Duffy himself is no stranger to the trials and tribulations of professional football after being released by the Reds as a youngster, almost giving up the game before working his way back up from non-league. Now, he was enjoying arguably the best spell of his career as United looked to continue their push for promotion, after being set a target by their manager to be within touching distance of the league's top sides around the festive period.

And that man Duffy was instrumental again on New Year's Day, as he helped to orchestrate an eye-catching 3-0 win over Wigan Athletic at the DW Stadium, to move United up to third and within four points of leaders Leeds United. But it was a rare day of individual focus for United as, after goals from David McGoldrick and Duffy had put the Blades in control, skipper Billy Sharp finished off a slick move, involving his two fellow goalscorers, to break Rickie Lambert's record and move clear as the highest-scoring player in the English leagues this century. The goal, in some ways, was typical Sharp; a strike from just outside the six-yard box after a good cross from strike partner McGoldrick. At the time, though, the United skipper was more concerned about not blazing the ball over the bar than any individual glory.

Earlier, former Blade Lee Evans had missed an incredible chance to open the scoring for Wigan before somehow putting his shot wide and appearing to receive a few choice words from United goalkeeper Dean Henderson. Afterwards, Wilder was full of praise for his skipper on his record-breaking day. "Billy leads from the front. He does what he does but he drives all the other lads forward as well," Wilder said. "He deserves all the plaudits that come his way because his record speaks for itself. But what I really like about him is that you know he'll want more... not only for himself, but for the team as a whole, too."

In the short space between the Wigan game and United's next fixture, an FA Cup third-round tie against National League side Barnet, it wasn't Sharp's past goal exploits that came under the microscope, but his relationship - or supposed lack of one - with former Sheffield Wednesday striker Gary Madine. Madine, by this point on the periphery of Neil Warnock's plans at Premier League side Cardiff City, emerged as a January loan target for the Blades as boss Wilder looked to equip himself with all the different options he felt would help plot a course towards promotion. United's forward line possessed many strengths and quality - Sharp had 17 goals by New Year's Day, McGoldrick chipping in with nine - but lacked a physical option to give them an 'outlet' when sides tried to press them and nullify their unique style of play.

It was that reasoning that led to James Hanson's arrival midway through the League One promotion-winning season - incredibly, his most effective display in a red-and-white shirt came in the Championship, and a remarkable 5-4 defeat to the eventual play-off winners Fulham - and this time around, with the prize of Premier League football on the horizon, Madine's name featured prominently on a shortlist of three on the desk of Wilder's Shirecliffe office. Unsurprisingly, though, United's pursuit of Madine wasn't initially popular among their fanbase - and, it later transpired, some members of the club's board, too.

The majority of Blades fans could forgive the connection with Wednesday - several former Owls had gone on to become popular at Bramall Lane, including McGoldrick - but it was Madine's reputation off the field that went before him. One item towards the more trivial end of his rap sheet was a video which emerged online of Madine calling Sharp 'a fat pig' shortly before his then-side, Bolton, were due to visit Bramall Lane. Madine was subsequently withdrawn from the Bolton side for the game at the 11th hour and later returned over the Pennines in a taxi.

More serious, though, were Madine's previous convictions for actual bodily harm and grievous bodily harm, for which he served five months of an 18-month prison sentence before being released in 2014. A court heard that Madine had punched two football fans, one a supporter of Wednesday and one of United, in separate attacks in Sheffield city centre bars, and among an outpouring of opposition to him signing for the Blades, some fans insisted they wouldn't cheer Madine's goals - or even return to Bramall Lane at all, if he was unveiled as a United player.

Wilder, however, had no such concerns about either the player's attitude or ability. The United boss is close friends with Steve Parkin and Lee Butler, who worked with Madine at Bolton Wanderers as assistant manager and goalkeeping coach respectively, and received encouraging reports from the pair about the striker, having been impressed with the centre-forward's stand-out display the previous season when he scored the only goal for Wanderers in a 1-0 win at Bramall Lane. The move for Madine may have seemed a brave one in some quarters but in reality, Wilder would not even have considered an approach for the striker's services if he sensed some kind of risk to the steadfast team spirit that he had carefully assembled at Bramall Lane.

The manager and his recruitment staff place a huge emphasis on signing good people as well as good players, and the emphasis is very much on the group effort. Two months earlier, United's assistant kit man and amateur boxer Adam Geelan stepped through the ropes for the first time in three years. At Woodseats Working Men's Club, Geelan was cheered on to victory over Doncaster's Chris Hartley by United's first-team squad and staff, including Wilder, with Brooks - now a Premier League star with AFC Bournemouth - also making the long journey north to support his friend. Another of Wilder's well-worn cliches sums up his approach: 'You're either in, or you're out'.

The notion of 'team spirit' has become almost a cliché in football - every team always seems to have a 'good set of lads', most often found 'in the changing room' - but at United, that carefully-crafted culture is almost tangible. After Wilder had pulled his skipper into his office and told him he was considering signing Madine - the best of the three options available at that time - Sharp insisted he had no issues whatsoever. There was no opposition from the rest of the squad either; many of whom already knew Madine from spells together at previous clubs.

The striker shared a house with Oliver Norwood when the pair were youngsters at Carlisle, played alongside John Fleck and David McGoldrick at Coventry and Wednesday respectively, and had his boots cleaned by a young Dean Henderson when he was a Brunton Park trainee. The biggest tick in the box, from Wilder's point of view, was Madine's determination to force through the move and play for United. The striker had appealing offers from other clubs in the second tier, but had first set his heart on a move to Bramall Lane towards the end of his time at Hillsborough. Madine became good friends with a number of United players and was a big fan of their striker, Ched Evans, often travelling incognito to watch him in action.

"The gaffer got everything right and didn't leave any stone unturned," said Sharp. "He thought about everything and did it for a reason. He brought in Scotty Hogan and Gaz to make sure me and Didzy didn't fall away and they more than played their part. The gaffer asked me if I'd be okay with Gaz signing - he didn't have to, because he's the manager and signs who he wants - and I said: 'Listen, if he's going to help us get over that line and make us all Premier League players, then I haven't got a problem with that'. It's not about me, it's about everyone. I don't think even Gaz could believe he was coming here, but fair play to him for showing the… *character* to come here and help us to get promoted.

"If the gaffer thought that it was a risk to bring him in, he wouldn't have done it. People questioned if it was going to work… I know someone who said he wasn't going to come to games anymore if Gaz was playing. I said to him: 'Why? He's playing for Sheffield United now, you're a Sheffield United fan. Come and support whoever plays'. And to be fair, he did. I played against Gaz loads of times and of course he used to play for Wednesday. Everyone knows that I hate Wednesday but I've also got a lot of respect for them. A few players have moved from there to here, like Leon Clarke and Caolan Lavery in recent times. Gaz was another part of the puzzle to make us click and like everyone else, played his part. It was a collective effort rather than an individual one, and everyone was brilliant."

Madine's controversial loan move was eventually completed in the aftermath of a rare low moment for United throughout the promotion season, when they slumped out of the FA Cup at the first hurdle to National League side Barnet. There were a few laughs in the pre-match press conference when Martin Cranie was asked if he had any good FA Cup memories - "well, I won it once," came the reply with a grin, referring to his time at Portsmouth in 2008 - but this was well and truly an afternoon to forget, as Barnet were good value for their 1-0 victory over a much-changed, yet sub-standard United side. A visibly angry Wilder summoned big-hitters such as Sharp, Duffy and Chris Basham from the substitutes' bench in an attempt to get back into the cup tie, before waiting to shake every single Barnet player's hand as they dragged themselves off the field after celebrating - deservedly - with their excellent travelling supporters.

Those Blades fans who remained inside Bramall Lane also gave Darren Currie's side a standing ovation, but Wilder's mood was not so hospitable when he eventually returned to the home dressing room and confronted his players. In a slight departure from one of his favourite sayings, Wilder advised his players to find a side door to sneak out of after a display he described as "arrogant" and "unacceptable". "I heard some boos at the full-time whistle," said Wilder in his press conference. "To be honest, I think the fans should have booed louder."

"I feel quite sorry for lads when that happens," Basham later reflected. "It's happened to me before when the gaffer changes the team, you haven't played too much with a lot of your team-mates and it's the other team's 'cup final', so to speak. The boys felt terrible after that but it's football and it happens. It was gutting at the time because we all want to win every game but maybe it was a blessing in disguise, because it meant we could focus on the league. The gaffer didn't see it that way, though, and he questioned us as men afterwards. Some boys really struggled and it really hurts him when we don't perform."

After Wilder's rare rant over his side's attitude, there was little surprise inside Bramall Lane when the teamsheets were handed in - ahead of United's next game, against Queens Park Rangers - and he had reverted to the side that had taken United to within touching distance of automatic promotion in the Championship table. Madine's name was greeted by a positive reception when it was read out before the game, but the striker didn't make it off the bench as McGoldrick's glancing header, from Norwood's sublime cross, sent United into the top two.

Norwood's exceptional form in United's midfield was made even more remarkable when it was revealed that he had been carrying a hernia since before Christmas. And after former England boss Steve McClaren had become the latest opposition manager to tip United for promotion, Wilder refused once again to hide away from talking about the potential prize in front of them. "We were in League One for six years and there was an awful lot of pressure every year that went by without promotion," Wilder said. "We were under big pressure to do the business in that division and the players didn't show heavy shirts then. It doesn't feel any different now, really. Whether we step out at Bramall Lane or away from home, I still expect them to play well. We are expected to win games at this football club, with the history here, and we want to keep doing that."

By this point, some of the initial noise that greeted Madine's arrival had quietened somewhat but another off-field storm was brewing just up the M1 as United's Yorkshire rivals, Leeds, became embroiled in a saga that later became universally known as 'Spygate'. Ahead of their January clash against Derby County, a Leeds employee was discovered attempting to 'observe' Frank Lampard's training sessions and in response to the growing furore, Leeds boss Marcelo Bielsa called a remarkable press conference at their training ground to reveal the depth of data he and his staff collect on every opponent. Analysis of each rival team, according to Bielsa, might amount to as much as 300 hours of work and the Argentinian also admitted that he had observed training sessions of a number of Leeds' other rivals up to that point - possibly including United, before their meeting in early December at Bramall Lane.

United train on a pitch away from the main road at their Shirecliffe training base and it isn't immediately clear where any 'spying' could take place from. But either way, Wilder held a different view on 'Spygate' to a number of his Championship colleagues. Eleven clubs wrote to the EFL demanding further action over the controversy but Wilder admitted: "I wasn't bothered about it. I thought it was quite funny and amusing, to be honest. I thought Leeds would do what they did in attempting to make out that the world was against them but I watched the game and they absolutely destroyed Derby. It really didn't bother me. Is it morally wrong? Maybe it is. Did he come and see us? Yeah, he might have done. Would I have done it? No.

"But I thought there was loads made of it. It then came out what Marcelo and his staff do in terms of analysis, but that didn't upset or surprise me because the level of detail that every club in the Championship, and even some in League One, go into now is enormous. I think the majority of Championship clubs wouldn't have been surprised by his presentation and were possibly saying: 'Well, we do that anyway'. As I say I thought it was quite amusing and good luck to Marcelo.

Although if we'd have caught his man in the back of a van at Sheffield United, I don't think he'd have been getting out."

The Blades boss was more concerned over a rare defeat for his side in their next game, away at Swansea City's Liberty Stadium. The victory secured the double for Graham Potter's men, but United improved after the introduction of Madine, coming off the bench to make his Blades debut, and could have been handed - literally - a route back into the game when the ball appeared to strike Mike van der Hoorn on the arm in the Swans' penalty area. But referee John Brooks - who aggrieved Wilder with his decision making all evening - was unmoved, and United made the long journey back from South Wales with nothing to show for their efforts. On the face of it, the defeat - if not the performance - appeared to be less than ideal preparation for the following weekend's trip to Carrow Road, to face automatic promotion rivals Norwich City.

But Wilder had been privately encouraged by his side's display at Swansea, and how they maintained their belief until the final blast of Brooks' whistle. That mental and physical commitment had become a hallmark of Wilder's time at United, even if Duffy did feel the need to speak out on social media against a minority of fans he felt were questioning his professionalism by doubting that he had the fitness levels to play for 90 minutes. "If that was true, there was no way the gaffer would allow it," Duffy said. "I just wanted to make sure that the people who were questioning me knew that I was working as hard as anyone. And that the reasons for me coming off could be tactical, or just that I wasn't playing well. Nothing to do with fitness levels at all."

At Carrow Road, the clash of two Championship titans was not only a seismic one in terms of that season's promotion race, but also in the context of the emerging rivalry which continued between the two clubs. Each of their three meetings since United's promotion back to the second tier had produced its own talking points, and the psychological warfare had been cranked up another notch this time around when City painted the away dressing room at Carrow Road in 'deep pink' - supposedly in an attempt to lower testosterone levels and increase levels of calmness in opposition players before the game.

Whether such methods actually work remains unproven - although Norwich's finishing position at the end of the season suggested it certainly did no harm - but, either way, United were taking no chances. So, with boss Wilder jokingly threatening to fine them for each flash of pink he saw, kit men Carl Hopwood and Geelan got to work from the early hours of the morning, covering the walls with white paper and then adding a final flourish; photos of United's players throughout the season, celebrating goals or winning tackles and headers. If that was United's own psychological ploy, it appeared to do the trick as they twice bounced back from a goal down to earn an impressive and deserved point.

Daniel Farke's Canaries began the contest well and a difficult afternoon beckoned for United when Onel Hernández finished off a good team move to put Norwich ahead after just 11 minutes. But on the stroke of half-time Sharp levelled from the penalty spot, despite goalkeeper Tim Krul's ridiculous attempts to put him off, after Enda Stevens had been clumsily bundled over by Emi Buendía. Sharp emphatically smashed the spot-kick past Krul and celebrated by producing a sock signed by wrestling star Mick Foley out of his shorts, before pulling it over his hand and performing Foley's signature 'Mandible Claw' move on teammate George Baldock.

To his credit Baldock - despite knowing where the sock had been kept for the last 45 minutes of the game - wilfully played his part, and the celebration saw Sharp and United make headline news all around the world - eventually attracting the attention of Foley himself, better known as 'Mankind' to wrestling fans. "I didn't realise all that was going to happen," Sharp admitted.

"I'd had a reunion with some old mates from my old Sunday League team, Middlewood Rovers, and I hadn't seen some of them since I was 12, so it was a great day. One of the lads was mad on wrestling and was begging me to do the celebration, for a laugh. So he bought the sock online. I think it cost him about 40 quid because it was signed. He was gutted that I gave it away!

"I agreed to do it and then I was thinking 'where am I going to put it?' I shouldn't have been thinking about that - I should have been focusing on the game! I was lucky that we managed to get the penalty because it was coming out at half-time. It was doing my head in. But it was a bit of fun and it was a bit surreal when Mick then turned up at my house! I just wanted to get on with the football again and keep scoring goals. I didn't really want all the attention that came with it."

United suffered a blow at Carrow Road when Teemu Pukki, the hosts' Finnish international, put them back ahead with a first-time finish but Sharp, who had earlier hit the bar with a header, had the last laugh when he nodded home substitute Duffy's delicious cross with 11 minutes to go. "We weren't at our best with the ball that day and it was one of those games when we thought we might have to dig in and show our character," Sharp added. "There was a lot of talk about the pink dressing room and things to try to put us off, but Hoppo and Adam sorted it out and did a good job. The gaffer and the staff are always doing little things, to help us. Then we have to try to repay them by performing out on the pitch."

From United's point of view, considering the context of the game and the opponents, the point from the 2-2 draw was a good one but the day's big winners were undoubtedly Leeds. They took advantage of the stalemate between their two nearest challengers to go three points clear of Norwich, and six clear of United, when they scored late on to beat Rotherham United at the New York Stadium. By this point West Brom - a point behind in the table, with a game in hand - were breathing heavily down United's necks. But, as the clock ticked steadily towards the end of January, and the transfer deadline, attention was momentarily diverted away from matters on the field. Scott Hogan, of Aston Villa, had been a long-term target of Wilder and when the striker was eventually given permission to leave Villa Park on loan, he told his employers that Bramall Lane was his preferred destination.

This time, there were no deadline-day fax machine hiccups and Hogan's signature on the contract was dry long before the transfer window slammed shut. His journey to Bramall Lane had been a whirlwind one. Five years earlier he was playing just down the road, for Stocksbridge Park Steels in the Northern Premier League, and graduated steadily through the leagues before making a £9million move to Villa Park, from Brentford. The memories of Hogan's time at Bracken Moor came flooding back when he drove past the Stocksbridge turn-off, en route from his native Manchester to complete his medical at United - and so, it turned out, did the recollections of the previous season, when he played for Villa against United at Bramall Lane.

"We sneaked a 1-0 but got absolutely battered," Hogan said. "I don't think we saw the ball all game apart from a bit of magic at the end from Robert Snodgrass. There are a few things that went wrong for me at Villa but I will take full responsibility for everything. Ultimately, I was paid to do something and I did not do it. I have to shoulder the responsibility, which I am fine with, but I'm looking forward now." United's January window work wasn't done there, though, as an unwelcome offer, from Premier League side West Ham United for midfielder John Fleck, landed in Wilder's in-tray. The bid, of £4million, was swiftly rejected.

Fleck told his agent that he was happy at Bramall Lane and had no desire to move, before meeting Wilder the following day and repeating that pledge to him. "He said he was happy with that as well and that was it, really. Done," the Scot said. "We have an incredible group here, and I include the manager and staff in that. Everything is the way you want it to be at a club and long may that continue. Whatever level you play at, it's everyone's dream as a footballer to play in the Premier League and now we'll all get the chance to do that for this club."

Like Hogan and so many of his United teammates, Fleck has also taken a circumvented route to the top-flight. He almost became a United player earlier in his career, before administrative errors scuppered a loan deal for Fleck and teammate Kyle Hutton, and in 2012 he declined to transfer his contract to Rangers' new company and moved to England with Coventry City. "It was a bit of 'head over heart' with leaving Rangers, in terms of my career," the boyhood Gers fan said. "I could have stayed there but I wasn't sure how much I was going to play, so I made the decision to take the step for myself. And it's proved to be the right one.

"When I left Coventry I had a few options but I knew United had some good players like Sharpy in the team, so I thought: 'Why not go and be a part of that?' I should have come here on loan a few years before but it fell through. It was about 10 o'clock at night and I was at home in bed when I got a call, to come to Ibrox and try to get the deal done.

"Me and Kyle Hutton were still there well past midnight trying to get it done but it fell through. Someone said something about the fax machine at the time but I don't know what went wrong. At the time I was gutted but luckily I got the chance to come again. I said to my family, as soon as I got the call to come and meet the manager at United the second time around: 'Maybe this is supposed to be'. You could look at it and say that it was fate for me to be here."

Don't mention the fax machine
by Dan Atkin

Sheffield United's January transfer windows have generally been something to be approached with a mixture of dread and pathos over the years, as well as a raft of obligatory fax machine 'jokes' doing the rounds on social media from New Year's Eve for the next 31 days. Every year. Without fail. Going into 2019 we had got ourselves into a position where, with the right additions in the right positions, we could launch a genuine assault on at least a playoff place. But that feeling was certainly tempered by the historical precedent that our good position would be derailed by one, or both, of either: flogging our best player(s) towards the end of the window - like the time we replaced James Beattie with Craig Beattie - or failing to strengthen our position with the requisite quality, as we did during our last sojourn into the Premier League with such world-beaters as Mamadou Seck and Ahmed Fathi.

Our league form in January was pretty solid on the whole. A comfortable victory at the DW Stadium on New Year's Day set the tone for the second half of the season - the highlight being Billy Sharp's goal, which sent him above such luminaries as Wayne Rooney, Jermaine Defoe, Sergio Aguero and Chris Porter - but the following game was a serious reality check. A very deserved 1-0 home defeat to a Barnet side who, at the time, were smack bang in the middle of the National League - or the Vauxhall Conference, for those of a certain vintage. The result, though, was of secondary concern in the grand scheme of things.

The real issue was the performance, or lack of it, from back-up members of the squad who we assumed would be ready to slot seamlessly into the first team should they be called upon. This was certainly not whitewashed by Chris Wilder in another refreshingly-honest post-match interview, when he called the players "arrogant" and said the fans were generous for not booing more. In reality the whole thing was a blessing in disguise. We were now free to concentrate on our league campaign, our players got a rocket up their collective a***s and it confirmed that we needed to press ahead with our January transfer plans.

A 1-0 home win over QPR moved us back into the top two and was much more of what we expected to see, but at Swansea a week later, we were given flashbacks about one of the litany of awful previous Blades managers. Nathan Dyer, a man whom Kevin Blackwell decided wasn't good enough for a permanent deal at the Lane but now has a Premier League winner's medal hanging off his fridge door, tormented us and set up Oli McBurnie to continue his irritating habit of scoring against us. In truth this was a game in which we should have taken something because we were by far and away the better side in the first half. In reality, we somehow contrived to let an extremely-average Swans side do the double over us.

For me, events on the pitch at Carrow Road showed how

close this incredible bunch of players are, and why they achieved what they achieved in 2018/19. As a barometer of team spirit and togetherness, some people would point to the fact that, in one of our toughest games of the season, we twice came from behind to draw. It's a fair point. However, for me, it was far more telling that George Baldock was quite happy to have a sock shoved in his mouth, as part of a WWE-themed goal celebration, when he knew it had been stored in Billy's undercrackers for 45 minutes!

Above all else, that proved to me that these lads were a true band of brothers and that, as a judge of character and when it comes to building a dressing room dynamic, Wilder has a skill which borders on alchemy. Although I had no idea what the celebration was about, it brought us to the attention of the national and international media for positive reasons again... something that has become a running theme during Wilder's time at the club.

After the Barnet game, there was a definite feeling throughout the fan base - and, I'm sure, the coaching staff as well - that we had a lack of depth in the squad. Like the season previous, our first 11, when fit, were a match for anyone but scratch the surface and a distinct and worrying drop in quality was evident - especially in the forward positions. As well as Sharp and David McGoldrick had done up to this point, it was looking more and more obvious by the week that Leon Clarke was struggling to hit the heights of the previous season, Conor Washington was nothing more than a body and Ben Woodburn was a boy trying to play in a man's league.

He reminded me a little of myself, playing in the Imperial League at 17 and getting absolutely monstered by blokes in their 30s (and keeping the scars to prove it). Quality was needed. Woodburn returned to Anfield and Leon was loaned to Wigan with our collective best wishes - and no doubt Wilder's final instructions about helping us out by causing chaos in games against our rivals later on in the season. Kieran Dowell arrived from Everton with a good reputation, following a loan spell at Forest last season - but also an awful haircut to rival Dean Henderson's early-season 'curtains' abomination - and there were hopes that Scott Hogan could replicate the really hot spell at Brentford which earned him his big move to Aston Villa.

Overall seven points from four games wasn't the worst January we'd ever had, and we strengthened our front line with quality additions. But one of our other January dealings was to prove the main talking point for the month; one of our most potentially controversial transfers in a long time. Throughout the years, as a club, I would say that we have a pretty good record of getting the best out of players who had previously played for our cross-city neighbours and, in a lot of cases, taking them to our hearts. Players such as Del Geary, Carl Bradshaw, Leon and others have genuine legend status at the Lane and others such as Richard Cresswell, Alan Quinn, Wilf Rostron and Leigh Bromby are still thought of with genuine affection by Blades fans.

The signing of Gary Madine, though, appeared to be one that had the potential to split not just the fan base, but the dressing room itself. Now most sensible Blades don't actually care whether someone has played for 'that lot' previously and personally, I love it when we bring someone to S2 who has worn blue and white in the past and get a tune out of them. For me, it's a victory of our coaching team and ethos over theirs. This one, though, had more potential opportunities for controversy than having a Steve Bruce impersonator at the end-of-season do!

The first I heard of the possible transfer itself was when a lad who sits just behind me on the Kop tweeted an online betting company, to ask for odds on us bringing Madine back to Sheffield. I initially assumed this was a wind up to get a few 'bites' on social media but in the following 24 hours, it became clear that this rumour had legs. It quickly escalated into a major furore within Sheffield with some fans happy with the prospect and some - including me, in all honesty - a little more sceptical and concerned.

Some doubts centered around his talent as a footballer and whether or not he slotted into our system; others were more focused on his previous misdemeanours off the pitch and, in particular, that video of him insulting Billy while, let's say, 'well oiled' a couple of years earlier.

Now for me - having seen Darius Henderson and Chris Morgan pretty much attempt to kill each other when on opposing sides for several years, yet have no problem being in the same team after we signed the former - I assumed that professionalism would come out in the end and everything would be fine between Madine and Sharp. That was pretty much how it played out, with Madine striking up a good understanding with Billy when they were on the pitch together. The man himself was fairly bullish about signing for us and, as Wilder attested, it showed some b******s to want to move to a club after you've scored against them for their most bitter rivals, insulted their legendary captain and been booed off the team bus 18 months earlier when turning up for a game.

In fact, the more I think about it, in terms of what we as a fan base demand from and gravitate towards as a player, Madine - without the baggage - is the sort who would be almost tailor-made to be a cult hero overnight at Bramall Lane. The fact that he will now go down in Blades' folklore as part of this exceptional side is a testament to both his and Wilder's attitude. Cult heroes at the Lane have always been players who, while certainly not without talent, have won us over with their work rate, attitude and commitment to the cause.

Players such as Geary, Bob Booker, Paul Beesley, Porter and, dare I say it, Wilder himself would be unlikely to feature in most fans' all-time Blades XI if the criterion was pure ability. But for the reasons mentioned they, and many others, hold a special place in most fans' hearts. And while I wouldn't expect Madine to be afforded a hero's welcome should he turn out against us in the future, you can bet your life the reception will be a damn sight more cordial than when he stepped off the Bolton team bus 18 months ago.

The whole episode was just more proof, if it were needed, that Wilder's connection with the fans is something extremely special and something unlikely to be repeated for a long time. He was quick to reassure us that, as usual, he had done his due diligence here and while acknowledging that the signing may not be universally welcomed, made it clear that we needed to trust him with running the show. And let's be right, given what he has done for us since he returned to the club... who were we to argue?

Breaking the records
by Billy Sharp

The season before the promotion campaign, I remember seeing a stat about how far off the record I was, and I just ticked people off as I went past them. From a selfish point of view, of course I wanted to get to the top of that list. Every player wants to hit targets, especially with Rickie Lambert at the top as an ex-teammate of mine. I didn't want an award for it or anything - I didn't know there was one, to be honest - but to break the record was phenomenal. I'm just glad it was with this club and team that I did it.

I owe a lot to my teammates because I'm not the kind of player who takes three or four defenders on or really dribbles. I rely on my teammates getting the ball in the box, and I have a good knack of getting on the end of it. At Wigan, I could see the 'keeper reading what I was trying to do and I couldn't hit it too hard because that's when you blaze it over. I just concentrated on hitting the target and it went exactly how I wanted it to. When I close my eyes, I can still see all the players running off to celebrate with the fans. That was a good day for us.

I went past an old mate in Rickie and I'm not sure who can catch me. He certainly can't! At the time I didn't realise what all the fuss was about, but Wigan was a good start to the year for us. It's a tough place to go and win and, in the dressing room, I started to feel and smell it, that we could do something special. We were a long way from the finishing line but I could feel the momentum building. We took four points from Norwich, the top team in the league and we went away to teams like West Brom and Leeds and won. I remember saying to my dad around that time that I felt like I was playing well.

I wasn't scoring goals, but I felt a big part of the team. To win at West Brom was huge and then when we won at Leeds, people began to talk about us. As the pressure built, we buckled a bit and then Leeds did. Over the Easter weekend, we got lucky with their results but we made sure we took care of ours. When we got the biggest chance, against the bottom of the league team at home, we took it with both hands. Now it's about time I tried to get some goals in the Premier League.

It has frustrated me a little bit, that I've never had a real chance in the top flight but I've never wanted to say anything. I believe I can play in the top division; I just needed a chance and hopefully, I can take it. If not, so what? I'll have had the opportunity. And really, I couldn't have asked for a better one; playing in the Premier League with Sheffield United, *my club,* in front of family and friends - and alongside friends on the pitch, too. It'll be nice, and I can't wait. We fell a little bit short the season before because we didn't have as much quality, and we felt we'd learned from that experience to make us stronger this time around. We had a real battle with Leeds and even dragged Norwich back a little, too.

What we had achieved in winning promotion began to sink in a little bit more when people like Brian Deane and Keith Edwards, legends of Sheffield United, said the nice things they did about me. It makes me so proud. I used to come to Bramall Lane and sing Deano's name, and now he's saying to me: 'Congratulations, you're a Premier League player'. It's mental. Everything's just gone absolutely brilliantly since I came back, and I'm so grateful that I had the chance to come back and be a successful United player.

I said in my speech at the *Sheffield Star's* Football Awards in April that I owe the gaffer here a lot. And I do. I still remember the phone call when he asked me to be his captain. I asked him why he was giving me the armband, and he mentioned my interview after the season under Nigel Adkins, when I was *really* hurting. I was like: 'Okay, that's fine'. I put the phone down and then it hit home. *I was going to be the captain of Sheffield United.* And looking back, it could hardly have gone any better!

Players need to play games - any footballer will tell you the same - and the gaffer has given me that. He's shown a lot of belief in me, and I've managed to repay him by scoring goals. He talks a lot about running the dressing room and that can be quite tough at times, but a lot of the boys have pulled me over the course of the season and thanked me. I told them not to thank me - I should be thanking them! I'm just the lucky one who wears the armband. The lads have been unbelievable and I'm very grateful to have been a part of it as well.

There were tough times, of course. Aston Villa away sticks out in my mind immediately and it's easy to look back at games like that, and Millwall at home, and think: 'If we'd have held on here or there it'd have been different'. But there were days when we nicked points at times as well. Against Millwall, when John Egan got sent off, I was in the physio room watching the game on TV and, at the time, I thought it was a good header! Then I saw the replay. It was still a good decision because they missed the penalty. But then they equalised. And after that, as a group, we were so, so down.

It was just for the one day, though, because we knew we had to dust ourselves off. It was a blow to lose myself, Egs and Chris Basham but that's why we had a squad of 25 or so. Any-one who stepped in, like Martin Cranie or Richard Stearman, has done his job and then been taken out, but they haven't once let the team down and they've played a huge part. Anyone who's played a part deserves the plaudits that come their way.

Stears hasn't played as much as he'd have liked but he's a fans' favourite and a big leader, on and off the pitch. My big mate Paul Coutts has had a frustrating couple of years but I heard Mark Duffy say he's one of the best players he's ever played with, and he couldn't get in our team. It was frustrating for him but he was brilliant, too. It just shows he did his job by pushing. All season he was one of the best trainers, day in, day out, making sure the lads are performing. You can't overesti-mate how important that is.

Egs made himself a legend of the club with his song at the player of the year awards, as well! I didn't know what was going on when he was like 'everyone come on stage'. I thought: 'What's he doing? Has he had too many drinks?' We all had, to be fair. And then he launched into this song and absolutely owned it. Unbelievable. The lads were all singing it as we celebrated until our voices were sore and I'm sure the fans will use it for years to come. Not only has he helped United get promoted, he's giving the fans songs now! I said in an interview soon after that we're a very unique group. I saw Kevin Gage say that we're the new Crazy Gang! But we are all unique characters who seem to link into one. The gaffer's a bit of a loon as well, which helps.

But we're all on the same page no matter what we're doing, whether that's in training or on a match-day or even socialising with each other. Times like this are definitely made even sweeter by the experience of the not-so-great times. We had an embarrassing season under Adkins, but that happens sometimes. As the gaffer says, he's done well at other clubs and he's obviously a good manager, it just didn't work here for him. He wasn't the right character for the fans and since the gaffer took over, whatever he's done has worked.

He's had promotions here now as a player and a manager and I've got huge respect and admiration for him. Giving me the armband changed me as a player and as a person, it made me a stronger character as a result. Everyone knows I've had frustrating spells in the past here as a player and I used to come and watch the team as a kid. I think I've sat on all four sides of Bramall Lane! I'm delighted it's worked out this time and we're going to go down in history for getting this club back to the Premier League.

I've been in good dressing rooms before, and won promotion before, but this one is a lot different from the others. We've been the underdogs for a lot of it and we weren't the biggest earners, with the biggest budget, but the gaffer and his staff put so much thought into everything we do. Alan Knill talks about the performance levels a lot. When the season was getting tense, I was thinking: 'It's all about the three points, surely?' but he was going on about the performance. We were improving every day and he knew that if we got those levels right, everything else would take care of itself.

We've got to try to step up again now because the gap from the Championship is so big. We have to try to close it. We'll have to take some things on the chin in the Premier League, but we can't get too down if we do because another game will be just around the corner. At the same time, we'll have some great days too, and I believe we can do all right. It summed it up for me when people like Tony Currie and Len Badger were asking US for photos. These are legends of the Lane! A few of the lads didn't know who they were but I obviously do, and I said to them you might only appreciate it in 20 to 30 years when we come back to functions at the club and we're all a lot older.

We're just trying to win football games at the minute. One of the best times in the celebration was when we were just sitting, having a quiet beer, the lads and no-one else. It meant we could tell each other how proud we were before we went out and got carried away with the fans, singing songs and all that! I did make sure I told all the boys and staff how proud I was of them. Each and every one of them are Sheffield United legends, no matter how many games they played throughout the season. A lot of them say that I am, but they are as well.

Although I do think I've got a lot left in me, when I do eventually retire I'll look back on an unbelievable United career, because of the boys and staff. We've achieved something incredible. I'd have never thought getting two promotions in three years was possible in my wildest dreams. One would have been enough, especially with this club. But to get two, and get back to the Premier League, is unbelievable. My teammates and the manager are the ones who've helped me and the club be successful over the last three years. I can't thank them enough.

chapter ten

The pain of Villa Park

February 2019

From the sublime, to the ridiculous. Months after September's 4-1 home hammering of Aston Villa, the biggest club in the Championship, had showcased everything that was good about Chris Wilder's Sheffield United side, it was the return fixture that was supposed to have been the beginning of the end for United's hopes of promotion to the Premier League. Leading Villa 3-0 with 10 minutes to go - Billy Sharp scoring a hat-trick that also saw him go past 100 goals for his boyhood club - United were cruising, and on course for a return to the top of the Championship table. On this Friday evening in the Second City, everything was in place for this to be a day that lived long in the memory, for everyone connected with United. It still turned out to be. Just for all the wrong reasons.

Nobody had really seen it coming, either. United had bounced back from a rare defeat, away at Swansea, the month before with a deserved, battling point away at promotion rivals Norwich, and Wilder's men then rediscovered that winning feeling with a comfortable 2-0 victory over struggling Bolton Wanderers at Bramall Lane. United's strikeforce of Sharp and David McGoldrick, both written off as 'journeymen' by one journalist before the season began, came up with the goods again to see off Wanderers, Sharp notching his 20th of the campaign late on.

Gary Madine received a pleasant reception, from both sets of supporters, when he made his home debut for the Blades against his former club, after coming off the bench to replace McGoldrick. It was markedly different from the 'welcome', in the loosest terms, given to some ex-Wednesday players when they made their United bows in the past, and Wilder caught journalists napping after the game when he breezed into Bramall Lane's media suite shortly after the final whistle so he could share a beer with Bolton's assistant manager Steve Parkin and goalkeeping coach Lee Butler before they boarded the coach back over the Pennines.

Butler, the man with possibly the strongest handshake in the game, had first impressed upon Wilder a lesson in not getting too carried away in football. During their playing days - they worked together at Alfreton Town and Halifax Town - Wilder made the mistake of celebrating what he felt was an inevitable victory before the final whistle had blown. Butler, his goalkeeper, gave him a smack around the head - which would be enough to leave a lasting impression upon anyone - and reminded him, in no uncertain terms, that nothing is over in football until it's really over. The headache may have subsided in the years since, but the lesson had not. And, as his side approached the final straight of the promotion race, Wilder was not about to lose sight of it now.

"That humility has always been in me as a player and, at this football club, the successful sides have never had that feeling of superiority over anyone else," Wilder said, on the eve of his side's trip to Villa. "Possibly the worst periods for the club have been when there's been that arrogance. Because of our upbringing, as players and staff, we always keep our feet on the ground. We know we've got to work hard for anything we get."

His side, though, were dealt their own reminder of the game's harsh realities in front of the Sky cameras at Villa Park - in a different, yet no less painful manner. Norwich had beaten fellow promotion-chasers Leeds the previous weekend - again highlighting how impressive United's point at Carrow Road had been - and so Wilder's men knew that three points against Dean Smith's Villa would send them top of the Championship, on goal difference. Not for the first time that season, United were seen as favourites against a club with vastly-inflated resources at their disposal but there was no denying that Villa had endured a difficult time of it in the Championship since their Premier League relegation in 2016. Under Steve Bruce, Wilder's former team-mate and manager at Bramall Lane, Villa had lost in the previous season's play-off final to Fulham and the hangover lingered long into the following campaign. Bruce eventually paid for Villa's poor run of form with his job in October, days after they drew 3-3 with the division's bottom club, Preston, and a fan threw a cabbage at the manager in his dugout. Some of the feelgood factor had returned to Villa Park, though, under Smith – also a boyhood supporter of the club he now represents.

Later in the season, as Smith took Villa to the play-off final again, he revealed that his father was, too, a proud Villa fan. But, suffering from dementia, Ron Smith didn't even know his son was the manager of the team they both loved. Wilder, be-fore completing his pre-match media duties and travelling with his squad to Birmingham, forecasted an "end-to-end game". "I know we've got weaknesses that other teams will try and exploit," the United boss said. "Just like they have. Both teams will go for a win. I don't think their managers, their players and more importantly their supporters will accept either side sitting on the edge of the box, playing counter-attacking football. I think it will be end to end. So possibly it could come down to who is more clinical in both boxes."

United certainly rose to that particular challenge when they stormed into a three-goal lead, from just five shots on target. Sharp opened the scoring with a typical poacher's effort which Tammy Abraham failed to clear off the line before he netted a controversial second. Villa protested vehemently that Sharp, who was also offside, had kicked the ball out of home goal-keeper Lovre Kalinic's hands. There was little doubt about the third, though, as Sharp headed home Kieran Dowell's deflected cross from three yards out to seal his hat-trick. With four min-utes of normal time remaining, and United 3-1 ahead, Sharp was substituted; his, and the team's, job surely done.

Villa had pulled a goal back when loanee Tyrone Mings got to a corner before United goalkeeper Dean Henderson and headed home, but only about half of the home fans in the 34,892 crowd remained inside this famous old ground to see it. The Villa supporters who did remain, though, were on their feet again soon after when Henderson could only palm Tommy Elphick's deflected shot into the path of Abraham. The England international made no mistake from close range, to make it 3-2 with four minutes of regular time remaining. But Wilder, believing his side were fully capable of seeing out the game and claiming a vital win, saw little danger.

Time was quickly running out for Villa to snatch an equaliser and as another move broke down, the ball looped up towards the dependable left boot of Jack O'Connell. United's centre-half had been excellent all evening, nullifying the threat of Abraham almost completely, and had the freedom of Birmingham to boot the ball clear. Instead, the defender mis-kicked his clearance straight to the feet of John McGinn, in the United box, and his cross was inch-perfect for substitute Andre Green. As Green headed past Henderson, Villa Park erupted.

Oliver Norwood and George Baldock sank to their knees in despair and the inquest into United's capitulation began. The debrief, which began on the field, continued in the away dressing room and then turned physical. Tempers became increasingly flared, and a couple of stray punches were thrown. Boss Wilder described the scenes as 'bits and pieces' and although the episode was made to sound like a full-on brawl in some quarters, several onlookers described the physical part of the row as over almost before it began. One player later pulled a teammate to one side to apologise for his part in the coming-together before the long journey home and, if nothing else, the incident at least demonstrated how much United's players cared about the club and their pursuit of Premier League football.

"I couldn't believe it," Sharp said months later. "I'd scored a hat-trick at Villa Park, we all thought we'd won the game and we would have gone top of the league. The second goal was also my 100th for Sheffield United, and it was so nearly the perfect night. It all changed very quickly and we were devastated afterwards because we threw away two points and that could have hurt us. Really hurt us. Maybe it was a blessing in disguise - we could have gone top and got a bit complacent, a bit big time. Who knows? But it was a kick up the backside that we probably needed, and it stood us in good stead to be where we are today.

"I wasn't actually in the dressing room after the game to see what happened. I just wanted to win the game, go over and celebrate with the fans - top of the league... brilliant. Then bang, all of a sudden it was taken away from us. We went over to clap the fans and I had to do an interview on Sky straight after, although I really didn't want to. I wanted to get back in the dressing room and start ranting. But as I walked down the tunnel, it was all quiet. I put the matchball and the man-of-the-match award on the floor outside the dressing room, because I didn't want to go in with them. Then I walked in. Everyone was silent and I started my rant. 'Lads what the **** are we doing? We can't....' Then the gaffer just said 'Bill, leave it - it's been dealt with'. I was told afterwards that a few things went off. But that's because all the players care."

Before United's players had even left the pitch, Sky Sports' cameras showed Enda Stevens gesturing animatedly towards Henderson in the aftermath of Villa's equaliser. "There was a lot of talk about what I said to Deano after the game, but it was nothing to do with him making mistakes or anything," Stevens said. "Mistakes are part and parcel of the game and when you look back, I don't think his 'mistakes' were actually that bad. They were blown out of proportion a bit. The argument I had with him was about a goal kick. For the last goal, he kicked the ball straight into their 'keeper's hands. It came back down the pitch and they scored.

"That was my point to him - he needed to kick it out of play or somewhere else. That was blown out of proportion, too, and I apologised to him for that because I didn't know the cameras were on me at the time. What was said was said, but I wasn't calling him out - although it did look like that. It looked terrible on my behalf. Emotions were high; we had people celebrating in our faces and we were very emotional, because it hurt us as players."

The pain didn't end when the bus pulled away from Villa

Park, either, as Wilder gathered his players in front of a big screen at United's Shirecliffe training complex the following day and made them sit through the last 10 minutes or so of the game again. In the hour-long meeting, and as the tape played, several members of Wilder's squad received some home truths from the manager. Basham later admitted he'd never been spoken to like that by Wilder before, describing it as "an eye-opener". "The whole meeting was painful," another player said.

Wilder impressed upon his squad that the Villa capitulation couldn't be allowed to derail United's season and then, according to those who were present, went a step further by openly questioning his squad. "Is this us now?" he asked them. "Is our season done? Are we just going to peter out?" His methods in that meeting proved a managerial masterstroke. Not that everyone present, in that room at Shirecliffe, appreciated them at the time. "Jesus..." remembered Henderson, puffing out his cheeks at the memory of the Villa game and the immediate aftermath. "I've never felt so bad, for days.

"Because I'm a confident boy, people look at me and say 'Ah he'll be all right. He'll be sound'. But deep down, I'm just the same as everyone else and sometimes, it does hurt. I didn't want to come back in after the Villa game. Then the manager called a meeting and I'm thinking: 'Oh no'. We walk in and the goals are on the big screen and I'm thinking again: *'Oh no'*. Honestly, I wanted the ground to swallow me up. With how I felt at that moment, I could have quit football. Retired on the spot. It's maybe something only goalkeepers will understand, but those moments are horrible.

"Looking back, though, it was the turning point of our season. I'm sure any of the boys would say the same... Aston Villa away made Sheffield United go to the Premier League. If the last 10 minutes didn't happen and we'd breezed that 3-0, I think we'd have taken our feet off the gas. Whereas in every game after that, everyone put 110 per cent in. We started keeping clean sheets and everything else looked after itself. For my part, I improved my concentration levels and tried not to get carried away. It levelled me out, definitely. I was starting to think it was

too easy. I did the same the season before at Shrewsbury. It got
to Christmas time and I thought it was too easy, and I wanted
to go and play in the Championship because a load of those
clubs were ringing my agent. So my head was getting swayed.

"I started doing stuff in games that I shouldn't be doing, like
side-volleying the ball instead of throwing it out to look good.
Then, when you play more games, you realise that's stupid and
I think I matured on the pitch as the season went on. I took my
foot off the gas at Villa and it was a good learning curve for me.
Karma came for me and I got punished for it. I take full responsibility for that day. But I like to think that I came back from it.
I got brought back down to earth a little bit and played a part
in keeping a few clean sheets. I only did that with the help of
my teammates of course, but I made some big saves in there as
well."

Wilder may have resisted the temptation to hold back on his
players when he gathered them at Shirecliffe for the debrief, but
he did disagree with his opposite number Smith's assessment
that Villa had pushed United back in the game. Instead, Wilder
attributed the defeat, on the whole, to "three seconds of individual neglect". "That happens in football and in sport sometimes," he added. "We win, lose and draw as a team and we all
take responsibility for what happened, but for me that was right
up there as one of the best away displays since I came to the
club. In terms of the team we were playing against, the stature
of the game, the crowd and everything else. If people think
we got pushed back and dominated then they saw a different
game. We attacked the game and created the better chances
but made three mistakes.

"We played Preston at home earlier in the season, and *they*
did push us back. As a manager, you sometimes feel you have
to do something to change the flow of a game, but I never felt
that at Villa. These things happen and it was important that we
got over it quickly but, apart from three mistakes, it was a really
positive performance, both collectively and individually, in terms
of shape and how we set the side up and the substitutions we
made. I'm my own biggest critic but when you make individual

errors like we did, you'll get punished. Especially against top sides. But on the whole, I thought we were in good nick and I was delighted with how it was going."

If United's confidence levels had taken any dents, they were sure to be sniffed out by their next opponents, just four days later; Tony Pulis' aggressive and physical Middlesbrough side. "I was sitting at home after Villa thinking: 'Oh my God, we're playing Boro next - who just lump balls into the box 24/7 and have all their big lads running onto them'," said Henderson. "In the build-up, though, I spoke to my old man and he said to me: 'You show 'em pal'. I thought: 'Yeah I will, don't worry'. I told myself that, no matter what, the first cross that came into the box was mine. My old mate Dael Fry, from England U21s, went down the line and put it into the middle, but he mis-kicked it and it went sky high. I thought, and this is the 'clean' version - 'thanks mate. Thanks a lot!'

"So I thought: 'Come on then Deano, time to test your b***s'. I heard the shout from John Egan - 'Deano!' - and I thought: 'Yeah, I'm coming bud. I'm here'. It was a wet night as well but I've come for it - big shout, 'KEEPER'S' - and the ball stuck in my gloves, like glue. And I thought: 'Yeah, I'm back'. Honestly, I'd thought about taking that cross for three days solid. And when it stuck, that's when I knew I was the character I thought I was. Again it's something only goalies will really understand but it was the best feeling in the world when I came and claimed that first cross. I thought: 'Aah, thank God for that!'"

United went into the Boro clash without the suspended Basham, after he had picked up his 10th yellow card of the season at Villa, and were dealt another blow on the eve of the game when O'Connell was ruled out with a hamstring complaint, bringing his incredible run of 106 consecutive league starts for United to an abrupt end. "I was devastated when I knew I'd miss the Boro game," O'Connell said. "I couldn't even talk to people about it. I'd never had a muscle injury before so I'd no idea what it really felt like.

"I just thought it was a tight hamstring after the Villa game, which wouldn't have been anything out of the ordinary. But I trained for two or three days after that and when I went to overlap during shape practice for the Boro game, I knew something wasn't right. I went for a scan and we discovered it was a little tear. I'm so angry when I'm not playing... I was being unbearable at home. Not playing is the hardest thing in the world at the time, to me. I just wanted to get back out there." Although Wilder had publicly toyed with the idea of deviating from United's tried and tested 3-5-2 system, he sprung something of a surprise when the teamsheets were handed in and Kieran Dowell, the young forward on loan from Everton, was given the task of playing at left wing-back for the first time in his life.

Stevens moved across to left centre-half as part of a makeshift defence also including Martin Cranie in place of Basham, and those plans had to be adjusted again during the game when Baldock limped off through injury. His replacement was centre-half Richard Stearman, who then proved the unlikely hero when he rose highest to head the winning goal from Norwood's superb cross. The goal was greeted by a cacophony of noise from the Bramall Lane crowd, and a celebration from Stearman which featured a mixture of elation and frustration; after making 30 appearances in his debut season at United, the Boro game was only Stearman's 13th of 2018/19.

Another player who impressed off the bench against Boro was striker Madine. He was then rewarded with his first start at Bramall Lane the following weekend against Reading, but it was right-back Kieron Freeman, back in the side for the injured Baldock, who got United off to a flying start before the Greasy Chip Butty chant, sung at the beginning of each half, had even finished. Freeman's 38-second strike was followed by two powerful finishes from Madine in the first half, before Fleck added a fourth goal in the second period via the help of a deflection.

Madine was substituted to a standing ovation with six minutes remaining and his dramatic personal turnaround was completed when United's supporters voted him as their man of the match. In a refreshingly-honest post-match interview Madine, clutching the man of the match champagne and his shirt from the game as a memento, admitted he "didn't get going at Cardiff" and "lost fitness, confidence and goals". "I wasn't in a good place," he added. "I was six hours away from home and I'm a bit of a home boy. I'm back home three or four times a week now and I think it's put a smile on my face while I'm playing. I'm buzzing.

"I've had my troubles off the pitch but if you ask anyone who's worked with me, no-one will speak bad of me from inside the club. I saw a few fans saying I'd rock the dressing room and things like that but believe it or not I am a nice lad. I think I get on with all the lads. Fair enough, I've had a bit of bother when I've had a drink in me. But day to day, I turn up, do my work and go home again. You won't hear a peep from me."

Later, on *BBC Radio Sheffield*, Madine risked spoiling a surprise party that night by revealing he was going to a 50th birthday celebration after the game and revealed: "I won't say I'll never have a drink again but I'm learning as I get older to pick and choose when to have a drink, rather than thinking I can go out on Saturday and Tuesday and then perform at a high level. That's probably why my career stalled a little bit and at this level, you have to be bang at it. I've learned the hard way. Sometimes you need good people around you. When I got promoted at Wednesday, the manager literally shut the door on me instead of putting an arm around me and saying: 'You need to do this and that better'.

"As a 21 or 22-year-old kid what else was I meant to do? Some people may have done things differently but I needed a release from football. So I did the only thing I knew and went to a bar or a nightclub. As I say you learn from experience and I've got good people around me now. I had one option that was probably better for my own head, to be even nearer home, but football-wise, coming to United was perfect. I believe we are the best team in the league and play the best football, so it's where I had to be for football reasons."

Despite Madine's belief, and with rivals Leeds breathing heavily down their necks, the tests kept on coming for United as they looked to strengthen their grip on second place. A week on from the Reading win, United were momentarily leapfrogged by Marcelo Bielsa's men when they beat lowly Bolton, ahead of United's televised Sky Sports game at West Bromwich Albion that evening. The Baggies' squad remained packed with international footballers, despite the blow of relegation from the Premier League the previous season, and Wilder was wary of another "huge challenge" his side faced at The Hawthorns.

Step forward another unlikely conqueror. 'A hero will rise, to head in the first' screamed the Gladiator-style front cover of Albion's match programme for the game, and Dowell just did that when he leapt highest to nod home Cranie's cross. The centre-half had bust a gut to keep the ball in play after Freeman overhit his pass and Dowell, restored to a more natural No.10 role after playing at wing-back against Boro, looped his header over Sam Johnstone to put United ahead. United were then forced into yet another defensive reshuffle when Egan was withdrawn through injury at half-time, before Jay Rodriguez was penalised for handling the ball into the net late on. By taking three points at the home of the Baggies United had passed another huge psychological test, yet the win really looked in doubt only as the clock ticked towards full-time.

Albion substitute Jefferson Montero raced clear after punching a rare hole in United's defence, but goalkeeper Henderson came up trumps when it mattered with a stunning one-on-one save. The three points again came at a cost - Egan and Cranie both came off with calf injuries, joining O'Connell and Baldock on the sidelines - but another makeshift backline, this time of Freeman, Basham, Stearman, Stevens and Marvin Johnson, saw out the game. "Boro at home was one of the most nerve-wracking games I've ever experienced in my career," Stevens said. "I was covering for Jack at that left centre-half position, which is a mad position because it's basically made up! But it was a good experience. We had me, Egs and Cranie with Dowell at left-back. He was excellent, and then Marv came in and stood up at West Brom after coming in against Reading."

"To go to a place like West Brom with a makeshift back five

was brilliant and I ended up with a better record in Jack's position, than Jack!" Stevens joked. "I reminded him of that, but I think he already knew. He wouldn't speak to me for ages and I think he lost a bit of weight because he was worried about his place!"

Defeat left the Baggies fourth in the table, four points behind United, but two weeks later boss Darren Moore - a big pal of United chief Wilder - was unceremoniously sacked. The United game was the first time that season that the Baggies had failed to score at The Hawthorns - mainly because of Henderson's big, last-minute save. "At that moment the whole of Sheffield United was looking at *me* to stop the ball going into our net," Henderson recalled. "That's what I love so much about goalkeeping. I'm the last line of defence and I have a say in what happens. Often I'm the only one with that say.

"The feeling when the ball hit me and rebounded to safety and it was like: 'Oh my God, I've done it'... wow. The little section of United fans at the other end of the ground went mad and we went on to win the game. Little things like that can be so important. We went to West Brom and won! With the atmosphere before the game, I thought: 'This is impossible to win' but we came home with the three points. The best feeling in the world. I've never taken drugs but I presume that's what it feels like. We came in the dressing room again and said 'we're really here'."

I started to believe
by Paul Commons

February. The end of the transfer window. Does that mean it's safe to plug the fax machines back in and come out from behind the curtains? In all seriousness, though, having been an avid fan of the Blades for 25 years, February often starts with a bitter taste in the mouth for most fans; none worse than the decision to sell both Brian Deane and Jan Åge Fjørtoft within 24 hours of each other in January 1998.

Put simply, February normally dawns with abject disappointment and an air of resentment. Why would this latest transfer window have been any different? With an increasingly souring ownership wrangle, anyone could have been forgiven for thinking the worst. To come into February having strengthened our options by signing Kieran Dowell, Scott Hogan and Gary Madine pointed to the enormous effort and meticulous planning that had taken part behind the scenes.

First up, Bolton at home. Outside of Sheffield and Greater Manchester, no-one would know a rivalry between United and Bolton exists. I myself am still unsure why it does - let's put it down to the 'inferiority complex' that Bolton's chairman Ken Anderson seems to exude every time he mentions our beloved Blades - but I can pretty much guarantee that there is little room in the head of Chris Wilder and Alan Knill for such things. Coming into the game off the back of a deserved point at leaders Norwich, Bolton proposed an altogether different prospect.

Since Christmas, this group had engineered huge expectations for themselves and the feeling was more like how many we would win by, rather than if we would win at all. I hate that. Always have, always will. It is, though, a perfectly honest reflection on the expectations this group had set for themselves. A nervy performance without much/any threat from the visitors eventually ended with a wave of relief. Job done.

Villa always looked a great deal tougher. Back in October, they went down the route of hiring Dean Smith, a lifelong Villa fan who had a proven track record of getting the most from limited resources by playing a high-tempo brand of football. There are certainly similarities to be made with our own manager. In fact, Smith even spent time playing his football in Sheffield... on second thoughts, let's not open that can of tuna. Sorry, worms. Can of worms!

I'm not sure whether it was the Sky Sports-enforced late kick-off - or perhaps the embarrassment of riches and unnerving amount of talent the hosts possessed - but visiting Villa Park, under the lights, started to feel as if it might be a season-defining game. 'We must not lose'. Chasing down the top two from a relative distance leaves very little margin for error. The old cliché, 'Cometh the hour, cometh the man' has seldom rung truer.

Within 62 minutes, Billy Sharp had us racing into a 3-0 lead. Unassailable, surely? You know what, though, that's when football is at its best. It might not feel like it at the time but it happens to everyone, every once in a while. Dean Henderson, still only a young lad who had amassed us an immeasurable amount of points in the season thus far, looked in shock at the end of the game. Again, he won't have felt as if there were any positives to take at the full-time whistle but no-one will convince me that his performances didn't mature from that point onwards.

When the dust settled on Villa, I have to say that a point on their ground very much needed to be viewed as one gained. The kick in the proverbials made it feel exactly the opposite, but there were some real positives to take ahead of Middlesbrough. Does anybody ever look forward to playing a Tony Pulis team? 'Pragmatic' is the word that springs to mind. Boro certainly weren't winning plaudits for their free-flowing football, despite fielding a Champions League-winning midfielder in Jon Obi Mikel who should still be considered in his 'prime'. Boro were still firmly in the play-off mix at that point - a win at Bramall Lane would have lifted them to within a point of us - but our sights remained firmly forward-facing.

Jack O'Connell's absence though surely meant a change in formation, and disruption to the system that had seen us bearing down on the top two at a rate of knots? I put out a tweet earlier in the year saying something along the lines of 'It's Chris Wilder's world, and we're all just living in it'. Who among us can honestly say they thought of playing Dowell at left wing-back? Not me. The youngster put in one of his most mature performances of the season but somewhat inevitably, the 'intensity' of the match - and the opposition's tactics - took their toll, as George Baldock gingerly limped down the tunnel.

I personally don't think that there is anyone I would rather turn to in a time of need than Richard Stearman. I once met him in a bar with the rest of the group in 2017, after United had dismantled a richly-assembled Hull team. Stearman was relatively new to the group and obviously happy, at the time, to avoid the limelight. Even though I was relatively inebriated, I managed to convey the growing feeling of a bond between supporters and players that we had developed since the change in management team, and how there was a feeling that we were seeing only the start of something special. Stearman, though, was quick to recognise everyone else's contribution to that, and how he played a relatively small part in it.

I distinctly remember recounting our brief, drunken chat as I watched him leap highest to give us a crucial win over a top-six rival. How fitting that a man who is quick to divert praise to his teammates, should be the match winner? The outpouring of passion in his celebration was there for all to see. If you ever need a yardstick to judge his character and influence, just have a look at how quickly he was mobbed by every single one of his teammates. That's the sort of signing we've come to love and expect from Wilder. Not all of them will go on to pull on the jersey every week, but you can bet the ones who don't are chomping at the bit to give their all for club and manager.

It seems almost incomprehensible that Reading finished third in 2016/17 and lost only in the play-off final on penalties, because their decline since that day at Wembley has been quite astonishing. It's certainly not been through a lack of resource. They signed Sone Aluko for twice the price of our record signing, John Egan. It's difficult to pinpoint where they've gone so spectacularly wrong, but I would be lying if I said I wasn't completely confident that we would get a result at Bramall Lane. I genuinely don't mean that in a disrespectful or arrogant way, but the expectation of the fans was seldom left unfulfilled by this group of players. Early goals always help calm nerves and, 3-0 up at half-time, there was only going to be one winner.

Reading actually ended the game with almost 60 per cent of the ball but to say they flattered to deceive would be an understatement. If anything it made me appreciate what we have under Wilder and Knill. We often have the lion's share of the ball but it's not without purpose. Give me overloading centre-backs and full-backs playing as wingers any day, over sideways passing across a flat midfield in the centre of the park. Occasionally cries of: 'Get it ******* forward!' can still be heard, only for a defence-splitting pass to occur in the next phase of play… and a wry smile creeps across my face.

It's a sign of how far we've come in such a short space of time. The tactics have been radicalised to the extent that some fans confuse patient, purposeful, build-up with a lack of intent. We've not only been dragged kicking and screaming into modern football; we've smashed through the other side with swashbuckling aplomb.

I remember waking up on the day of the West Brom game with butterflies in my stomach. A cauldron of nerves and excitement. As a Blade, it can often feel only as if it is a matter of time before something good comes to an end. A flash in the pan. I remember the reverse fixture at Bramall Lane where we were beaten by the better side. I came out of the ground thinking 'We never win the big games'. Capitulation down the road at Villa was fresh in my mind. But something changed that evening at West Brom, and I can't place it.

We played largely the same way we always do - as shown by the build-up to Dowell's winner, and the players involved - yet somehow we felt more mature. Before the game, Baggies fans had been far from complimentary about United but heaped praise on us afterwards. The old adage about being gracious in victory and humble in defeat sprung to mind. Maybe they genuinely still thought of United's top two aspirations as a pipe dream. Until that day I think, subconsciously, I did too.

I've got a long-standing tradition of a half-time pint with a good friend of mine, Alex. He is a long-suffering Blade too and we've been conditioned to expect disappointment with United B.C. - Before Chris! I'd frequently message him saying 'it's happening, we're going up' - perhaps in an attempt to persuade myself, more than anything else. The final whistle at the Hawthorns was probably the first time I'd genuinely believed it. He's more pessimistic than I am and, for the first time, his lack of tempered response told me one thing. The dream that most of us believed was nigh-on impossible, was actually far from it.

Enjoying my football
by Dean Henderson

Winning promotion to the Premier League with Sheffield United has been the best thing ever to happen to me in my life, up to this point. I remember looking up at the Blades badge at the top of the stand after the Ipswich game and thinking: 'This is mad, we've actually done it'. I'm only young but I've come on loan and we've got promoted to the Premier League. I think stuff like that will go down in history. It's pretty mad, but I'm delighted about it.

Promotion sort of sunk in for me pretty quickly, because I thought it was going to happen all season. So I almost got used to the fact we were going to do it anyway. But the way it happened was really good; it's not been given to us and it's not been easy. We could have run away with promotion at stages, but it's sometimes good to have little upsets. They make it even sweeter when the success does come in the end. Growing up at Manchester United, you learn to become a winner but you also learn to work hard for everything you've got. I remember in my days at Carlisle when I had to buy all my training kit, and my parents had to travel to take me everywhere for games.

We come from a town called Whitehaven, so to get to the Manchester area to play teams like Bury and Oldham took us like three hours. And my mum and dad were doing that when I was 12! Those were the humbling days which help to keep you grounded. Everything I've worked for hasn't come easy, so I try to enjoy the good moments when they come. Because you never really get them back. I've had to sacrifice a lot; when your friends are going out partying at 17 or 18 and sneaking off from their parents to house parties in school, I've never really done that.

It's funny because when you're doing well, a lot of faces come out the woodwork. But my circle is really small and my family deserve a lot of credit because none of this would be possible without them. If I was to get ill tomorrow I know they would be there for me, whereas a lot of people wouldn't. People can try to stab you in the back and get you down when you're doing well. It's jealousy at the end of the day. People try to get involved and try and tell you where to put your money, for example, and it goes wrong.

But it's the family who have always been there, looking out for me and not wanting anything back. When we had nothing, they were driving me everywhere; who else would have done that? Certainly not the people who want me to buy them drinks in nightclubs, or whatever. Being a footballer can be frightening like that at times. It's a mad sport. Everyone wants a piece of you; wants this, that or the other from you. You've got to be pleasant but know the restrictions, really. The game's a bubble, though. And people don't understand the effects mentally.

I'd say it's 80 per cent mental, especially as a goalkeeper. You win on a Saturday and come in buzzing, emotions so high. The fans love you, the gaffer's smiling. Everything's great. Then you lose on the Tuesday. No-one likes you, they think you're a... well, they're not happy with you. It's like constantly living in a bubble and the effect can be huge. That's why this group at Bramall Lane is so special. We all look out for each other and we're mentally strong; we're like brothers in the changing room, and that's why we were so successful in 2018/19.

For me, going out on loan is where you really learn about football. It's like driving, I think; you learn more from getting out there on the roads on your own, than you do in the car with your instructor, telling you how to use the clutch and all that. You naturally get better by getting out there and making your own way. I said when I first came here, there's no point in sitting in a jacuzzi at Manchester United saying you're good. Go and show that you're good! Go and prove it.

There was no point in sitting in the under 23s at Old Trafford, third choice to the first team, saying 'I'm going to play for Man U' because you're not. Which Man U manager is going to put you in the first team, with no first-team experience? None. I needed to go and make my path slightly different. I showed character, went out on loan in the last year of my contract, with no security. I backed myself and it reaped rewards. You've got to believe you're great, or you never will be.

How are players going to be able to play in front of big crowds if they don't back themselves? No-one else will if you don't. I went from strength to strength from there, agreed a new deal at Man U and then came to Bramall Lane on loan. To be honest, I'd felt ready to play Championship football for a while before and I feel the Premier League will suit me more than any other league, because I've been brought up that way. I make my saves, good distribution with both feet, that kind of thing.

The lower I've been, the harder it's been for me. Stockport was the hardest time of them all. Teams kept lumping balls in the box and at 17, I just kept getting smashed. I actually found it easier as I moved up the levels. There was more football than long-ball stuff, smashing it a million miles and seeing what happens. But those experiences have made me a better player. Put it this way, could you put Hugo Lloris in Grimsby's team and expect him to do well? Questions would be asked, whether he's strong enough to deal with this, that and the other. Could you stick him in Stockport's net, or Shrewsbury's? I've been through all the leagues and proved that you can chuck me anywhere, and I can do it.

I think it'll be the same in the Premier League, if and when I get the chance. It might take me a few weeks to get going, but once I've done that I'll go on and prove I'm one of the best 'keepers in the Premier League that year. I'm confident it'll happen, too.

Being a goalkeeper's such a specialised position. As a kid I just thought 'this is class', diving in the mud and that. There's obviously a lot more than that to it, but mostly it's about loving having loads of footballs being smashed at you and being brave. You know how people say you have to have a screw loose to be a goalkeeper? It's absolutely spot on! When the gaffer here first expressed an interest, he spent 45 minutes on the phone with me and told me he wanted a goalkeeper who could come in and win points. He said Jamal Blackman did really well last season but didn't quite win any games; he let in the goals he should have and made the saves he should have.

But he said he wanted someone who could make match-winning saves. When he said that, I was thinking: 'That's me all over - he'll love me this guy!' When we met, he was great. I sat in his office and we just chatted about football and what we were going to achieve that season. I mentioned promotion and said to him: 'Listen, I just want to reach the Premier League. It'd be unbelievable. What a feeling!' Towards the end of the season he pulled me to one side and asked if I remembered that chat. I told him: 'Yeah, it's mad isn't it?' Then I said: 'I told you!' I think he thinks I'm psychic.

My goalkeeping coach at Bramall Lane, Darren Ward, has been outstanding. The best goalkeeping coach I've ever worked with. He's brought me on leaps and bounds in every aspect of the game - mentally, physically, tactically - and the sessions are brilliant. I look forward to coming into work every day, and long may that continue. If I could work with Wardy for the next couple of years, I really think I can elevate myself to being one of the best goalkeepers in the world.

In a weird way, I feel Wardy was more in charge of me at United and the gaffer is outstanding with that. He said to me at the start: 'Listen Deano; I won't be chewing your ear off every day. Darren's your coach, he knows what he's talking about and I don't have a clue about goalkeeping. I'll speak to you before games or whatever, but he'll look after you because he's the specialist'.

The gaffer has real good trust in his coaches. So the 'keepers go off and do our little thing in the corner. He's always keeping a watchful eye over us and making sure we're doing well though, not letting our standards slip. His standards are so, so high. But it's been a pleasure working with him. Sometimes I feel that I can get away with murder, but he doesn't let me. He's the only guy, apart from my dad, who gets on at me and doesn't let me get away with anything, but does it at the right times. He also wants to have a laugh and I've got massive respect for him.

He's been great for my learning; he's put me in my place when I needed it, and put an arm around me when I've needed that as well. He's got that balance right. After the Rotherham away game, when we conceded in the last minute, I came out and said to the press that we were the best team in the league. We didn't quite win the league in the end, but I honestly believed we were.

I didn't fear anyone. I was looking at teams thinking: 'They won't beat us, they won't beat us'. I honestly believed it. When I say things, I mean it. I remember when Paul Hurst rang me about going on loan to Shrewsbury the season before I came to United. He was saying: 'We're going to get relegated, we've got no budget, we want you to keep us in the league'.

I said to him: 'Are you mad? If I'm coming we're getting promoted.' I was in Mexico when I said it to him, I remember it now. We got so close, too, losing to Rotherham in extra time in the play-off final. But I believed what I was saying, and I think that rubs off on people in the changing room. Look at George Baldock, who grew throughout the season, and sits next to me. And Enda Stevens next to him who became more and more confident by the game. Whether it's rubbed off on them from me, I don't know, but I'm always confident. All the boys have helped me as well, so we've improved as a unit and the season was so, so enjoyable.

I think I got better and better as the season went on, and the scary thing is that I'll keep getting better and better. And better and better, to the extent where I'll be the best. I'm a passionate lad and I wear my heart on my sleeve for any football club that gives me an opportunity. I just love playing football and I'm just like a young kid really, enjoying my life. I back myself, I'm not scared of anything and I wouldn't want to go into a game with anyone else's ability other than my own. I've got to go out there and enjoy it, because it doesn't last forever.

chapter eleven

All roads Leed-s to promotion

March 2019

After their superb victory at fellow promotion-chasers West Bromwich Albion, Sheffield United entered March well-placed in the race for the Premier League. The month began with United third in the table, just two points behind second-placed Norwich City and only three adrift of leaders Leeds United, who had played a game more. Despite United's good position, though, manager Chris Wilder felt somewhat conflicted.

It was nothing to do with points and places but rather the identity of his side's next opponents and, more specifically, their manager; Sheffield Wednesday, and Steve Bruce. Four days before Christmas, United's city rivals had finally pulled the trigger and sacked their manager, Jos Luhukay, after a poor run of form left them 18th in the Championship, and just six points above the relegation zone. Luhukay lasted 11 months at Wednesday after replacing Carlos Carvalhal, who was sacked on the previous Christmas Eve, and on January 2 Wednesday confirmed that former Blades player and manager Bruce would take the reigns.

Bruce had been out of work since he was sacked by Aston Villa in October - after a run of one win in nine games, including a 4-1 defeat at Bramall Lane a month earlier - but showed he at least retained his sense of humour when he bumped into Wilder's wife Francesca towards the end of his time at Villa Park. "She didn't know him but he came over and had a word," Wilder revealed. "He told her: 'Your husband nearly got me the sack!' He was joking and it shows he's down to earth. I've got a lot of respect for him and we'll definitely have a drink afterwards.

"I know there has been a couple of different opinions from opposition managers over the last couple of years. I think Carlos said 'It's just a game' which I didn't get and the other guy [Luhukay] said he's played in bigger derbies, which I didn't get even more. But Steve hit the nail on the head, being the man that he is. Being brought up in the north-east and having been involved in Manchester derbies and so-called derbies between Liverpool and Manchester United, he gets it. I get it, our supporters get it, their supporters get it, and the players get it. It's great to be involved in."

Wilder's description of Luhukay as 'the other guy' suggests their relationship was not a lasting one, but the same cannot be said of Bruce. The pair worked together briefly at Bramall Lane in the late 1990s and Wilder, despite his obvious feelings towards Wednesday, gave his opposite number the ultimate badge of honour by describing him again as a 'proper' football man in the build-up to the derby. "Steve was here as a player-manager, then a short period as manager," Wilder remembered. "That was the first time I got to know him. I wasn't really playing regularly, so it wasn't a big relationship. But, as he has said, he has taken note of my career, and I don't think you cannot take note of Steve's career as a manager and what he has done.

"He is a proper football man and a proper guy. He is a man who I have an enormous amount of respect for. He says it as it is, and he has certainly galvanised a really good group of players, at a powerful football club. But still, we don't want them to do well and they feel the same way about us. I wasn't sat there cheering them on when they were in the play-off final a while back and they won't be cheering us on and hoping we go up. That's just the way it is in the city."

Wilder wasn't wrong about that, but in modern times the rivalry between the two sides has become more hate-filled than ever. Vile chants, aimed at female relatives of both Wilder and Owls owner Dejphon Chansiri, could be heard from both sets of fans at the last derby in November, while supporters of both clubs united to condemn a disgusting message, posted by a

Wednesday fan on Twitter, which mocked the tragic death of United skipper Billy Sharp's newborn son back in 2011. "It has changed since I was a player," Wilder said. "I used to go out in town and see John Sheridan and Jon Newsome, another pal of mine, regularly. They both played for Wednesday but it was never a problem.

"There's always been that Saturday-night bit between supporters. I'm not trying to be confrontational about it; that's what happens, young men having a bit of rough and tumble on a Saturday night. But the other part has changed in the last five to 10 years, and I don't think the social media stuff has helped. We never used to get any hassle going out. The managers definitely never got any hassle going out. It happens in Glasgow, it happens in Liverpool, it happens in Manchester and it happens in London, that rough and tumble stuff. It's a passionate city but hopefully people behave because women and children will be going as well and this is for them too. This is a game for everyone."

Wilder's words, though, weren't heeded and this time it was the turn of United goalkeeper Dean Henderson to be targeted with sick abuse. The slurs began when Henderson posted a video on his public Snapchat page - visible to anyone who follows him - about his good night's sleep before it was recorded and re-posted on Twitter by a 17-year-old boy, who falsely alleged it had been sent directly to a girl. The tweet was shared widely online, before it was later deleted when it was pointed out that it contained both untrue and libellous accusations. But the damage had already been done and Henderson was subjected to vile taunts before, during and after the Hillsborough derby; both at the game, and on social media.

The on-loan goalkeeper, though, had the last real word in a game typically high on intensity but ultimately low on real quality. As the rain teemed down and soaked the Hillsborough pitch, former Owls man Gary Madine forced a good save from Keiren Westwood in the first half before Henderson denied Sam Hutchinson in the second. Hutchinson sneakily shouted 'Keeper's!' as a cross came in from the left and John Fleck pulled his foot away, before Henderson blocked the Owls' midfielder's shot well.

"You don't want to know what I had planned if we'd scored that night," Henderson reflected at the end of the season. "They're done, so I don't have to worry about them, but there was something there, for sure. They think that I was scared that night in front of them but we'd have seen who the real men were if we'd have scored. I would have been all over it, like. Honestly, I was blowing the ball in. I couldn't think of anything better than to celebrate in front of them."

Henderson may be a confident individual but the scale of the abuse he endured - continuously on social media as well as at Hillsborough and, later in March, at Elland Road - took its toll, to such an extent that he felt like driving his car off the Snake Pass. "I felt sick," he admitted. "If people were being racist then something would be done but instead, they can say stuff like that to me and get away with it? Honestly, it was horrendous. Some kid took the video off my Snapchat story and tried to stitch me up because he's a fan of another club? Stuff like that shouldn't be going on. Some of the things people were saying to me were the most sickening things in the world. I couldn't be called any worse.

"It was the first time, really, that I realised people are out to get me, hurt me and stab me in the back. I did nothing wrong and then for something like that to blow up, it was the biggest shock I've ever known. I thought 'Jesus Christ, what's that all about?' It was nothing at all, just about me having a good sleep. My old man told me I had to learn from it, deal with the consequences of people shouting stuff at me, move on and put it to bed. It just makes you a better person. From my point of view, it's all put to bed now. I just had to focus on my football and let that do the talking. That kind of stuff always blows over because that's football, isn't it?"

As a spectacle the derby was disappointing, and United left Hillsborough knowing they had lost ground on Norwich after dropping two points against their rivals - but the vast majority of Blades fans were left hoping that this would be their last visit to the home of their nearest rivals for some time, as they geared up for the final straight of their promotion push. "They had no interest in playing against us, did they?" said United midfielder Oliver Norwood. "It takes two to tango and they said they tried to come at us at Hillsborough, but it was embarrassing to be honest. In a derby game, too.

"To play the way they played, I'd be quite embarrassed if I was one of their players. Listen, they got two points out of us over the season, didn't they? But I'm a football fan as well as a player and you want to see good football. You don't want to see a team sitting on their own crossbar and celebrating a 0-0 draw because it's easy to do that. It's so much harder to go on the attack and try to win the game. We tried everything we could to get a goal, but it wasn't to be and it was a bit of a damp squib in the end.

"Two poor games, really. In the home game we were good but in the away one, we got dragged down to their level a little bit. I've been brought up on derbies between Burnley and Blackpool and I know what it's about. And it makes it a bit more special when clubs have proper history, and proper rivalries. United is a proper football club and it's a privilege to be a part of it. Hopefully I'll be here for many more years to come."

Norwood, who had been partly culpable for a calamitous last-minute equaliser for Rotherham United at the New York Stadium earlier in the season, then got the chance to lay some of those demons to rest when Paul Warne's Millers visited Bramall Lane the weekend after the Hillsborough stalemate. Jack O'Connell put United ahead from a clever corner routine in the fifth minute - United knew the visitors had an aerial presence, so devised a clever set-piece which saw the defender side-foot home - before Millers skipper Will Vaulks became embroiled in a 'Towelgate' row on the South Stand touchline as he prepared to hurl one of his trademark long throws.

Vaulks then launched himself, with the same gusto, into a shocking challenge on the breaking George Baldock on the other side of the field, earning him a deserved straight red card from the referee Geoff Eltringham, before Mark Duffy scored a superb second goal with his left foot to put the game to bed in the second half. The Millers didn't have a shot on target throughout the 90 minutes and one of their better performances of the afternoon came in the post-match interviews from boss Warne - a popular manager on the circuit and without a doubt one of the most genuine.

"It's a journalists' dream isn't it, a story about a towel," Warne laughed. "We put the towel out and there was a complaint about it, so I said: 'It's there for both teams'. The ref said we could have it and the next thing we know, it gets thrown into the crowd. And then we're in all sorts of trouble. I asked the fourth official to walk another one down but he wouldn't - so that was brave of him - and I wasn't going to because I'd have got cups and all sorts smacked at my head.

"Then the ref decided to send Will off so we didn't have any more towel issues, and it was an absolute win-win really. To make matters worse, it was our towel! So that'll probably come out of my wages. I remember a Stoke player had something put in his shirt to help him to dry the ball but it worries me if we did that, something would go wrong. It'd end up being the heaviest towel ever or something and he wouldn't be able to run. It was a bit of a blow for us. But we'll get another towel."

Victory sent United second in the table - at least until that evening, when Leeds won at Bristol City - and also gave O'Connell further evidence for his theory that Duffy only ever scores when he does, denying him a man-of-the-match award and confirming the topic of conversation in the car home as the pair drive back to their native Liverpool. But O'Connell, a former Brentford man, was forced to revert to his bread-and-butter instincts of defending in United's midweek clash against the Bees, when he received the only ever 10/10 mark ever given by the writer currently tasked to rate United's players for the *Sheffield Star*.

Brentford arrived at Bramall Lane 13th in the table - a position which rather belied their reputation as arguably the Championship's best team from a technical perspective - and United went ahead when Norwood, again skipper for the day in Billy

Sharp's absence, calmly fired home from the penalty spot after Yoann Barbet had brought down Baldock. But the game turned in a moment of madness from striker Madine, who lunged recklessly at Brentford defender Ezri Konsa on the halfway line and was sent off with just 35 minutes on the clock. Madine later insisted that he'd tried to 'nick the ball' and that it could easily have just been a yellow; one of his teammates more accurately described it as a 'kung-fu kick'.

Either way, United got through to half-time without conceding and after Madine apologised to his teammates, the players had five minutes to themselves before Wilder entered the dressing room. 'Think back to the weekend and the game against Rotherham,' was the message, 'and remember how they didn't simply lie down after having a man sent off'. United, the players reminded themselves, were actually in a better position, with a lead to hang on to. What followed was one of the best defensive displays in recent memory at Bramall Lane as United - and O'Connell, fellow ex-Brentford man John Egan and Fleck in particular - bravely threw themselves in the path of everything that came their way.

One block from O'Connell, as he charged down Emiliano Marcondes' goalbound shot, actually burst the ball and although Neal Maupay and Kamohelo Mokotjo had good chances to level - the latter hitting the post with a well-struck effort - still United continued to hold out, against a Brentford side that ended the game with 70 per cent possession and 29 shots at goal. Then came the key tactical switch, as Wilder summoned striker Sharp from the bench and send him on in place of right-back Baldock, to encourage his side to play further up the pitch. It worked.

From Fleck's right-wing corner, as United enjoyed a rare foray forward, O'Connell headed the ball into the path of half-time sub David McGoldrick, who swept the ball home to an almighty roar around Bramall Lane. The tension and relief lifted in an instant, and it became an evening when the Blades really began to believe. "That was when I knew we could do something special," Norwood later admitted. "One hundred per cent. The number of clearances and headers that Jack and Egs made was incredible. I think we could still be playing now and we still wouldn't have conceded. And what a clever bit of management from the gaffer to bring Bill off the bench and leave Didzy on, even when we were down to 10 men.

"It was mental. I was thinking: 'What are we doing here?' But it got us up the pitch and helped us press better. We got a corner, Didzy stuck it in and we were away. The feeling after the game was like: 'We can get through anything'. When he scored, the noise made the hairs on the back of my neck stand up. In moments like that, your character comes into play. Down to 10 men, it's a case of: 'How much do you want this? How much do you want to get to where we want to be?' We knew it would be tough. If there's a team you don't want to be a man down against it's Brentford, because of how they play. But we weren't to be denied that night."

O'Connell enjoys that type of gritty, 'backs-to-the-wall' performance more than any other and believed that United demonstrated their growing maturity by seeing games out when they were under the cosh - something he admits they failed to do on occasion the season before when they ultimately fell short of the play-offs. After the disappointment of the Aston Villa capitulation, the Brentford game was United's sixth in a row without conceding a goal and Henderson's England U21 teammates had started to call him 'Cleano'. By this stage, with just nine games remaining, third-placed United were seven points clear of West Brom in fourth but two behind second-placed Leeds - their opponents the following weekend, away at Elland Road.

Little wonder, then, that Leeds defender Pontus Jansson described the game as the 'biggest of their lives'. "We need you more than ever," the defender said in a call-to-arms to fans, posted on social media. "So we ask you to come to Elland Road one hour before the game and be with us already from the warm-up and create an atmosphere that hasn't been seen at Elland Road before! So everyone with a ticket on Saturday, spread the word and see you on the warm-up. Together we will do this!"

Leeds' famous old stadium, though, wasn't even near half full an hour before kick-off as the rain fell incessantly from the West Yorkshire sky, peppering the tarpaulin covers which had protected the Elland Road pitch overnight. The conditions did little to add to the spectacle from United's point of view as they struggled to get to grips with the game. Sharp summed up his side's start rather succinctly when he admitted Leeds "battered" United for the first half hour or so.

The visitors did enjoy the best chance of the half just before the whistle, when Chris Basham rounded Leeds' former Real Madrid goalkeeper Kiko Casilla but couldn't take advantage, and Sharp sensed some frustration at half-time in the away dressing room. The United skipper reminded his players that they had actually pulled off a classic 'away-team' display so far by weathering the Leeds storm early on, with boss Wilder adding that big chances would come his side's way in the second half. Jansson missed one of his own when he somehow poked wide a cross from the right-wing when it seemed easier to score, before the breakthrough eventually came... from an unlikely source.

Basham, who has reinvented himself as a marauding centre-half in Wilder's unique 3-5-2 system at United, was redeployed in midfield for the trip to Leeds in an attempt to give the Blades some extra steel in the middle of the park. But he struggled and Wilder later admitted, only half-jokingly, that he was in danger of being substituted after about 25 minutes. But Basham did emerge for the second half and showed typical bravery, determination and energy to get forward in support of Sharp, who was battling for the ball between Jansson and his old mate, Liam Cooper.

As Basham arrived, leaving Barry Douglas trailing in his wake, Sharp laid the ball off for his teammate and Basham found Casilla's bottom-right corner with a curling, clinical, first-time shot. His subsequent celebration, sliding on the wet turf in front of the jubilant Blades support, became one of the defining images of United's season. And Blade Keiron Salt almost missed it, among the carnage in the away section down one touchline at Elland Road. "I started about ten rows from the pitch but the surge took me right to the front - which was much lower than pitch level," Salt recalled. "I couldn't see a thing, and then Bash's head popped up over the advertising boards when he got up after his dive. Absolute carnage, and quite surreal."

Leeds were later reduced to 10 men when Casilla had a rush of blood and fouled Sharp, and Wilder pushed away a Sky Sports camera that had encroached into his technical area as the full-time whistle loomed.

After what seemed an eternity of injury time it eventually arrived, to an explosion of joy from the away section of Blades fans; delight from goalkeeper Henderson, who was targeted incessantly with vile abuse again; and then criticism from Leeds striker Patrick Bamford. "Hearing the fans and hearing the Sheffield boys," Bamford said, "it was as if they already think they're up."

It was nonsense. Yes, United celebrated the victory - as well they should, too, after winning at the home of their nearest promotion rivals, at that stage of the season - and knew they had taken a big step forward in the race for second place, by leapfrogging Leeds into the automatic promotion places. But eight games still remained in the regular Championship season and United knew that nothing had been decided on that glorious day in West Yorkshire.

"I heard 'Leeds this' and 'Leeds that' throughout the season and a few things wound me up, and a few things came back to bite them in the a**e while we went about our business," said Sharp. "Their fans put up a mosaic in the stand before a game saying 'Believe', as if we didn't believe. It helped us a little bit. You could tell in the gaffer's reaction and in interviews that he was frustrated too, but they were a great team throughout the season. I honestly wished them luck in the play-offs. Although I was glad we weren't in them."

Jansson later deleted his post-match Twitter post and there was also a healthy amount of schadenfreude directed his way on social media at the end of the season, when Leeds fell in the play-offs and he was shown on Sky sitting disconsolately by the side of the Elland Road pitch. Enda Stevens, the Blades defender, summed it up nicely. "There was talk of Leeds fans turning up for the warm-up," the Irishman said. "We turned up all season."

Basham's strike at Leeds was eventually voted as United's 'goal of the season' - Kevin Cookson, United's head of media, joked with Basham that it was the first tackle ever to win the award - and on the way back from Leeds the defender tried, with varying degrees of success, to convince anyone who would listen that the slide as he hit the ball was intentional, to shape it away from Casilla, rather than him simply slipping on the wet turf.

"Did I have any doubts when the ball fell to Bash at Elland Road? Yeah!" joked Norwood. "Bash was incredible all season. What a player and what a person. I was thinking when it broke to him: 'Please Bash, just score'. We all thought he'd slipped but he told us afterwards, 'I slid to draw it out of the 'keeper's reach!' If anyone deserved to score that goal, for the service he's given to the club, it's Bash. There are no airs and graces about him and he works hard every day, like the rest of us. And it was a good slide tackle!

"To win there was a great feeling because we'd been written off and told that they were going to beat us. There was a lot of noise from the Leeds players and all the pundits and every-thing else. So yeah, it was nice. Leeds seem to get promoted in August every year, don't they? I think it's incredible. I say that without being arrogant or putting the club down because I think it's a fantastic football club. They have a fantastic stadium and a great history. I had a few bits of stick on Instagram from Leeds fans and I was desperate to write back at times. Myself and Bill got some new suits from a company when we got into the team of the season, and a Leeds fan commented, saying 'I hope you've got your suits ready for the play-offs'. I was so tempted to give him a little message at the end of the season, saying he could have mine for the play-offs if he wanted... since we wouldn't be needing them."

After leaving Elland Road, United's staff - and the players

who weren't on duty with their countries - decamped to Valencia for a warm-weather training camp during the international break. Wilder and his coaching staff made the decision to fly to Spain based on a 'gut feeling' - United had many tired bodies, the weather forecast in Sheffield was hardly promising and they needed to get away from their training base.

Instead, they swapped Shirecliffe for the renowned Parador de El Saler resort - as soon as United checked out, the Spanish national team moved in - and although their training gear, bibs and cones were packed for the flight, the trip was about recharging batteries as much as it was about technical or tactical work. United's players were also permitted to enjoy a beer during their downtime, although the trip didn't have the immediate impact the coaching staff would have hoped for as they returned to England and lost their next game, at home to Bristol City.

Andreas Weimann netted a hat-trick as he became the first player to score at Bramall Lane in the league since Harry Wilson, for Derby on Boxing Day, and United's 10-game unbeaten run came to a grinding halt despite them twice leading, through Sharp and Scott Hogan. Wilder refused to blame the warm-weather camp for the defeat, though, and instead took some solace in the statistics from the game, which confirmed that Lee Johnson's City had made more sprints and covered more miles than any other visiting side at Bramall Lane all season.

"We felt we needed to get away during the break," Wilder said. "You never know if it's definitely the right thing to do - we came back, got beat by Bristol City and we were thinking 'Should we have done it?' But we felt it was the right thing to do. We looked at the last eight games and knew we were in a good position after the Leeds game, if we kept our nerve. Looked after our business and accumulated points. We thought that if we could take two points a game from those last eight games - which is promotion form, especially at the business end of the season - we'd be okay.

"There was a lot of hype about the Leeds game but we were a tired group. We'd played 60 minutes with 10 men against

Brentford, a side who moved us about all over the place, and then we had to pick a side to face Leeds. When they played West Brom and Derby - especially West Brom - Leeds battered them in the first 15 or 20 minutes, so it was important that we established a foothold in the game. Yet again it was another organised, resolute performance and we got the goal. We were keeping clean sheets but we still had an attacking threat.

"I have an enormous amount of respect for Leeds and Marcelo Bielsa, because they're a really talented group. We felt we didn't deserve to lose the game against them at Bramall Lane and they will probably feel they were marginally better at their place, but that's how it rolls. We weren't big-time after it, although Bamford annoyed me with his comments about us celebrating like we were already up. They were so predictable, and I've never done that in my career.

"So I had that in the back of my mind if it did go wrong for them, but that was just him as an individual and nothing to do with Marcelo or the football club. We never said anything, went over to our fans who followed us up and down the country all season, got back in the changing room, and then on the coach and off to Valencia, while the international boys were away. It was so predictable for a player to deflect from his performance to try to start the early mind games… which didn't pan out well for him or Leeds."

As a veteran of so many promotion campaigns previously in his career, Wilder stressed the importance of keeping level-headed and consistent to his staff and players but one thing, from his point of view, did change. In the build-up to the City game Wilder warned members of the press at Shirecliffe that his media briefings until the end of the season may become 'boring' and that, as a keen cricket fan, he intended to adopt the Geoffrey Boycott approach and meet questions with the straightest of bats. The United manager also revealed his dislike of the phrase 'twists and turns', which had become something of a cliché when used to describe the yo-yoing battle for promotion between Leeds and his Blades.

But the race did indeed take a twist and then a turn on the

dramatic afternoon that saw United lose to City, while Leeds were in action at home to Millwall 30 miles up the M1. At one stage, with United 2-1 ahead and Leeds losing by the same scoreline, the 'as-it-stood' table had United four points clear of Bielsa's men; then Weimann levelled the scores at Bramall Lane, and Luke Ayling equalised for Leeds.

The turnaround was completed when, within a period of a minute or so, Pablo Hernandez sealed the points for Leeds while Weimann broke United hearts.

For the first time, United's international players began to show signs of fatigue. Kieran Dowell, who had played in both England U21 games during the break, was due to be rested against City until Mark Duffy picked up an Achilles problem in training, while O'Connell sparked an injury scare by limping off during the game.

"The boys who went away looked a little bit sluggish," Wilder admitted at the time. "Looking at some of them, they ran their nuts off for their national teams and so they should. But it was always gnawing away at me, that we had to try to get through this game."

Striker McGoldrick was another who fell below his usual high standards, on the back of a superb display for the Republic of Ireland against Georgia and a standing ovation which he described as a career highlight. "A lot of people sit and think about their story but generally I don't," said McGoldrick, when asked to reflect on his rise to Irish golden boy less than a year after being released by Ipswich Town. "I'm just day to day. Whatever happens happens.

"God led the path and I'm just on that path. I always felt like I could play at the top and it's been a crazy season, but it could all change in an instant. So I'm just day to day. My faith is quite important to me. I was brought up with religion in my life, so I believe that everything happens for a reason. I thought my international career was probably over but my old boss from Ipswich, Mick McCarthy, got the job and got in touch soon after. It was a pleasure to get back involved. I love playing for my country, and long may it continue."

McGoldrick was born in Nottingham and was adopted as a young child, but qualifies for McCarthy's side through a maternal grandparent. "McGoldrick is my adopted name and there is Irish ancestry in my adopted family as well, but to play for Ireland it has to be through your blood," the striker revealed.

"I've never met any of my blood family. When you're adopted you get a file telling you about your background but I wasn't interested in that, because in my eyes the woman who adopted me has always been my mum.

"So the FAI and I had to do some digging to get me a passport, through my birth mother's parents. It's crazy when you think about it, but that's how I qualify. Everyone has their own backgrounds and I don't ask too many questions about it, but I was a baby in a foster home for a bit. A lot of people ask about it and find it interesting. But for me, it is what it is, and it's the path I've taken so far."

McGoldrick was named man of the match as McCarthy's men beat Georgia 1-0 in Dublin, and the home sections of the Aviva Stadium stood to applaud him as he was withdrawn late on. "I thought I had a good game and it was a really proud moment for me and my family who were watching," McGoldrick said. "For the year as a whole to go how it has - to cap it with a promotion, with this set of lads who I hang about with every day - it couldn't have worked out any better."

McGoldrick was regularly joined on international duty by Blades teammates Egan, Stevens and Hogan throughout the season, and McCarthy hoped to make that quartet into a five from Bramall Lane when he instructed FAI officials to investigate O'Connell's ancestry. "I couldn't do it anyway," the defender revealed. "It can only go as far as your nannan or grandad, and my great-grandad was Irish. Maybe they just looked at the surname! But I always get asked. They asked me when I was younger, when I first got picked for England."

O'Connell played for England U18s and U19s earlier in his career and now has his sights set on a call-up to the full squad. "A lad who I used to play with at Brentford, James Tarkowski, has made that step-up with Burnley and played at international level, so it has been done," O'Connell said.

"You've obviously got to be playing in the Premier League to be considered for England and there are definitely players ahead of me in the queue, the likes of Conor Coady at Wolves. But if I have a good season in the Premier League, I don't see why not."

Basham's arriving...
by Matt Casbolt

Sheffield Wednesday away is always the most dreaded fixture of all if you're a Blades fan, a trip to the deepest north of Sheffield. It's always an odd one going to Hillsborough, travelling there and walking outside the ground as, in a strange way, it feels more distant than a visit to somewhere such as Swansea away. I think it's because we're genetically wired, almost from birth, to dislike everything about the place. To make it worse, South Yorkshire's finest agreed to switch the game to a dreary, dark and rainy Monday evening, which reminded fans once again of their place in the pecking order for almost everyone, including the police and Sky Sports. Right at the bottom.

Wednesday had started to turn a corner after Jos Luhukay departed while the confidence levels of United fans were almost unnervingly high, after a hugely impressive victory at West Brom a week before. The whole of Sheffield, it seemed, was geared up for a truly memorable game. That meant, of course, that a third successive 0-0 draw was virtually inevitable and United couldn't find that bit of quality to decide the game. It felt as though United were dragged down to their level at times and the only bright spark of the second half was the introduction of David McGoldrick, who was a class above everyone on the pitch in the final stages of the game.

Thank the Lord we don't have to venture there again for at least a season, cup draws dependant. I'd also imagine it may take a lot of convincing from the powers-that-be for Sky to select the next Steel City derby - whenever it next appears on the fixture calendar - after the three previous uninspiring 0-0 draws. There is more of a friendly rivalry between the Blades and Rotherham United, and Paul Warne's club is one for whom the Blades have always had a bit of a soft spot. United began like a house on fire before one of the more humorous moments of the season concerning Will Vaulks and his towel. Presumably, it all got a bit too much for the Millers skipper as moments after giving away possession, an overzealous lunge on Baldock meant an early bath for Vaulks. Presumably it was compounded by the fact that he didn't even have his towel to dry himself off in the changing room!

As always, Warne dished high praise on the Blades after the game with a string of superlatives. I think all Blades fans would agree that the guy oozes class, and is generally one of the good guys within the game. After that, on to Brentford; one of the most infuriatingly brilliant sides I've ever seen at Championship level. They really are great on the eye and play an exciting possession-based style of football, but often lack that punch at both ends of the pitch when it really counts. If only they had a backbone of strong, commanding centre-halves like John Egan and Jack O'Connell... maybe they could find themselves closing in on the play-offs!

Even after the early goal, in true United fashion, this crucial game was never going to be plain sailing. Gary Madine left the ref with no other option but to show a straight red card, and we feared the worst. From then, Brentford were at their blistering best, moving the ball about with ease and causing United problems all over the pitch. Half-time proved a bit of respite before much of the same followed, with United camped in their own half - true backs-to-the-wall stuff. United's defence, though, admirably stood up to the onslaught with, for me, the colossal Egan particularly impressive against his former side.

Then came the change, George Baldock making way for Billy Sharp before a characteristically-tenacious performance from the skipper dragged United further up the pitch and away from their own box, to cause Brentford problems of their own. There aren't many managers in this league - or any league, for that matter - who would have the guts to swap a defender for an attacker while a man down and clinging on for dear life, but that rather sums up Wilder's fearless approach. What followed will be remembered in Blades folklore and for me was a season-defining moment, when McGoldrick sparked an eclectic and electric mix of joy and relief across the Lane.

I'd urge anyone reading this to dig out the highlights on You-Tube, and just listen to that roar from the Kop when that ball hit the back of the net. Spine-tingling. While the trip to Leeds would deliver arguably the key goal of the season, that McGold-rick header was symbolic of a side who could stand up to pres-sure, cope when things got tough and went against them, and come out fighting, attacking and with three valuable points. It felt like a true turning point and was a symbol of Wilder's tenure. This team was special and wouldn't collapse when the going got tough.

What a way to go into the Leeds game, intensified by the pompous attitude of Pontus Jansson. His rallying cry proved about as successful as his side's promotion attempt. Again Sky treated us to an early kick-off and the atmosphere was already lively at Sheffield train station by 7am, as Blades fans were packed in like sardines on trains shuttling up to Leeds. West Yorkshire Police had advised us, through social media, to drink in a bar just five minutes walk from the station. Several hundred United fans duly obliged and followed their advice, only to find it wasn't open until mid-morning and were left herded outside in the pouring rain. What's that saying about organising a get-together in a brewery?

Turns out it's not just their colleagues in South Yorkshire who are incapable of doing so. The welcome didn't extend to Elland Road - with just three turnstiles for 2,500 Blades to file through after queuing in the pouring rain - or when the game kicked off, either, as United again were forced to defend like warriors for much of the first half.

Marcelo Bielsa's men squandered several decent chances early on as the atmosphere built from both fans, United drown-ing out Leeds' bizarre 'Champions of Europe' song - which the home side still sing, despite the small problem of never actually being champions of Europe.

Then came Basham's moment, the most memorable of his career and arguably of United's season. The famous belly-slide, an iconic image, and those immortal words from Sky Sports commentator Daniel Mann: 'Basham's arriving'. A moment to remember, for so many years to come. Poor old Pontus put aside his hobble to go in goal when Kiko Casilla saw red for bringing down Sharp, and the scenes in the away end were simply phenomenal. We'd gone into the lions' den and beaten our promotion rivals when it really mattered. And yes, we let them know about it as well.

There just aren't enough superlatives to describe United's remarkable defensive performance that afternoon, in keeping a seventh consecutive clean sheet, and that game goes down with the *'Bouncing Day Massacre'* as one of my favourite-ever Blades away trips. Then it was back down to earth against one of our bogey sides in recent seasons, Bristol City. What a chaotic ending to the game.

The run of seven clean sheets came to a juddering halt as United's defence looked uncharacteristically rocky and even though United took the lead twice, the afternoon belonged to Andreas Weimann.

I thought the main turning point came with 15 minutes left, and United 2-1 up, when O'Connell limped off. Wilder has made some superb signings for United but the marauding centre-back has arguably been the best of them all and, if he has a successful Premier League season, he will soon find himself in the England setup.

I feel the same way about Jack as I did about Harry Maguire, Phil Jagielka and Kyle Walker before him; he's simply just a class above any other defender in the division. It was no surprise that, after he was forced begrudgingly to depart play, both City's equaliser and late winner came from down his flank. Both would've more than likely been prevented, had O'Connell been able to see out the game.

Another defeat after an international break, too; another curse which I'm sure Wilder will manage to banish. It was an afternoon of twists and turns, but ultimately ended up with Leeds gaining the advantage as they came out on the right side of a 3-2 scoreline against Millwall. It was hard not to feel a little despondent at full-time when that result came in, coupled with a rare home loss for the Blades. But deep down, I think we all knew it wasn't quite over yet.

Moment of the season
by Chris Basham

Promotion, for me, did take a while to sink in but around the time of the open top bus parade, seeing so many fans come out and cheer us on, it began to feel 'real'. A lot of people said that we looked like brothers while we were celebrating and it felt like that to us, too. We've achieved something we never thought was possible, but the gaffer had belief in us and it's worked out brilliantly. Personally, I'm more of a thinker than a believer but as the season went on, I started to believe more and more. We went to big places like West Brom and Leeds and weren't just getting results, *but winning*. And that became more and more infectious.

I remember telling my wife and family: 'This could actually happen here'. We pipped Leeds just at the right time, because we had a bit more momentum than they had. It became a two-horse race but we were always going to win it. Obviously it'd be hard for me to pick any other game than the Leeds away game as my highlight of a season that had so many. West Brom definitely comes close, but against Leeds it was vital that we didn't lose. Even a draw wouldn't have been great for us because of how the table was at the time, although they really went off the boil towards the end of the season so we might have caught them anyway. But things don't always work like that in football and if you get confidence, it's easier to just keep going and going and going.

Their place can be unbelievable at times too when the fans get going, so we knew that if we'd got beat there we'd have really struggled. I remember the build-up was like it was the biggest game ever. I normally try to keep myself settled on social media before games but I couldn't get off it in the week before we went to Elland Road. It was lashing down with rain and an early kick-off, and I didn't enjoy the first half at all. I struggled and they're a really good team, but in the second half, we grew. The gaffer gave us belief at half-time, saying we just had to keep plugging away and we'd get the goal. Then Billy passed it to me and the rest is history, really! It was certainly up there with the moment of the season, for me. The aftermath was huge and the fans seemed to have the best day ever.

I had a chance in the first half but screwed it up, just before the half-time whistle, and this time I thought 'just hit it as hard and low as you can'. And if I had to slide to go with the ball, then so be it. I didn't slip, but I did slide with it! It nestled lovely in the bottom corner, and then my emotions went.

Cheeks puffed out, slide on my front. I must have watched that goal about a million times since! And I bet every United fan did as well. I did the Klinsmann-style dive a few seasons before when I scored away at Bradford. It was a bit surreal to be honest, to score that goal, and it's hard to describe the feelings and emotions in words. If you could bottle them, I'd be sitting on a yacht in Marbella I think!

You can't reach that pinnacle anywhere else. Especially because I'd come from a two or three out of 10 in the first half, to making history in the second. I came from root bottom, not enjoying the game at all, to that ecstasy. It all turned around so quickly. Normally I can settle myself down in games and be a solid seven or eight out of 10, but that first half was tough. That's what football is like, though. We might go through some tough times in the Premier League but it can all turn around so quickly. There was such an emphasis on the game at Leeds, and the prize, so to go and get that prize of three points in their backyard was so sweet.

We all knew what a few of their players were saying in the press about us celebrating, but it meant so much to us and the gaffer. By then, we were counting down the games and how many points we might need. To get there was just an unbelievable feeling, especially after we lost our first two games of the season. I thought at the time: 'Here we go, we might be in a dogfight here' but when you go on a run of results, as I say, it's infectious. When you get momentum behind you at this football club, I don't think anything can really stop you.

Then, there's the gaffer himself. He's so demanding and you have got to be on the ball every day, because he's a 100 per cent man. All or nothing. It's because of him that we've done so well because he drives everyone on, every day. He's a perfectionist and goes over tactics and opposition in so many ways, putting us in a little shape box on Fridays and telling us who and what we'll be up against. The gaffer and Alan Knill nit-pick everything to make sure we're ready, and the staff and players follow him all the way. Like a few of us players, he also started his managerial career at the bottom and I think that makes us a special group.

We haven't been brought up with silver spoons in our mouths, but to fight for what we want rather than wait for it to be handed to us. For me, that meant working at McDonald's after leaving Newcastle United at 16. I didn't do it because I wanted to do it but because I had to do it. I had a scooter and stuff to pay for! So now I'm very grateful for what I get out of football. I thought my chance of turning professional had gone. Definitely. I was so old in football terms - I was 18/19, and not many players start their careers that late. But Sam Allardyce and Gary Megson believed in me and what I could do, the positions I could play and the motivation I could give the team. That has stayed with me throughout my career.

When the move to United came about, my agent said to me 'Chris, this is a great opportunity here - if you get the club promoted you'll go down in the history books as they've tried for so long'. Two years down the line when we were still in League One, I remember thinking: 'What's he going to say next?' But I didn't want to leave the club down in League One. It was a big decision for me to drop down because I'd just played a full season in the Championship with Blackpool. We had a bit of success with United under Nigel Clough but nothing compared to what's happened over the last three years. The plan was to take one step back to move three forward when I came here and under Chris Wilder, I think we moved about 20 steps in 2018/19 alone.

I was one of the players the gaffer inherited when he took over from Nigel Adkins, after the season we had. I felt sorry for Nigel a little bit because he'd had success elsewhere and it was disappointing that he couldn't replicate that here. It wasn't a nice time for anyone.

I was coming home from training or games and I wasn't how I should have been. We were being beaten by teams who, as a Sheffield United player, you shouldn't be getting beaten by and although everyone says you shouldn't bring work home with you, I'm a proud man, a man who cares. So that was difficult. If you read the 'paper or things on social media, it was hard to escape from and that affects everyone in your life.

It did hurt me very badly and if things aren't going well at work, it's horrible and it can depress you a little. But it's all worked out in the best possible way in the end. The gaffer came in then and I don't think he had many players left, but he wanted those he had to wear their hearts on their sleeves and I'm truly grateful to him for giving me the best days of my career so far. It was always going to be a difficult job because, no disrespect to Nigel, the club was on its knees. I'm still pinching myself now at how good a job he's done, to be honest. And under him, the boys have turned themselves into legends. It truly has been remarkable.

Chris has got more out of me than any other manager – things I didn't even know I had myself. It's down to the belief and confidence he has in his players, I think. And the formation we play also suits me down to the ground. He has his philosophy and it's been nothing but a success really, once everyone got on the same page. I remember when we changed the formation and he said to me that he didn't just want me to be a defender, he wanted me to attack as well as we needed to create the overloads.

That suited me to a tee as I'm one of the fittest players in the team, running-wise, and I always preferred to play centre-half because you're facing the play, rather than looking over your shoulder in midfield.

He told me to just drive with the ball as much as I could and if I had an assist in me, try and get the cross in. I loved it straightaway. Just get the ball, run with it and keep on running! The opposition find it really hard to track me because of the way I run, and Jack O'Connell - who has been amazing since he came into the club after a rocky little start - is the same on the other wing. It looks so good when we're in full flow but I'd absolutely hate to play against it. One million per cent. I don't think I'd be able to deal with it!

Every day Billy Sharp and the gaffer and Knilly and the rest of the staff are behind us, and that belief and morale have been big factors in our success. I think the decision to make Billy captain of the club was a masterstroke by the gaffer. Crucially, too, we enjoy our football. This year's been immense in that we haven't conceded too many goals - it hasn't been a case of 'You score three, we'll get four'. Instead we've kept clean sheets and scored two or three, which has been so important.

We brought in a bit of experience in John Egan - which is no disrespect to Richard Stearman, who is as good as anyone - and we were better players and staff for a year's experience in the division, too. We realised that the Championship wasn't as good as we were told it was when we first came up from League One.

The manager had an old saying when we went into games - 'We're not playing Real Madrid' - and he was right. We were a little bit anxious at first but we weren't playing Real, we were playing, say, Middlesbrough or West Brom.

Teams who had been relegated or been stuck in this league for so many years. I'm looking forward to playing in the Premier League again - it's a different league but I'm also a better player from when I played there before. I also scored for Bolton at Stamford Bridge, and I am so happy that my time in the Premier League isn't done. There are a few more memories to be made yet.

chapter twelve

Blades on the brink

April 2019

As winter turned to spring and the first glimpses of sunshine began to break over Sheffield United's Shirecliffe training base, boss Chris Wilder summoned his players into a room at the complex's top building for a rare meeting. United, by the manager's own admission, are not the type of club "to have a meeting about a meeting" because he fears they would lose their impact, although the two previous ones - after a 3-0 defeat at Middlesbrough early in the season, and the Aston Villa capitulation in February - did harness the positive response that Wilder and his staff were looking for.

This time, though, the mood was not confrontational and as he outlined the areas where he felt his squad could still improve, Wilder also took the chance to reinforce the things they had done right during the course of the season to that point. There were plenty. Despite the blow of a rare home defeat in their last outing, to Bristol City, Wilder's men began the month of April still well-placed in their pursuit of promotion, just two points behind second-placed Leeds - although leaders Norwich had opened up a seven-point gap between themselves and the Blades in third.

The latest shot in the mental war between United and Leeds had been fired the week before, when Tyler Roberts claimed the Whites were 'back where they belong' in the automatic promotion places. "I knew there'd be noise and nonsense from managers and players alike," Wilder responded. "There always is at this stage of the season. Where they belong? I know that's got to be earned. If anyone wins five out of seven or six out of seven, then I'll make a phone call to that manager saying well done, because they'll have deserved it. With everything that's going off, they'd deserve all the praise in the world if they did that."

Despite his measured response, though, Wilder could have been forgiven for flashing a wry smile in Roberts' direction the following weekend, when the promotion race took yet another turn. As Marcelo Bielsa's men went down 1-0 at Birmingham City, United beat Preston North End by the same scoreline at Deepdale, with David McGoldrick the hero. After an eye-catching run of form, which culminated in a man-of-the-match display for the Republic of Ireland against Georgia the month previous, his teammates and manager had jokingly christened McGoldrick 'Ballon D'or winner'.

"We didn't get too excited after Leeds and to lose to Bristol City was disappointing, but we knew there was still a lot of football to play," said McGoldrick after the game. "Now there are 18 points left to play for and anything can happen. There will be ups and downs. Will it change again? No-one knows. It might change right through to the end of the season. But there's a lot of experience in the group. We have level-headed boys who have been around the block and we're a real tight-knit group with a lot of characters. The young lads are level-headed, too. They know what needs to be done. We learned a lot from Aston Villa and how we chucked it away then. Against Bristol City we took the lead and needed to grind it out. Now there are six games left. No-one is jumping up and down now and celebrating."

That no-celebration policy was relaxed a little the following evening when Wilder, Billy Sharp and Oliver Norwood travelled to London for the English Football League Awards. Sharp and Norwood had already been named in the Championship team of the year, with Wilder selected as its manager, and on the night Sharp and Wilder were honoured with inclusion in the overall EFL team of the season. Sharp also picked up the 'moment of the season' gong, after he broke Rickie Lambert's record to become the highest scoring player in the English leagues since the turn of the millennium.

As the great and the good of the EFL mingled at the Grosvenor House Hotel on Park Lane, Sharp passed on his thanks to former teammate Che Adams, then of Birmingham, for scoring against Leeds, and caught up with his good friend Liam Cooper. The Leeds skipper, Sharp remembers mischievously, wasn't in the mood to talk about football 'for some reason' but Cooper's side were then handed the chance to put the pressure back on United when the fixtures were reversed in midweek. Leeds travelled to Deepdale while the Blades faced Birmingham, at St Andrew's, 24 hours later.

A month before, Wilder had warned journalists that he was about to become 'boring' in pre-match interviews to avoid giving unnecessary psychological ammunition to United's opponents and rivals. And the United manager was true to his word ahead of the meeting with Garry Monk's Blues, who were still reeling from a nine-point deduction handed down by the EFL for breaking their profit and sustainability rules. City posted losses of almost £10m higher than the permitted amount during a three-year period and their punishment could have been more severe, after they signed defender Kristian Pedersen from Union Berlin in the summer of 2018 while under an EFL transfer embargo. The hearing, though, decided that Pedersen's arrival should "not be treated as an aggravating factor" in the case.

"He's a bright and intelligent man," Wilder said of Monk. "Managers use whatever they can, be it people making outrageous comments or something happening to the team, to provoke a reaction and foster a siege mentality. They're a tight-knit bunch and have found themselves in a situation which obviously isn't ideal. But that's not a group of players who should be fighting relegation… not with the people in charge and the talent they've got at their disposal."

Wilder avoided a diplomatic crisis by revealing what many observers suspected were his true feelings about the EFL's financial rules as a whole, and his team travelled to St Andrew's out of the top two once again after Leeds beat 10-man Preston 2-0 the evening before. Any Blades hopes of a blistering start to the game were dashed by City's curious tactics - the Blues' strikers simply stood off Norwood, and gave him the freedom of the

West Midlands when he had the ball - before United took a big step towards reclaiming their top-two spot, when Enda Stevens lashed his first goal in 13 months through the grasp of home goalkeeper Lee Camp.

Moments later Blues captain Michael Morrison equalised after the ball dropped rather fortuitously into his path from a corner and United, despite enjoying more than two-thirds of possession, could not find a winner. As their players trooped into the dressing room after applauding their supporters in the away end, there was an undeniable air of disappointment among them at only taking a point - especially given the psychological impact of Leeds' win the evening before. Then Wilder got to work, reinforcing his well-worn message both to them and to the media. The promotion race, he reminded, would be about an accumulation of points. United also had the chance to strike first blood the following weekend, when they faced Millwall at home hours before Leeds played Wednesday in the day's televised, late game.

Three points at home over Neil Harris' struggling Lions would make Leeds' clash with Wednesday, with faint play-offs of their own, a must-win, pressurised game. That was the theory. It just didn't turn out that way. Both United and Millwall had escaped from the clutches of League One in 2016/17, and defied early-season predictions of struggle by threatening a promotion push in their first season in the Championship; eventually finishing 10th and eighth respectively. Harris' Lions ended 2017/18 only three points off the play-offs but with second-season syndrome very much taking hold, they arrived at Bramall Lane the following season just two clear of the relegation zone.

Both sides, for differing reasons, began a little cagily and Wilder attempted to raise the intensity levels by taking the positive approach when Chris Basham succumbed to a hamstring complaint early on, throwing on striker Gary Madine in place of the injured defender. Madine later relieved some of the tension in the second half when he put the Blades ahead, with a calm finish after good work from John Fleck. But United suffered a further injury blow when top scorer Sharp departed, also clutching his hamstring, and seemed to become increasingly nervy as the minutes ticked by.

Millwall steadily grew in confidence before the introduction of Tom Elliott completely changed the complexion of the game. United's reshuffled backline simply couldn't cope with his physical presence and, sensing blood, Harris' side continued to knock on the door until, with five minutes remaining, they thought they had finally got an answer. Elliott rose highest to meet Shane Ferguson's cross and send a powerful header towards the top corner of Dean Henderson's goal. The United stopper was completely beaten by the flight of the ball and, like the rest of Bramall Lane, could only watch on helplessly as defender John Egan desperately attempted to clear it off the line.

Realising he couldn't get to the ball with his head, Egan instead diverted it over the crossbar with his hand. The defender knew what was coming as he lay prostrate in the United goalmouth, head on the turf, and was shown the inevitable red card when he eventually dragged himself off the ground. But Ben Marshall, the former Wednesday loanee, stepped up and smashed the resultant penalty into the Millwall fans, via a deflection off the top of Henderson's crossbar. Egan's decision looked to have been vindicated. Bramall Lane seemed to breathe a collective sigh of relief as the home players looked to gather their thoughts, regain their shape and see out the game.

Then, disaster struck. In the fifth minute of stoppage time Elliott again caused havoc, forcing a good reaction save from Henderson, before Jake Cooper, Millwall's giant centre-half, poked home the rebound. United had dropped two vital points in the cruellest of circumstances, and the mood inside the ground changed in a heartbeat. Some fans kicked out at seats in frustration, others simply headed for the exits as if a part of them suspected this would happen. Many just stared straight ahead, at nothing in particular, with head in hands. All wondering if their top-two chance had finally gone.

"I remember getting back on the line after anticipating the header, and I'd done something similar for Brentford against QPR when I flicked it away with my head," Egan recalled at the end of the season. "This time their lad bulleted the ball off his head and before I knew it, it was past me. I jumped up to try and head it clear and my hand flicked up, instinctively. I didn't think 'I'm going to handle this', it honestly just happened. I fell to the floor, had a quick look at the ref to see if he was reaching for the red, and I was like 'Ah crap, I did handle it'.

"In the heat of the moment, I wasn't sure if I actually had. I was absolutely gutted and eventually, I dragged myself up and stood by the tunnel, waiting for the penalty to be taken. Thinking 'Please miss, please miss'. He blew it over the bar and I just thought, *'Promotion'*. In my head, it was a sign. I went to the physio room to watch the rest of the game with Bash and Billy, and it really felt like a kick in the stomach when they scored in the 95th minute. Everyone was down and I felt really down for a while afterwards, to be honest."

When the final whistle blew, Wilder raced onto the pitch to remonstrate with referee David Webb after he inexplicably failed to blow up for a foul on McGoldrick, by former Blade Ryan Leonard. The incident occurred right in front of the referee and seconds before Cooper's dramatic intervention, but Wilder was calmer after making the long walk up to Bramall Lane's media room. Instead, he then channelled his disappointment towards the approach taken by his players. "The thing I'm struggling with is whether they thought that was the best way to play," he said. "I think it was a mindset more than anything.

"It was a decision from players not to get forward and run forward to get up the pitch. The instruction didn't come from us. We all know, if you are 30 yards from goal, it gives the opposition more chance to ping a dangerous ball in. It's a thought process more than anything else. I told the players what my thoughts were and it wasn't an open house. I'm not bothered what they feel and what they think… I think it would have been someone quite brave to have taken me on 20 minutes ago. They've done fantastic but we want the big prize and you can't go backwards to grab that."

James Shield, the *Sheffield Star's* United correspondent, summed up the mood around the club in his match report when he wrote: "On the evidence of Saturday's contest, United appear inhibited rather than inspired by the prize on offer. And, although neither Fleck nor his manager would admit it, the debris of an uncharacteristically subdued display threatens to cast a shadow over their remaining fixtures." For that evening at least, the whole city of Sheffield was praying for a Wednesday win at Elland Road.

United's miserable day, though, was compounded when the Owls failed to hold out against Leeds, and only the inspired performance of goalkeeper Keiren Westwood made the game a contest. Again, the momentum in the promotion race had taken a big swing, this time up the M1, and that evening, as United's players and staff attended the supporters clubs' player of the year night, the mood was understandably subdued. The morning after, before training, the players took it upon themselves to gather for an impromptu meeting and despite the previous day's crushing setback, the mood was defiant and the message consistent: 'Leeds will give us another chance. They won't win every game and we'll get another opportunity. When we do, we're taking it and not giving it them back.'

"At times I thought we'd blown the chance," skipper Sharp later admitted. "We didn't want the play-offs. That'd be a killer, especially for the team who finishes third after being in the hunt for so long. I remember seeing a stat that said Leeds were in the top two for the most consecutive days, but I said to the lads: 'Forget about that. Whatever happens will happen. Make sure we're in with a chance going down to the last few days'. After Millwall, we were just hoping for another chance. With the kick-offs at different times, there were a few anxious days, just waiting and hoping."

By this point, United were three points adrift of Leeds - with only four games remaining - and the more pessimistic factions of United's support were convinced their hopes of automatic promotion were over. Some began to book hotel rooms for Wembley, where they had suffered so much heartache before, and one fan went a step further by staking £2,500 that United wouldn't be promoted. His rationale? If United went up, he would be too happy to miss the money and if they didn't, the disappointment would still be gut-wrenching - but he'd have £6,000 in his pocket, to spend on a holiday and try to numb at least some of the pain.

Despite United's various setbacks over the years, though, some optimistic fans do remain at Bramall Lane and they looked at things another way. In their final four games, United were scheduled to face Nottingham Forest, Hull City, relegated Ipswich Town and Stoke City - none of whom came with a real sense of dread - whereas Leeds had Brentford and in-form Villa to come, between easier-looking fixtures against Wigan Athletic and Ipswich.

Every eventuality and hypothetical scenario relied on one caveat, though; United had to take care of their own business first when, in an added twist to the drama, they kicked-off in three of their last four games hours before Leeds thanks to Sky Sports. The first was Good Friday's clash with Forest - a lunchtime kick-off ahead of Leeds' clash with relegation-threatened Wigan later that afternoon - and in the build-up to it, Wilder came out fighting. In the week after the Millwall blow, Wilder had one of his regular chats with Dave 'Harry' Bassett, the legendary former Blades boss who led United into the top flight while Wilder was still on the United playing staff.

"There was a bit of doom and gloom around the fans and the media and everything else, and Chris and I had a good chat," Bassett said. "I pointed out that when we were going for promotion in 1990 against Leeds, and we went to Elland Road and got hammered 4-0, we still ended up going up that year. I told him he couldn't listen to what was going on around him; he had to do what he thought was right. Players have to believe in themselves, and that success can be achieved. Sometimes the benefit of those experiences can help. And all of a sudden they can turn around and say 'Christ, yeah... he was right'."

United didn't quite adopt a siege mentality after the Millwall game, but it wasn't far off. Mark Duffy posted a quote from legendary former Liverpool boss, Bill Shankly, on social media - 'if you can't support us when we lose or draw, don't support us when we win' - in response to what he felt was unfair criticism of his teammates. "They were a minority of fans but I felt we needed to stick together, no matter what," Duffy said. "We give it our all when we go out there in every game, and in training every day. The lads here work as hard as any people I've ever come across in my life.

"We were all hurting so when I saw them getting criticism, I wanted to speak up for them. I care about them all and wanted the fans to know we were giving it our all. I'll just say it how it is, and there's nothing wrong with that for me. Everyone knows where they stand then. I've had managers in the past who'd look me in the eye and tell me one thing, and then go around the corner and say something different. I'd rather just be told straight, as the gaffer does. Black and white. Ask me a question I'll give you an honest answer and if I feel something needs saying to someone then I'll say it to them, not in corridors or behind backs. Resolve the problem, and go from there."

Perhaps in an effort to retain some perspective, Wilder sat with analyst Mikey Allen in the Bramall Lane changing room and discussed how far the club had come since he had taken over, when United had just finished 11th in League One. "He's been here a long time and sometimes, you have to take a step back and look at the progress you've made," Wilder added. "It's dangerous to write us off, as a team and as a staff. I know there are people out there who think we're done. I'll accept some of our own supporters probably think we're done. But I'm not done and these players aren't done either. These boys care. They care as much as any supporter and they care as much as me. And people know my background here. This is a huge weekend for us and, no doubt about it, we've got to win some games."

Oliver Norwood, the United midfielder, went a step further when he strode into the small interview room at Shirecliffe, and insisted he still felt promotion would be secured. "I don't care what people think about us," he said. "It is just noise. I do not care about the opinion on Twitter of John, who is 45 and still lives at home with his mum. It is completely irrelevant. I have seen it all in my time.

"Compliments, and the negativity when you draw or lose. It is what it is. Part of football."

Although some interpreted the comment about 'John' as a dig at United supporters, Norwood later clarified his point. "It wasn't directly aimed at United fans… it was aimed at the general consensus of the public, that 'if something doesn't go right, let's get on social media and vent our frustrations'," he said. "My point was that as footballers, with what we want to achieve, we can't worry about comments - good or bad - because we've been taught from six or seven years old to have thick skin. Yes, there will be negative comments and yes, there will be setbacks, as plenty of us have had. We've all not made the grade at a certain level and had to go away and rebuild… some more than I have."

Norwood singled out Mark Duffy as a 'prime example' to any young player who has experienced rejection in their lives, and so it was somewhat fitting that the former Vauxhall Motors and Prescot Cables forward should deliver a moment of magic against Forest, by curling an eye-catching effort past the substantial reach of their giant goalkeeper Costel Pantilimon. After a goalless first half, the visitors went down to 10 men when Yohan Benalouane brought down the advancing former Forest striker McGoldrick and was sent off. Four minutes later Duffy curled home, before full-back Enda Stevens ran half the length of the pitch with five minutes remaining to smash the ball into the bottom corner and seal the points.

Duffy faced the media afterwards but as he was being interviewed, almost everyone in the room - the Blades star probably included - had at least one eye on the television on the side wall, showing live updates from Leeds' clash with Wigan. By the time that Duffy had finished his interview commitments Wigan were already a man down, and a goal behind, and Leeds had also missed a penalty. The writing, many felt, was on the wall. But The Clubhouse, a Blades pub on London Road, erupted when Wigan's Gavin Massey equalised just before half-time, and Massey went on to score a second, assisted by United's on-loan striker Leon Clarke. After learning about Leeds' early goal, and

Cedric Kipre's unjust red card, Wilder decided against watching the game on the big screen in his office before being informed of the score with five long minutes remaining.

Toby Perkins, the Blades fan and Labour MP, was keeping up with events from Elland Road at the other side of Bramall Lane, in the John Street stand's International Bar. "Alan McInally informed us that Leeds had a penalty and Wigan had a man sent off," he remembered. "They missed the penalty but Patrick Bamford gave them the lead soon after, and every one of us began to fear that a rampant Leeds might erase our goal-difference advantage in a single afternoon. By the time we got to The Lescar at Hunter's Bar, Wigan had, to our amazement, equalised.

"We were still all convinced that it was a cruel trick, designed to get our hopes up, but were at least hopeful that the equaliser would at least mean Leeds wouldn't score a hatful. The sunny afternoon in The Lescar beer garden took an even more excitable turn as news came through that 10-man Wigan, the team with the league's worst away record, had actually gone ahead. We heard of their second goal when a nearby table of lads all suddenly celebrated. We all decided that their news was lucky news, so no-one was allowed to look at their phone and we were able to receive updates only from the lads on the first table.

"We unsuccessfully tried to find other things to talk about instead of studying our phones, for fear of breaking the lucky spell that had been cast over Elland Road. By 10 to five we were beside ourselves, but eventually heard the cheers that confirmed the season's biggest shock. It turned into a very big evening. As if by magic, at around eight o'clock, two of the lads popped to the chip shop over the road from the Porter Cottage, and who should come into the chippy but Chris Wilder and his wife Francesca? They got a selfie with him, and a magical - and ultimately decisive - day and night had ended in the most fitting way imaginable."

Clarke's excited jump after Massey's decisive goal was recognisable to anyone who remembers his legendary brace in the Steel City derby the season previous and the striker, who remains close to a number of United players, spoke to McGoldrick on FaceTime after the game from the away dressing room at Elland Road. His job was done and in what felt like a seismic shift in the race, United were now back in control; just as their players had predicted less than a week earlier.

That didn't stop a number of articles from appearing in the media about Bielsa's men, though - 'Why Premier League needs Leeds United' screamed the headline of one, in *The Times* - and in his press conference after the Forest game, Wilder was asked if he felt there was a groundswell in national support for Leeds in the race for promotion.

Despite his previous reticence to hand Leeds any more psychological ammunition, the answer was an unequivocal yes. "That wasn't a negative or anything, just an honest opinion," Wilder later said. "I'm not being funny, but would you rather have the kid from Sheffield or the Argentinian who's well-publicised and internationally-known, and very successful in everything he's done?

"You've got to admit that Leeds are one of the biggest football clubs in the country, never mind this county, in terms of the support they get and their history. If you talked about putting the Premier League together based on history, tradition, players and honours, Leeds would be in the top 10. So nationally, I get why that would happen. It was just an opinion borne out of the facts more than anything, really."

Behind the scenes, and with skipper Sharp still sidelined with the hamstring injury he picked up against Millwall, Wilder and his coaching staff were impressed with how McGoldrick subsequently stepped up - both on and off the pitch. "I said some words before the Forest game and I think the boys respected it," McGoldrick said. "Without Billy I felt I had to speak up and that's what I'm about. I'm a team player. I'm laid back normally but on match-days I come alive and find my voice. I don't think it was down to my speech though! I maybe added half a per cent onto what we already knew we had to do."

With just three matches remaining United were now ahead

of Leeds in second, by virtue of their superior goal difference, before they completed their Easter double-header by making the short trip to the KC Stadium to face Hull City. The Tigers' faint play-off hopes had all but been extinguished by the time that United came to town but Wilder was keen to warn against any complacency - pointing to Adkins' previous ties with United as just one factor that would motivate Hull to get a positive result.

United's destiny had been placed back in their own hands, but there were still some nerves among the players; even if they were only temporary. Defender Egan, available again after completing his one-match ban against Forest, remembers a pre-game walk before the Hull game and feeling "a bit of butter-flies. I lifted my head up and saw Didzy in front of me, Flecky to my left and Enda to my right and thought: 'What am I nervous for? We're going to blow these away. Look at this team... no-one is going to stop us'."

United did indeed blow Hull away, inspired by a command-ing two-goal display from their talisman McGoldrick. The first was ridiculous by Hull's standards - the striker left completely unmarked in the box to head into the top corner, past ex-United goalkeeper George Long in the Hull goal - but the second was nothing but sublime, as McGoldrick picked up the ball in acres of space and curled a superb effort past Long and into the far corner. Stevens then continued his own mini-scoring streak with a third before half-time, nonchalantly heading in George Bal-dock's right-wing cross to put United 3-0 up at the break.

One small corner of the KC Stadium had been rocking all afternoon - mainly to the sound of Stevens' new chant, to the *Heartbeat* theme tune - and a memorable day for the wing-back was completed when he won a personal bet with Jack O'Connell by scoring United's third. O'Connell owed Stevens a small amount of money from a card game and in the tunnel before the game, the pair arranged a 'double or quits' deal if either of them got on the scoresheet. Stevens' header meant O'Connell owed him twice the original amount - although the significance of the goal, and the win, probably tempered

O'Connell's disappointment a little when he eventually settled the bet.

United might have added a fourth in the second half when Long saved brilliantly from Fleck and were every bit as comfortable as the 3-0 scoreline suggested. Even if Wilder did disagree, to say the least, with Adkins' dismissive post-match view that United had only four attempts at goal all afternoon. "I can only imagine the feeling in the Leeds dressing room before the Brentford game, when they saw we were 3-0 up in the first half," said Baldock. "It must have been heartbreaking for them at that point. From our point of view, it was a really good, strong performance under pressure… the kind of performance the gaffer loves. When we stand up and be counted, and really put on a show."

Again, it was over to Leeds to respond as they took on Brentford at Griffin Park. The game wasn't played on the television screens on United's team coach but a few players watched it on their phones and iPads - so even those who didn't want to keep up to date with events from West London, including McGoldrick, had no real choice. It didn't matter too much in the end as goals from Neal Maupay and Sergi Canos gave the Bees three points. But, more importantly from a United perspective, put the Blades on the brink of promotion to the Premier League.

With just two games remaining, United were three points ahead of Leeds with a superior goal difference; so three points in their penultimate game of the season - at home to relegated Ipswich, in front of a packed Bramall Lane - would all-but guarantee them top-flight football. Victory over Paul Lambert's men would definitely be enough, if Leeds failed to beat Villa on the following afternoon. Some weeks earlier, on the flight back to England from their international break training camp in Valencia, Wilder confided in those around him that he felt United would secure promotion against Ipswich but, now that he was actually on the verge of greatness and his pre-match press conference was noticeably busier than usual, he markedly refused to utter the P-word.

"Knowing how the fixtures fell, we felt like we could take

a big step forward over the Easter weekend," reflected Wilder at the season's end. "And we certainly did that. It was quite a surreal week. We didn't have the Brentford game on the bus but people had seen the result and were running about when we got back to Bramall Lane. We still had a job to do in terms of the game against Ipswich, though. It was a great performance against Hull but after that, it seemed quite a long week. It should have been a short week from Monday to Saturday and normally that would fly by, but the week seemed to last an eternity before the day finally arrived."

Staff at Bramall Lane remember seeing Wilder jog from his home to Bramall Lane on the morning of the Ipswich game as the tension grew. Scott Hogan netted in the first half to calm United's nerves a little before O'Connell put the result beyond doubt in the second, sprinting into the box to head home Fleck's cross seconds after retreating to the dugout for some sustenance. The noise that greeted O'Connell's bullet header almost took the roof off Bramall Lane and Sky Sports' Daniel Mann summed it up perfectly on commentary, as the ball clipped the underside of the bar and nestled in the back of the net. "That's the one," Mann said. "Forget the maths... *the Premier League beckons for Sheffield United.*"

To overtake United now, Leeds would have to win both their remaining games and hope United lost at Stoke on the final day. And a 13-goal swing in Leeds' favour was also needed. It was, as the old phrase goes, all over bar the shouting. Wilder, who later helped to take down the goalposts long after Bramall Lane had emptied, gathered his players in a huddle at full-time on the pitch and Mark Duffy's reaction said it all, as he stood with his hands on his head; in apparent disbelief at what had happened.

For others, though, it was a time to remember those who weren't there to share in the moment. Blade Adrian Bell's mother and father passed away within six weeks of each other earlier in the year, closely followed by the death of his Wednesday-supporting brother-in-law David. One of Adrian's biggest regrets about United's promotion was that he couldn't wind David up about it. "I've always regarded promotion seasons as special, with 1990, 2006, and 2017 sitting pretty at the top," he said. "But I felt somewhat conflicted about 2019. At the end of the Ipswich game, the chap who sits in front of me turned around and said: 'It's been an emotional year for you, Adrian'. I found myself giving him a big hug and bawling my eyes out. I then proceeded to hug anyone who came near me, and cried all over them as well.

"Then, just as I thought I'd got myself under control, and with the stadium almost empty, I was making my way up the Kop steps and stepped to one side to let a Blade, of a similar age to myself, pass. He was helping his aged father, resplendent in his red and white scarf, down the steps. Off I went again – tears of joy, tears of sadness, tears of pride. It was some day. It had quite possibly been the best season ever, and this is arguably the BEST EVER time to be a Blade. But I don't half miss my dad phoning me up after we've lost and launching straight into… 'Were they rubbish?'"

Wilder also felt emotions of a different kind from a year earlier, when he walked in front of the Kop and wondered if his time as United manager was coming to an end. Staff and players were joined on their lap of honour by their families and Norwood's young son, Pierce, lapped up every moment as he stood next to his father, clapping United's fans with 'Daddy, 16' printed on the back of his shirt. Henderson then sparked further excitement when he grabbed stadium announcer Gary Sinclair's microphone and channelled his inner Jordan Belfort, from *The Wolf of Wall Street*, by announcing that he 'wasn't f******leaving' Bramall Lane.

Henderson was later spotted on the shoulders of a fan, singing United songs, as thousands of Blades supporters turned London Road into a sea of red, white and Stone Island for an impromptu street party. One Blade's evening ended prematurely, though, when he fell through the roof of a bus stop and was rushed to hospital, somehow escaping serious injury. The atmosphere was a carnival one and United had taken what Wilder would call 'a huge, giant leap' towards the Premier League.

But still, the job was not *mathematically* done and the celebrations couldn't *fully* begin just yet.

"We were accused by a couple of players of getting ahead of ourselves earlier in the season, which couldn't be further from the truth," defender Baldock said. "The gaffer put his stamp on that comment and I felt it was a bit disrespectful actually, because that's not us at all. We're a real level-headed group and we never once got ahead of ourselves. Even after Ipswich at home, everyone saw the celebrations on the pitch but I can tell you that it was a strange atmosphere in the dressing room because we're so level headed.

"We were 100 per cent promoted at that point because we were never going to lose by enough goals to miss out, but the atmosphere afterwards was like 'We've done it, but we haven't'. It was weird. I spoke to the press afterwards and said the same... we really wanted to celebrate properly, but we couldn't. I think that showed just how level-headed and humble every single person in the group is."

Even considering United's history, though, a turnaround of epic proportions would be required to see them miss out by this stage and even O'Connell, one of the more superstitious players who declined to be interviewed about promotion until it was officially confirmed, could also contemplate a summer holiday with his partner, Manchester United captain Alex Greenwood. By avoiding the play-offs with United, O'Connell could go away with Greenwood before she joined up with Phil Neville's England squad for the Women's World Cup.

Greenwood, also a defender by trade, was a key member of the England squad that reached the semi-finals in France and scored a goal, in a bad-tempered clash against Cameroon, that was almost a carbon-copy of O'Connell's, against Rotherham United earlier in the season. "Alex has been a massive part of my journey," said O'Connell, who met fellow scouser Greenwood when the pair studied at Savio Salesian College in Bootle. "She has been the one who has been there, through all the ups and downs. And seeing her doing so well motivates me to do the same."

The defender, and his three older brothers, were raised by mum Sharon, as a single parent in Merseyside, and joined Liverpool County Premier League side REMYCA United at the age of 16. "I used to play for anyone who'd have me before I got signed by a club, so I'd play on a Saturday morning and then jump in a taxi to play Saturday afternoon, and then play on Sunday as well," O'Connell said.

"We didn't grow up with our dad in our lives so it was hard for my mum, with four boys. We all played for the same team but at different times, so I'd be the first and she'd be there for about five hours watching us all. It was tough but I think that helped make me the person I am now."

"When I was a kid, my mates weren't really allowed out because they were too young, so my mum let me out with my brothers - which meant I've always played football with people who are older than me," added O'Connell, who flew to Madrid to watch Liverpool beat Spurs in the Champions League final in May. "I think that stood me in good stead as I grew older. I idolised Steven Gerrard and Jamie Carragher when I was a kid watching Liverpool but I had John Arne Riise's name on the back of my first shirt, for some reason. It'll be strange going to Anfield and places like that, but an incredible experience for everyone connected with the club."

After their victory over Ipswich, O'Connell and his United teammates were on the brink of Bramall Lane immortality and, less than 24 hours after their 2-0 win, gathered at the stadium's International Bar to watch Leeds' clash with Villa - knowing anything but a win for Marcelo Bielsa's side meant they were in the Premier League. "I thought it would go all the way to the last game of the season, to be honest," admitted skipper Sharp, "because of what happened over the last few months of the season. We went second, and then Leeds went second, and vice-versa.

"We sort of threw it away a couple of times, they threw it away and then we talked in the dressing room about the position we'd put ourselves in and how hard we had worked. So it was about us making no mistake and taking our chance while it was there. We did that with a professional performance against Ipswich - no disrespect to them, but we could have beaten them 4-0 or 5-0 if we needed to - but the win was the main thing, and I was personally delighted to be a part of it after injury."

United never seem to do things the easy way, though, and events on that afternoon weren't exactly straightforward either. Leeds went ahead in controversial fashion when Villa's players stopped, expecting Leeds to put the ball out of play following an injury, before Mateusz Klich instead rifled home - and Patrick Bamford, hardly the most popular footballer in Sheffield at that point, embarrassed himself once again by falling to the turf and clutching his face, after being flicked on the arm in the melee that followed Leeds' opener. Anwar El Ghazi, the Villa forward, was sent off, the goal was given - and, as it stood, United's promotion party would be delayed for another week.

Then, Bielsa intervened. The Argentinian ordered his side to let Villa walk the ball into their net and level the scores - despite Pontus Jansson appearing to defy his manager's orders - and the equaliser was cheered as loudly in this corner of South Yorkshire as possibly anywhere else in the country. Some wondered out loud whether Bielsa would have been quite so sporting if Leeds didn't require a mathematical miracle to overtake United but it was a gesture nevertheless appreciated by Wilder. Bamford's theatrics, though, didn't quite attract the same praise.

Debate about the legitimacy of either goal at Elland Road quickly sparked but United couldn't have cared less with, as the seconds ticked agonisingly towards full-time, the ultimate prize almost in their grasp. The final whistle in the game was greeted with a mass explosion of joy, relief and Corona 30 miles down the M1, and then the celebrations *really began*. Baldock dodged air-conditioning units on the roof as he ended up on Gary Madine's shoulders; not for the first time, Martin Cranie stripped to his underwear. Duffy, who had been a notable absentee from the gathering after being excused to visit his ill grandad, was showered in beer as soon as he arrived, alongside his partner Alexandra.

Outside, Chris Basham kicked a ball around on the Bramall

Lane turf with his son Luke while Henderson - who had earlier appeared more and more nervous as the Leeds game went on, the hood of his Stone Island tracksuit pulled over his head - celebrated by sprinting the length of the pitch.

Striker Clarke, who had done so much to advance United's promotion cause while on loan at Wigan, joined in the celebrations via FaceTime to McGoldrick and Wilder and his wife Francesca then went on their own lap of Bramall Lane, hand-in-hand, before enjoying a private moment of reflection on the otherwise-empty Kop.

When he returned to the party Wilder chanted United songs on air, during an interview with Sky Sports' Richard Graves, before spraying him with Birra Moretti, his new tipple of choice after the Peroni-fuelled celebrations that followed United's last promotion. As the beer dripped from Graves' suit, Wilder stood with his arm around Sharp's shoulder and sang the praises of his skipper, admitting he felt Sharp's remarkable goalscoring record was underappreciated outside this corner of South Yorkshire. Not here, though; Wilder broke off the interview, mid-question, to chant his captain's name as KC and the Sunshine Band played in the background.

When the realisation of what he had achieved later sunk in, an emotional Wilder struggled to compose himself in another interview, when he described the day of the Ipswich game as the best of his life - before collecting his thoughts again, and then taking aim at Bamford. "We've had one defeat in 13 and I've got muppets from Leeds talking about the pressure being on us," he said. "Bamford and [Adam] Forshaw and a couple of others. 'It's over to you' and this, that and the other.

"They got beat seven times since Christmas. We've been beaten once. We've set it up from Christmas to be in the race and we've steamrollered it. After the international break, two points a game. That's promotion form right the way through in the pressure part of the season. Listen, don't mention anything about bottle and b******s or about us dipping out. Full respect to Marcelo as well for the way they handled that today. Not full respect to Patrick Bamford, obviously.

"But the way we've gone about it, I think it has gone under the radar. It's not got enough credit in terms of media coverage. Everybody wanted Leeds to go up. And we've just come absolutely steaming through and deserve to play Premier League football. It'll be a fabulous experience for everyone at our football club. We had a lot of pelters for six years when we were in League One and a lot of crap to put up with, for a long long time. Now, it's our time. We've got to enjoy it. We'll enjoy this period and we might take a few thumpings. But everyone said that in the Championship, as well. Two years, in and out.

"In, year, out. See ya."

'Superstitious minds'
by Sam Parry

I am not especially superstitious. Being neither spiritually or religiously inclined, my brain usually takes more of a 'cause and effect' approach. *Usually*. But our ascent from the Championship felt more like a miracle, a phenomenon. Promotion might be a question of mathematics; you win games, accumulate points. Yet I still believe it was an achievement of otherworldliness, something inexplicable.

Rubber-stamp it: the 2018/19 season was a miracle. The writing was on the wall. But who scrawled it there? Chris Wilder and Co. were the public faces of United's promotion. The coaches and players prepare meticulously for games. As fans, we cling to inexplicable rituals and ceremonies to try to do our bit. All bound up in the nerve-popping consciousness of being a superstitious (and often pessimistic) supporter. The question I want to ask you, fellow Blade, is: What part did you play in promotion?

Tom was convinced that he was cursed. A footballing devilry stuck to him like an unwanted tattoo, when the Blades were on the telly. If he tuned in, we could not win. This had gone on for years and, of course, he'd long-since stopped watching us on the box. His Sky Sports subscription was burning a hole in his pocket and, one Friday evening, United were on Sky, away at Villa. Instead of tuning in, Tom followed the game on his smartphone; dragging his thumb down the touchscreen to refresh the vidiprinter. By the time Billy Sharp had scored his hat-trick to put United 3-0 up, Tom believed *even he* couldn't wreck this one.

Then, his mate texted him. "Hope you've switched this one on pal," the message read. "Best performance of the season. UTB." Tom tuned in. There were 10 minutes to go. Suffice to say, Tom's self-imposed Blades blackout was observed for the remainder of the season; he had learned the hard way. You may be reading this and thinking, "Luck's got nowt to do wi it". If that's the case, then I ask you; would you invite him over to watch the game?

It can work the other way. A few years earlier, Jenny and her daughter had heard Elvis Presley's 'Blue Suede Shoes' on the car radio on two consecutive match-days, on the way to the games. United had won both, so the ritual was born. Neither Jenny, nor her daughter, were particularly fond of Elvis' music, but she bought one of his CDs to keep the superstition going. As the pair set off for Preston, her daughter asked 'what about Elvis?" Jenny rumbled through her glovebox, found the case and stuck the disc in the slot. Nothing. Fearing the inevitable defeat, Jenny gave the disc's shiny side a hot breath, wiped it with her shirt and tried again. 'Suspicious Minds' began to play.

You might not believe that Jenny and The King, together, had anything to do with United's subsequent 1-0 victory. Your scepticism is noted. But one should always err on the side of persevering with a lucky ritual, rather than turning one's back on it. Take Nick, who was sadly at fault for our draw at Birmingham in April. Bad defending didn't cost us two points; it was bad luck. In 2016/17, during the League One promotion season, Nick discovered a lucky pair of grey, repeatedly-worn under-crackers.

It was a matter of a clothes-washing routine (AKA 'fate') that meant these particular pants turned up in his drawer on Saturdays. It was pure coincidence (AKA 'destiny') that he wore them three times in a row and watched United win three times. After that, Nick was converted and the rest was history. United won the league with 100 points, and Nick retired the pants. It was a bad move. With United desperate for a win at Birmingham, Nick found the pants in his spare room and wore them to St Andrew's.

His casual disregard for the laws of superstition must have angered the footballing gods; United had been a goal to the good before uncharacteristically conceding from a corner. With Millwall up next, destiny was no longer ours to control. Leeds needed only to keep winning to secure second spot. To Bramall Lane and Millwall. A game that ended 1-1, despite the Blades' domination. We had led the game in the closing stages when a Millwall chance looked destined for the net. Cue John Egan. A limb, a save, a red card, a penalty, a miss, a celebration. Then with seconds left on the clock, it happened. Fate, and Jake Cooper, stepped in and drenched us in misery. An equaliser that meant we relied on Sheffield Wednesday to beat Leeds in the late kick-off. Of course, they did not.

For us to concede to Millwall as we did, and for Leeds to win, someone must have messed up. Was it you? Did you not drink your morning coffee from that lucky Blades mug? Or were you in a rush and failed to pass through the same charmed turnstile you always do? Did you just 'forget' about your lucky jersey/ bobbles/badges/keyrings? Perhaps I am being unkind. Perhaps it was just written. I know a fan who parks near Heeley City farm and walks down to Bramall Lane with his son. When they pass the station, if they fail to see a train go by, then they know that the result won't be the one they are after. They can't have clocked a train that day against The 'Wall.

With four games to go, there was still time for luck to play its part. While many were grateful for the Bank Holidays over the Easter weekend, all Blades knew that our fate might be sealed by the Monday evening. It was my favourite kind of superstition that saw United over the line against Forest; the 'superstitious contract', when a fan enters into a binding agreement with the footballing gods. You've tried it at some stage, right? Callum from Crookes did so that weekend. "If I pass my driving test," he told himself, "then the Blades beat Forest." It was all in Callum's hands now. Six failed previous attempts at passing would not deter him; this time the stakes were higher.

It worked. Zero majors and nine minors later, Callum passed, and the Blades won 2-0. Simple business, in hindsight. What happened to Leeds United, however, was not. Level on points with United, Leeds conspired to lose against Wigan. Leeds led, were awarded and missed a penalty, Wigan were down to 10 men, Leeds had 30 shots. They lost 2-1. We were now in second place, on goal difference. Three to play, and a sort-of Yorkshire derby up next. On paper, Hull away was our toughest remaining fixture. A former manager to face, Jarrod Bowen and Kamil Grosicki to keep quiet, a near-impenetrable home record to overcome. But the game isn't played on paper... is it?

Claire routinely bets on United to lose. The habit began during Nigel Adkins' reign and continued under Wilder, albeit with the stake reduced. It's her way of discreetly paying homage to the footballing gods. This is no online affair; that wouldn't count. It's the local bookies, paper and ink. And Easter Monday was no exception. What might have gone wrong if she'd failed to back a Hull victory? Maybe David McGoldrick doesn't go on to score that screamer. Maybe the Blades don't win 3-0. The fact is that she did put her quid on. Didzy did score that goal, and United did win. The pressure piled onto Leeds ahead of their late kick-off against Brentford. Quite suddenly, on the anniversary of the day of resurrection, everyone turned to superstition.

Fingers and toes were crossed. Prayers were said. Old rituals brought back. New rituals created. Contracts made - "If I make it to the shops and back before half five, Leeds will lose." Blades fans turned off televisions and radios and sat in a quiet room. *'Don't tell me the score'.* Luck gets luckier the more people believe and, as the half-time scoreline came in, those superstitious Blades began to believe. Brentford led by a single, wonderful goal to nil. Early in the second half that scoreline doubled, and the Bees held firm. Whatever you did that day to secure that result, I salute you.

Victory at Ipswich would all-but seal promotion. As thousands of Blades descended on the Lane, the 'old classic' came to the fore: the lucky parking spot. (My spot adjoins Sharrow Lane… please keep clear.) It is likely that several groups of fans aim for similar spots each match-day. With the highest attendance of the season beckoning, many missed out on theirs. Including me. Who knew what wild constellation of dumb luck would be thrown up as a result? It was best not to think about it… and so I didn't. I turned my back on superstition.

Everything that fortune, favour and good luck provide to help me stumble through every 90 minutes, Wilder and this Blades team have trumped. Inside Bramall Lane, as the game kicked off, the brief moments of silence were deafening; at once an insular and collective experience. The players sliced through their opponents and the belief that 'We're Sheffield United, we could still mess it up from here' melted away. The superstitious Blade inside me disappeared; and that is as big a compliment as I can pay to this heroic team.

Promotion was sealed the next day when Leeds drew with Villa, and the final game, away at Stoke, barely mattered. No hoodoo now could affect Wilder becoming a top-flight manager, and United regaining their status as a top-flight club. Wilder, Alan Knill and the players obviously got us there but every superstition adds up. Yours especially, whatever you did. We can't necessarily do the sums; we can just about discern the equation. If every single superstitious Blade had given up his or her small rituals, do you really think this season would've been the same? I'm not so sure it would. It is, after all, the little things that make the big things matter more.

Running down the wing
by Enda Stevens

It's been a long journey personally back to the Premier League, which I had a bit of a taste of earlier in my career with Aston Villa, but it's been an enjoyable one as well and I've had the most fun in my career in the last two to four years. I had a good season at Portsmouth when we won the League Two title, and then we've achieved something on a different level here at

United. It's all experience, isn't it? And the memories will last forever. Once you get that taste for success, it just leaves you wanting more. In United, I knew I'd joined a team with a winning mentality, after the lads had won League One the season before I joined, and the manager suited me as well.

He just wanted us to grasp the opportunity ahead of us and we did that. You could see what it meant to everyone, the joy and happiness on everyone's faces... the whole club was bouncing. Just like, from how it looked and sounded on the pitch, that away end at Hull City near the end of the season! I really enjoyed that because it was the first time I heard a song being sung about me. The atmosphere was ridiculous from our fans and it made it feel like a home game, even though there were under 2,500 in the away end. It was one of the best away followings I've ever seen and the place was really rocking.

I had mates and family members sending me videos of fans singing my name in pubs and whatever, and it was nice to see. It's good to get that appreciation because it's what you play the game for. You want to leave something behind you so that in 10 years, when you look back at your career, you're remembered for what you have achieved. For me, that's what being a footballer is all about. It's been a long time since I was in the Premier League with Aston Villa, and a lot has changed.

There's obviously so much money flying around and the scale is so much bigger, but I'm also much more suited to go into it now under Chris Wilder and Alan Knill. I've learned so much under them and they really get the best out of me as a player, and that's what I'm really looking forward to.

I made my Villa debut at Sunderland after two left backs were injured and we won 1-0, and then after that I played against Manchester United, Manchester City and then Arsenal. Welcome to the Premier League! I then got injured against Reading but that was my real big taste of the big league. I had a loan spell at Doncaster Rovers in the Championship but it was a move to Northampton Town under Chris that really gave me a kick up the a**e. I knew I wasn't playing well and I wasn't fit... I was a bag of s***e, really. The gaffer finished my loan early and signed another left-back, and I went in and had a heart-to-heart with him so he could tell me what I needed to do better and where I was going wrong.

I was honest with him, telling him that I was in a tough spot and I didn't know where my next move was going to be, because my contract at Villa was up in the summer. I drove back to Birmingham thinking to myself 'I don't know what's going to happen here, I might have to move back home.' But then the phone call from Portsmouth came, with Paul Cook interested in taking me.

It was a scary one to go from the Premier League to League Two - it felt like pretty much my last chance and if it didn't work out, I don't know where I would have gone - but luckily I met the right man at the right time. Paul got me back focused, got my game back on track, and brought it to another level before United came in for me.

It was tough at times but that's what football is like - there are more bad times than good sometimes in your career. It was more a feeling that I'd let everyone down, my family and friends. At Pompey I fell in love with the game again and the manager backed me. I was surrounded by good people and got my career back on track.

But I'll never forget the chat with the gaffer at Northampton. It must have been about an hour in his office, and I didn't go looking for an argument - I just wanted to ask the question of him and get his advice on what I should do next and where I should go. I didn't know where I was going and he gave me some good advice, telling me that my career wasn't over yet and that I still had a chance.

I just had to get back focused and luckily I did, so, when there are moments to celebrate, I make sure I savour and cherish them. In my first season at United I was coming into a new team, and the team itself was new in the division, so there were always going to be ups and downs. We got off to a similar start and had momentum before we lost Paul Coutts to injury and never got back to where we were. But we learned a lot by looking back on games when we made mistakes and things went wrong, and asking ourselves: 'How can we improve?' I thought we did that on a massive scale throughout the season.

You grow as a player with the more games you play, and it's not the easiest position to be learning in - especially with the way we play at United. It does take time; you've got to learn how to play against other systems and how to overcome what the opposition are trying to do to us. And we've done that this season. I remember when we went to play Fulham and Wolves when they were in the division and I was thinking 'Jesus, they're a class above'. In the promotion season, we didn't have that; we didn't come up against a team who outplayed us or ran over us.

The biggest challenge for me was getting used to the fact that someone is going to overlap me. I don't think that's ever happened to me anywhere in my career before I came to United! Every single lad who's come in has that first challenge of learning how to play in this system and they've all done it so well.

We're all on board with what the manager and Knilly want from us, and that has given us a consistency level all the way through. There's so much work that goes into it, it's not just off the cuff or a case of thinking 'ah, I'll run over to the right wing now'. It's a case of looking around to see where John Fleck is, where Mark Duffy or Jack O'Connell are, and bouncing off them.

We have a strong relationship on and off the pitch and that's the biggest thing about our team. The back three have it together, Flecky and Ollie Norwood have it, Duffy links with everyone and then the wing backs, me and George, link with Jack and Chris Basham. It might look a bit mad but that's how we play the game and there's a method and intelligence to it.

If there wasn't, we'd be getting hit on the counter every game - but we actually finished with the best defensive record in the league. It's a credit to the discipline and the honesty of the lads and how much they're willing to work for the team. You won't see a centre-half in the league get anywhere near the distances that Jack and Bashy cover. It's unheard of. So for them to do that, and then get back and defend the back stick or put in a last-ditch tackle, is some going. Luckily, I get a bit more of a breather than Jack and my run back isn't as long as his!

The biggest thing for me as a footballer is fitness and once you have that, I think everything else just falls into place. A couple of times I had to fill in for Jack in his position and it might not seem it from the stands, but there's a big difference. I'm nowhere near as comfortable attacking from that position as he is. He and Bash play it so, so well.

There aren't many who'd be able to play it but they look like naturals. The only one who's not really involved in the attacking side is John Egan, although I've seen him get carried away and go forward a few times, and even our goalkeeper Dean Henderson got himself an assist! Everyone feels like they can play a part in creating a goal and that honestly makes the system so, so enjoyable to play in.

We play on the front foot for as long as we can, and we take the game to every team we play; there's no sitting back, or anything like that, and that suits us down to the ground. It's how you want football to be played and how it should be played. It's how every kid plays football; to win games, score goals and achieve something.

And the work I put in here will hopefully continue to reward me on the international scene. I have a hunger and a drive first and foremost to play well for Sheffield United and in turn, that will hopefully help me with Ireland.

To be recognised and represent your country is one of the biggest things you can do as a player, and I'm just so happy that it happened. Now, though, I want more of it, for club and country, and I was delighted to sign a new deal in the promotion season. I see United as a club that wants to go places and I'm grateful that they want me to be here while that happens. I honestly think we have a good thing going on and long may that continue. We spend a lot of time together away from football and all the lads are mates, which I think is helpful.

We're not a team of superstars but I think that's important because we're all about the group. Every footballer wants to play well because that's how we impress the manager and stay in the team, but my first thought, when I go out across that white line, is to help the lads around me.

That's why we achieved, because we're a group rather than a bunch of individuals and it's all about the dressing room. It's the best one I've ever been in and it helps when you're settled around the game so you can produce on the pitch. The missus and I have moved up here and we're settled, which is so important for me and just helped me concentrate on the main goal of promotion.

We did get overshadowed a bit in the run-in because people perhaps thought it was all done with Leeds and Norwich. But we always knew we had a chance because we were mentally strong enough to challenge. And our form backs that up. We lost one of our last 17 games and that saw us over the line. As soon as the final whistle went against Ipswich, I knew we'd done it, because of our goal difference, and it was quite an emotional moment. The day after was just a case of getting all the lads together and seeing Premier League football be officially confirmed. But this isn't 'Job done' for us. We don't feel as if the story is over just yet.

chapter thirteen

'Now we're going on a journey...'

April/May 2019

Hours after Sheffield United had become the Premier League's newest football team, the celebratory party was still going strong at Bramall Lane but, by now, many of the players had made the short journey to the Copthorne Hotel to drink in the moment - literally - with supporters who had gathered in the bar. Skipper and top-scorer Billy Sharp had jumped on top of a truck in the car park on his way over to the hotel; one of his teammates, who shall remain nameless, couldn't manage the same journey without throwing up.

Sharp was later filmed topless, on the shoulders of a supporter, 'heading' a lightshade; defender Richard Stearman threw beer over himself and turned the empty pint glass upside-down on his head, coining a new verb among United fans: 'to get Stearmaned'. One member of staff joked that Kieran Dowell, the young Everton loanee, had probably consumed more beer in his short time at United, than in the rest of his life before he arrived at Bramall Lane. "For the players," said manager Chris Wilder in a later interview, "there was no escaping the fact that they had to drink alcohol."

Wilder is big on celebrating success. His reasoning is that, in football, you never know if and when you will taste it again; so squeeze every single drop out of it while it lasts. It's an approach that has served him well, ever since he cut his managerial teeth at Alfreton Town all those years before, and Wilder wasn't about to abandon it now he was a Premier League boss. Conveniently, Sunday, April 28 - the day United's top-flight promotion was confirmed - was also the evening of their official player of the year awards night and the players - those who were able to, at least - continued their celebrations long into the evening.

David McGoldrick, a remarkable free transfer signing who scored 15 goals and delighted fans with his all-round ability, was named player of the year after a supporters' vote - although a number of his teammates would also have been worthy winners - while Chris Basham walked away with the goal of the season award, for his crucial strike against promotion rivals Leeds back in March. Dean Henderson - who refused to take off his 'We're going up!' flag since promotion was sealed, and wore it proudly over his suit - took home the young player and community player of the year awards and, desperate to return to United on loan and play in the Premier League, placed a bid on an auction prize for a place on the following season's official team photograph. The mood in the room was understandably buoyant, but the atmosphere was turned up a notch or two when John Egan grabbed the microphone and invited all United's players and staff onto the stage. "If you go to a pub in Ireland, you have to have a song," Egan told his audience, as many of his bemused teammates looked on nervously. "And if you don't have a song, you may as well not go to the pub at all. So in January, I said to my better half, I said… 'I have got a song'. And I said: 'We are going to the Premier League. And when we get to the Premier League, I'm going to sing this song'. It goes to the tune of a Liverpool song; we've got a few Scousers here…"

We are Sheff United, they call us the Blades.
We've got Billy Sharp, he's a legend at the Lane
Basham and O'Connell, overlapping down the wing
*Duffy, Fleck and Norwood, with his ******* ping!*
Allez, Allez, Allez… (x4)
Chris Wilder is our gaffer, he leads us all the way
Playing proper football, the Sheff United way…
Allez, Allez, Allez… (x4)
He stuck that paper on the wall, they called us 'journeymen'
*Now we're going on a journey, to the ******* Prem!*
Allez, Allez, Allez…

It became an instant hit. Egan formed his own version of the song, originally sung by Napoli fans, within 10 minutes earlier in the season, but refused to sing it until promotion was confirmed - although one teammate did hear a sneak preview before its official release. "I'd had a few drinks with John and he said 'I've come up with this song, what do you think?" fellow defender George Baldock revealed. "I told him he had to sing that song, and he'd regret it if he didn't, but he said he'd only do it if I came up with him. I thought 'Yeah, I'll go up and be a puppet for you', to give him the courage to do it. As soon as he was up there he went into a world of his own and belted it out like a real showman. I was so happy that everyone enjoyed it, because when I first heard it, I loved it. John is a massive character and played a massive part throughout the season."

The 'paper on the wall' reference was classic Wilder. The United manager had plastered the walls of United's training ground with an article which tipped Derby County, Leeds, Aston Villa and Norwich City to challenge for promotion from the Championship that season, and dismissed United's chances because of their 'journeymen' strikers, Sharp and McGoldrick. The pair ended the campaign with 39 goals between them as United finished five points behind winners Norwich, but six ahead of Leeds, 13 ahead of eventual play-off winners Villa and 15 in front of Wembley runners-up Derby.

After Wilder led United back into the Championship, one of their first games was away at Neil Warnock's Cardiff City and after a battling defeat, the United manager remembered a patronising comment by one of City's coaching staff who told him 'well, I don't think you'll go down'. Wilder had those words put on a sign at United's training ground, to fuel their promotion push. Earlier in his career, when he was at Oxford, promotion back to the Football League reignited a rivalry with Swindon Town, managed at the time by Paulo Di Canio. The former Wednesday striker made a series of disparaging remarks in Oxford's direction, describing Swindon as a much bigger club and suggesting that James Constable, Wilder's striker, was a Town fan.

Constable scored twice in the first meeting between the sides that season - Oxford's first victory at Swindon in nearly 40 years - but was sent off after just 11 minutes in the return derby at The Kassam. Wilder's 10 men won 2-0 to secure a memorable double and before the game, Wilder tasked Mark Edwards, sports editor of the *Oxford Mail*, to mock-up a front page of his newspaper with Di Canio's arrogant quotes. "One of the things Chris was great at was using adversity to create spirit," said Edwards. "He'd grasp onto that sort of stuff to foster a sort of siege mentality. "You often hear the cliché about stuff being pinned on the dressing room wall for motivation in team talks… Chris literally did exactly that."

It works. "We know that the 'journeyman' tag is the complete opposite with Billy and Didzy," Baldock said. "Billy… I've never seen someone enjoy scoring goals as much as he does. Even if he's just walking in from training and there's a ball lying near the goal, he'll put it in. In training, when we're playing at a snail's pace, he'll blast the ball in the bottom corner because he lives for scoring goals. Didzy is probably technically the best player I've ever seen. I don't know how he's never played in the Premier League, because he's that good. The way he manipulates the ball, and his vision, is ridiculous. To think we got him on a free is incredible. I'm just so happy he's getting a chance of the top-flight now. And with us."

While many groggy Blades fans reluctantly returned to work on Monday morning, though, the partying continued for the players. A group of them met up again in the Copthorne bar and were seen buying Jägerbombs in the afternoon while Paul Coutts, a huge snooker fan, was invited to the Crucible to watch the World Championship clash between Ding Junhui and Judd Trump. Coutts was still feeling the after-effects of the night before and lasted just one frame from his front-row seat before falling asleep, taking a swig of referee Marcel Eckardt's water and then leaving.

Coutts was last seen heading in the direction of West Street on an evening when Sharp, Wilder and Chris Basham were all honoured at the *Sheffield Star's* annual football awards. United were voted as the region's team of the season by the newspaper's football writers while Wilder was named manager of the year, and Sharp once again picked up a special award for breaking Rickie Lambert's goals record since 2000. But it was Basham who picked up the ultimate accolade of United's player of the season, from a shortlist also including Sharp and midfielder Oliver Norwood.

Although the defender admitted privately that he felt an unworthy winner of the award, James Shield, *The Star's* United correspondent, felt that Basham exemplified both the attitude and ability of the group who had made history. When he went on stage to collect his gong, Basham raised a chuckle from the audience when he replied to the question: 'On a scale of one to 10, how drunk are you right now?' with '11', and Sharp ended the evening in the Viper Rooms nightclub. Then, the following morning, United returned to training and, after a long weekend of celebrating, went back to work.

At Bramall Lane, rather than their usual Shirecliffe base, United's players were put through a session which largely resembled pre-season as they looked to get back into some sort of condition ahead of the weekend's final game of the promotion campaign, away at Stoke City. Norwich had sealed promotion a day before United, but had rather stumbled over the line and after a stuttering run of form, Wilder's men travelled to Stoke with an outside chance of winning the league on goal difference.

To do so, United had to beat Nathan Jones' Stoke and hope Norwich lost to Aston Villa, and Wilder's men made the trip to the Bet365 Stadium after being congratulated on promotion by their bitter rivals Wednesday. In a statement on the Owls' official website, chairman Dejphon Chansiri wrote: "Few things in life unite and divide opinion like football. But one thing at this stage of every season is undebatable and I would like to offer the warm congratulations of everyone at Sheffield Wednesday to everyone at our neighbours Sheffield United for their achievement of promotion.

"We may be rivals but we are friends of the same city that holds such unique tradition in the football world. Recognition in the Premier League can only benefit Sheffield and we wish United well, whilst promising our loyal supporters that we will be giving our absolute best to ensure Wednesday will be tasting the same success this time next year." Although Baldock and Sharp, appearing on journalist Alan Biggs' *Sheffield Live* television show, admitted they thought the gesture was classy, Sharp also suspected it also contained an element of psychology from the Owls chairman - an attempt, perhaps, to motivate his players to emulate the feat of their rivals.

There were certainly no such mind games from Norwich manager Daniel Farke, though, when he sent Wilder a text message - which the United boss described as 'lovely' - to congratulate him and his team on joining City in the top flight the following season. Wilder had sent a similar message to the German after Norwich confirmed promotion and said: "They've got respect for us and I think that's brilliant.

"It's appreciated and reciprocated. I always say that whoever finishes first will have deserved to finish first because it's all about what you do over the course of a season. Not patches here and there. I really like how they go about things, too. I admired what they did over the course of that season because, like us, they've got their own way of doing things. We're different, but that's football and that's not a bad thing either."

That goodwill between the two managers, however, did not dampen Wilder's determination to wrestle the Championship title from City's grasp - an achievement that would have completed the set for the United manager, after winning Leagues One and Two earlier in his career with United and Northampton Town. Wilder's relentless approach is well documented and when United won the League One title in 2017, with three games to spare, he demanded even more from his players, challenging them to reach the 100-point mark for the first time in the club's history. Wilder was even more amazed, given that the players dragged their celebrations out for a period of several weeks, that they managed to do so.

This time around, the festivities were more condensed. "We celebrated but it all got nipped in the bud quickly by the gaffer," said forward Mark Duffy. "He reminded us that there was still something to play for and it would have topped off an unbelievable year if we went up as champions. But the main thing was getting promoted. Every time we go out there on the pitch, we want to win. It doesn't matter what the occasion is or what is at stake, we always want to come out on top. It's part of the mindset here and that's helped to carry us through.

"After promotion, I told some of the younger lads to grab it and enjoy it because you never know when something else like this might come around again. We had the big blow against Millwall with the manner and timing of their goal, and then Leeds beat Wednesday that evening to give them an extra boost. But we knew we had to keep going. We asked each other if we thought Leeds could win every game, and we all said 'No'. And they didn't.

"We thought they were a bit flaky, away from home especially, and all we could do was take care of our business and see where we ended up. If they did win every game then we could look them in the eye, shake their hands and say 'Well done, we'll do it through the play-offs'. Because we looked at the teams in the play-offs and fancied our chances against them too. But they were flaky, like we said, and did drop points. So it worked out brilliantly for us."

Duffy has a tattoo on his bicep which reads 'One of the greatest pleasures in life is doing what people say you cannot do' and his journey, from the depths of non-league to the highs of the Premier League, has been fuelled by the desire to prove people wrong. "There was a lot of talk about how well Leeds play and about Marcelo Bielsa and the tactical side of things… it is what it is, really," he added. "We just went under the radar and when it came to the crunch, we stepped up. And they didn't. Since I came here we've done our talking on the pitch. Once we'd been promoted, everyone in the media wanted to speak to us and wanted a piece of us. We knew that if we did our talking on the pitch, the rewards would come.

"It didn't bother me one bit, that all the focus in the media seemed to be on Leeds. Genuinely, not one bit. I knew how good we were so I wasn't bothered at all if people said we were the best football team in the world, or the worst. What the gaffer says, what Alan Knill says and what the staff and players think - that's all that bothers me; because they're the people who matter. If someone on Sky Sports says that Leeds play better football than we do, so what? It doesn't affect us at all. We were happy to just go under the radar and see where we ended up. And we ended up in a nice position in the end."

Not everyone shared the same view though and Duffy's teammate Baldock felt some media coverage was disrespectful at times, flinching at suggestions that United were a team who relied on togetherness and hard work, still riding the wave of promotion from League One. "People always talked about togetherness and hard work when they spoke about us, but we have some fantastic players and a brilliant manager and assistant," Baldock said. "Look at Manchester City. I'm in no way comparing us with them, but they work as hard as anyone. When did you last hear a pundit speak about that? Every successful team works hard so I did sometimes find it a bit disrespectful. We laughed about it, but it did give us a bit of extra motivation to push on and get the job done."

United eventually fell just short in their title push as they could only draw 2-2 at Stoke, although the result was rendered irrelevant anyway when Norwich beat Villa to finish five points clear of Wilder's men. United's celebrations looked to have caught up with them as they began sluggishly at Stoke, and they went behind to a volley from their former striker Sam Vokes. But the Blades were denied an equaliser only when Ryan Shawcross handled Sharp's goal-bound volley on the line, which was missed by the match officials, and began the second period brightly after some choice words from Wilder at half-time.

Sub Dowell netted United's equaliser minutes after coming off the bench, but United were behind again when Shawcross - who was fortunate to still be on the field after his earlier handball - took advantage of some sloppy defending to convert a corner from close range. Enda Stevens then continued his fine streak of goalscoring form with a powerful run and finish, and claimed the honour of being the final goalscorer of United's promotion season when the game finished level at 2-2. Egan's *Allez, Allez, Allez!* song had rung around the stadium all afternoon, sung proudly by those United fans lucky enough to be a part of the promotion party, and Wilder's men certainly didn't let the disappointment of not winning the title dampen their festivities after the final whistle.

After a private moment of celebration in the away dressing room, United's players reappeared, in special T-shirts commemorating promotion, to share the moment with their supporters behind the goal. McGoldrick gave away his match shirt to a fan who had dressed as the striker for the day while Henderson summoned his mum and dad, Dougie and Yvonne, out of the away end to share the moment as he was presented with the Championship's golden glove award. Henderson kept 21 clean sheets throughout the season, the most of any goalkeeper in the division, and wanted to involve his parents as a thank you for their support. "They've been rocks for me, driving me up and down the country," he said. "I couldn't do anything without them."

Wilder later received a spontaneous ovation from the assembled journalists in his post-match press conference, after admitting: "It's a real tough one for the players after the emotions of the weekend as well as drinking every pub in Sheffield dry for four days. We've left some very big and powerful football clubs in our wake. A couple of things didn't go for us, including a great save from Ryan on the line, but the second half was much more like it. I was delighted with the way we turned it around in the second half, against some very, very good players."

When United's players and staff finally dragged themselves off the champagne-soaked pitch at Stoke, the party continued on the coach back to Bramall Lane where thousands of fans had gathered to welcome home their heroes. Egan was encouraged to lead another rendition of his song on the coach's microphone and Baldock reckoned it took the coach 90 minutes to get from John Street into the main Bramall Lane car park, because of the sheer amount of supporters who had congregated. When the coach did eventually weave its way carefully through the crowd, United's staff and players were crowd-surfed into the ground and Baldock was almost choked by a fan, who ripped a shirt off his neck as a souvenir. If anything summed up the madness of United's promotion, it was surely the sight of 54-year-old, 6ft 4in Alan Knill being passed above the throng of fans, his long limbs flailing everywhere. Someone even nicked one of his trainers.

Striker Gary Madine's rendition of the 'mind the gap, Sheffield Wednesday' song was well-received, considering his previous allegiances, and the players were serenaded by a Mexican band once they made it into Bramall Lane, after collecting their promotion medals from Tony Currie. Currie, officially United's greatest ever player and now a club director, conducted an emotional ceremony inside the home dressing room and choked up as he spoke of his pride in the class of 2019. Then, before getting his hands on the trophy, skipper Sharp addressed his teammates - telling them they would all be legends of the club forever more.

The United skipper admitted there was a belief, in pre-season, that United could achieve something special. "You have to have that," Sharp added. "I'd be lying if I sat here and said I thought we'd be challenging for the title, because of the other teams in the division, but we talked about that as well. It's not about the names or the club you play for, but it's the individuals who make a team and a squad and which ones knit together best. And we've done incredibly well to beat all those powerful clubs in the division to promotion.

"I maybe didn't believe as much after the first two games of the season! But there have been certain periods when I thought: 'We can really do this' and then something would come along and hit us in the face, and you think 'Maybe not'. But a few times - and I haven't found out yet if he was joking or not - the gaffer said things like: 'Some of the staff are writing you off, they don't think you have the character for it' - or words to that extent. If it was a bit of clever management then fair play, but it certainly drove us on.

"We had bits and bobs stuck up on the wall all season, as John's song says… pundits, managers and people in the game writing us off - or worse, not even mentioning us at all, when they talked about the best teams in the league or who's going to get promoted. It all added a bit of fuel to the fire. It riles the manager up but he's the best motivator I've played under, so he must be doing something that works. We all knew how good we were but sometimes it's good to prove people wrong and to see people who are highly respected in the game writing us off did, for me, give us a bit of extra motivation.

"Football's a funny game, though, and throws your emotions all over the place. After the Easter weekend, we couldn't believe our luck. Wigan go down to 10 men away at Leeds, go 1-0 down and then win the game 2-1, with one of our ex-players running around after setting the goal up. Leon has gone away from the club because he wasn't playing as much as he wanted, but that shows what he's about. He wanted to play football, he went and helped Wigan stay up and also played his part here. He scored goals and won us games.

"I don't want to leave anyone out because honestly, everyone has chipped in to help us to win promotion - whether they played one game, no games or every game. Jake Wright is now a double promotion winner with Sheffield United, even though he says it was different this time around and hard for him because he didn't play too much. But he, like all the lads, know they might never experience promotion again, so enjoyed every minute of it. Every person in the dressing room deserves a huge amount of credit. Because they're Sheffield United promotion winners, and will go down in history."

As they did after winning League One in 2017, United's players jetted off to Las Vegas to continue the celebrations - Stevens later admitted he was surprised everyone returned alive - while some members of staff booked a holiday together to New York. But before the passports were dug out and Premier League preparations could officially begin, there was one more official club engagement to fulfil - an open-top bus parade around Sheffield, and a civic reception at the Town Hall. Two years earlier, with the bus scheduled to leave Bramall Lane at 5.30pm, United's players met up on Ecclesall Road some hours before that after being told that the last to arrive had to buy all the drinks.

This time around, it was a more sedate affair for the majority of players... apart from two who had begun drinking on London Road earlier that morning, before stumbling the short distance to Bramall Lane to get on the bus! The parade was a fitting end to what had really been a champagne season for United. The bus itself had been impressively decorated with United livery and images of key players and Wilder on the side - it was, ironically, designed by a Leeds fan - and every eventuality was thought of; including a replacement number plate 'SUFC UTB' to stick over the original, which featured the initials of their city rivals Wednesday.

The Tuesday evening rain fell on the thousands of fans who had turned out to hail their heroes, but nothing could dampen their spirits. From the media's vantage point on the bottom deck of the bus, the roof above reverberated as United's players bounced to the tune of *Allez, Allez, Allez!* and later, as he took in the sight of thousands of jubilant Blades singing the song he'd given them, Egan appeared genuinely emotional. In the summer of 2019, Egan returned to his home town of Cork and sought out the statue of his late father, a Gaelic football legend. The defender placed his promotion medal around the statue's neck, and wished his father a happy birthday on the day he would have turned 67.

The open-top bus trip from Bramall Lane to the Town Hall passed relatively incident-free - apart from a smoke-bomb falling down the stairs and filling the lower deck with thick red smoke – and, after some members of United's squad had caused a health and safety heart attack two years earlier by hanging off the balcony of the Town Hall, the decision was made to present the Premier League's newest squad to their adoring fans via the safety of a makeshift stage instead.

Before they were introduced to the assembled thousands, United's staff and players were invited upstairs in the Town Hall to a reception by the outgoing Lord Mayor, Magid Magid. A Blades fan since he arrived in Sheffield as a refugee from Somalia, Magid was presented with a United shirt bearing his name before joining manager Wilder in a rendition of the Greasy Chip Butty song. In 2017, Wilder borrowed the then-Lord Mayor Denise Fox's hat during the reception, but couldn't quite persuade her to part with her ceremonial chains; this time Magid had no such reservations and handed them over as the two posed for a photo. For a moment, the chains belonged to Wilder and, for this night at least, the city did too.

The thousands of fans waiting patiently outside the Town Hall were rewarded when United's players and staff were introduced to them in groups, according to their position. Wilder and Sharp attracted the loudest cheers when they were beckoned on stage individually before Martin Cranie, who had become a cult hero at United for his displays both on and off the field, led supporters in a slurred singalong of Robbie Williams' *Angels* on the microphone. The raucous Town Hall celebrations also left Baldock with a sore head, but not just from the beer; on stage, as Egan performed his song again, a teammate's swinging medal had caught Baldock just above the eye, leading to a frantic search for a plaster as the celebrations continued.

Amid all the carnage on stage Alan Knill, Wilder's genial right-hand man, stood back and simply struggled to take it all in. Here was a man who once marked Marco van Basten out of the game when Wales faced Holland, never to be called up again; who rattled buckets as Rotherham United manager when they faced going out of business and went without wages at Northampton Town. Now a coach in the Premier League. Similarly remarkable tales ran all the way through United's group, a special bunch of people and players who had achieved something extraordinary. For some, though, the promotion parade was where their Bramall Lane stories ended. The day after the Town Hall scenes, and before they flew to Vegas, Wilder met with players individually and some, such as Cranie and Paul Coutts, left the club when their contracts expired.

All, though, departed with the best wishes of the entire football club for the part they had played while, behind the scenes, work gathered pace to bring Bramall Lane in line with Premier League requirements, with new media facilities, new wiring and even new floodlights needed. Supporters were left counting the days until August, when their top-flight adventure could begin. Visiting places such as the Tottenham Hotspur Stadium, the Etihad and Anfield; mixing it with Pep Guardiola's treble-winners and Jürgen Klopp's champions of Europe.

Wilder's three years at the club had brought almost unprecedented success but many fans recognised that, in the world's richest and most popular league, tougher times lay ahead. They were just happy to be a part of it; the achievement of promotion made all the more remarkable considering how low the club had fallen just three years earlier. For one night, Sheffield really was red and white and, after their heroes had boarded the bus back to Bramall Lane, fans poured into pubs and clubs all over the city centre. 'We're on the march with Wilder's army," they sang, long into the evening.

'We're not going to Wembley.'

chapter fourteen

The greatest ever?

by Alan Biggs

We all love to compare teams, players and managers from different eras and although opinions are one thing, the truth is that it's an impossible task - by the simple nature of those eras being, well, different. So what follows is not meant to be taken in any way other than a point of view. From a decent vantage point, though. I've been lucky enough to see, first-hand, the four best Blades sides of the modern era - from the legendary days of Tony Currie and Alan Woodward to the heroes of 2019. That early 1970s side remains the best in my view. For now, at least. But I still can't tell you who was the best manager from a field of John Harris, Dave Bassett, Neil Warnock and Chris Wilder. What I CAN argue in favour of the current group is that I've never known a more together dressing room. Or a manager who has had a bigger, quicker impact. And who has the ability to top the lot.

In those two areas - and rapport with the fans - Wilder's bunch stand out for me. And it's no coincidence - of course, it can't be - that Sheffield United have been ruled in the board-room, manager's office and dressing room by the holy trinity of Kevin McCabe, Wilder and Billy Sharp. Three born-and-bred Blades, carrying all before them. That has to be unique, not only at Bramall Lane but across the land. There is no more power-ful chemistry at a time when foreign players and foreign money have become the main currency of top football in this country. Blades fans have never followed their standard bearers with such fervour. Never have they been so rapidly reconnected with their club than after the disillusionment of the 2015/16 season.

Within the club, I think it goes deeper to the question of trust. One of my criticisms before the revival was that United, as an organisation of many chiefs, hampered managers they were trying to help. The process of expediting transfers became unwieldy, they seemed to be handled on a piecemeal basis rather than as parts of a plan, and each one went through stages of approval that, in some cases, saw targets lost. Wilder, effectively installed by McCabe, was given, and fully earned, more trust than some of his predecessors. No manager can be hands-on with everything in 2019 - the job is too big - but the prevalent ownership model from abroad has left them too detached. Clubs should ask themselves one question.

Who is the most knowledgeable football professional they possess? If the answer is not the manager, then what is he doing in the job? If they are not using him as their lead on transfers, in and out, they are undermining him and diminishing his chances of success. It's all so obvious now. Who needs a sporting director or a director of football when you have a manager such as Wilder? But it is giving him that trust in the first place - at the head of a tight-knit recruitment team including the chief executive - that has turned the club around. It's not to say that Wilder could keep anyone he wanted in the face of good offers (David Brooks, for instance) or that he could dictate his budget. But he was free to work within it, as not all managers would appear to be these days. And look at those signings. You don't need me to name them.

The baton of trust was handed down by Wilder to Sharp. That sparked a debate and I'll admit I raised half an eyebrow when Bill was made captain. Not because I doubted him as a player or character. Even then, in his third spell with his beloved club, it was apparent that no player cared more. Foolishly, though, I reverted to the default thinking of the rarity of strikers being captains. And wondered whether, as the team's best player carrying a weight of burden for scoring the most goals, it was asking a bit much. In fact, asking a lot was the masterstroke. Billy rose with huge pride to the challenge, as his boss knew he would, produced the best form of his prolific career - and, in one interview, shot down my earlier concerns about striker/captains in two words. "Alan Shearer!"

McCabe and his board, albeit split on other matters, trusted Wilder; Wilder trusted Sharp; the assembled players, recruited for character as well as ability, were trusted by the manager and captain. They policed themselves and they produced. Within that, I'll repeat I've never known a Blades boss have a more rapid impact. We can all see the reasons why and the logic looking back; in fact, it's been inspirational, beyond all logic in terms of budget. So it was for Bassett. His achievements can never be belittled or allowed to suffer by comparison. Although he did not, or could not, have the same impact, arriving in a bleak midwinter and starting with a relegation, he worked his miracle (nothing short) in two bounces, back to back.

Also work to do for Wilder in that Bassett, his manager as a player in those days, kept United in the Premier League for four seasons - and not hanging on for most of it, either. Has the football been better under Wilder? You'd have to say a resounding 'Yes' in being pleasing to the eye (of which more later) and yet I'm always wary of this sort of comparison. What is good football? Does anybody have a definition? If it's attacking, being on the front foot, creating lots of chances and scoring bundles of goals, Bassett's boys played 'good football'. It wasn't as flowing but it produced excitement where it mattered. His direct methods, fashioned in the fairytale of Wimbledon, were as innovative in their own way as Wilder and Alan Knill's overlapping centre-backs.

As for their teams, the promoted ones that is, I think that Chris' has been better than Harry's one-to-11 and better covered in depth. Not a weakness in sight. For all Sharp's 24 goals and the 15 of David McGoldrick, that pair won't become as singularly synonymous with this success as Brian Deane and Tony Agana were in 1990 - and beyond. That said, in terms of ethic, that was a team without stars also. A real parallel between the two and no coincidence considering an association between the managers that continues to this day. They speak regularly, although Bassett insists he is "not a mentor" and credits Wilder with being his own man. One he recommended for the job, mind you. And another theme, the importance of your goalkeeper. For Alan Kelly and Simon Tracey, read Dean Henderson and his unsung understudy, Simon Moore.

Although United have been deprived of success for long stretches of their modern history, there have been some outstanding figures at the club. For Wilder to be rated - indisputably - as one of the best managers in the club's history is some accolade. He may even become THE best from this point. It can, with the right conditions, be just the start of his story. He's a sponge. That's in the nicest possible way. A sociable bloke (especially with a drink!) who happily absorbs ideas from a whole range of people, inside and outside football. At Oxford United, he'd invite them into his office post-match - men such as Bassett and Jim Smith - to dissect a performance. They'd do it brutally.

He'd listen. Just as he's sought out and lent an ear to past greats of the Lane. There's a little bit of a lot of people in his methods; occasionally the explosiveness of a Bassett, sometimes the ability to be philosophical and take the pressure off. Always knowing instinctively which psychological buttons to press, while never being less than honest whichever way that view is expressed. You can imagine, too, the depth of conversation within his management team. Not always agreement, which is vital. Assistant Knill, coach Matt Prestridge and recruitment chief Paul Mitchell have contributed hugely to the club's success, as Wilder is the first to acknowledge. Ultimately, only one person can call the shots and Wilder is one of those people who seems to do it naturally; unflinchingly, never afraid to make a big decision or take responsibility for it.

In my experience, all the best managers have that. The worriers are consumed by the responsibility. It's been a pleasure to know Chris since his playing days at Bramall Lane, and a thrill to see him succeed in such a big way; a bigger way than I think any of us could have envisaged to this point. But the relentlessly upward trajectory of his career, from the very bottom and now to the very top, should have told us it would happen. Winning instant promotion from the third tier was one thing; leaving behind the Championship in two bounces quite another. Those two levels have never been further apart.

Now to the ultimate challenge. Let no-one make the same mistake again and follow the bookies in predicting an immediate drop from the Premier League. I have to confess I did not expect automatic promotion at the start of this last epic season. Top six, yes, without a moment's doubt. Anything more, I felt, was an unfair pressure considering a lower table budget. That was still my view during a casual chat with Chris back in December. He reckoned the January window would get him the extra impetus he needed.

And after that, you sensed he had total belief that the top two could and would be achieved. He clearly transmitted as much to the players. You could see during their nerveless finale to the season that their mentality was fixed on it. Beyond that, these last three seasons have been as enjoyable to witness as probably any spell within living memory. It's been a pleasure to come to Bramall Lane knowing that win, lose or draw, you'd see a team having a right go.

I've loved covering it for TalkSport with some national newspaper commitments thrown in. And there's never been any shortage of inspiration for my *Sheffield Telegraph/Sheffield Star* column which I used to finally see the light in mid-March and declare that the Blades WOULD be in the top two. The entertainment has been unstinting; the football back-to-front a joy. Expect more of the same in the Premier League - and not necessarily of the one-sided variety many pundits will tip! Chris Wilder isn't an animal who goes forward to go back. And, under his leadership, neither are United.

chapter fifteen

Roll of honour

2018/19 season

David 'Didzy' McGoldrick walked away with the official Sheffield United player of the season award after a memorable debut campaign at Bramall Lane, which saw him score 15 goals - including many vital strikes, at crucial times. During their exclusive interviews for this book, United's 11 leading appearance makers during the promotion season were asked for their own 'player of the year' choice.

Dean Henderson: I voted for *Billy Sharp* but I think since Christmas, John Egan has been outstanding and an absolute rock at the back.

He really grew into his role as the season went on and got better. So John for the second half of the season and Billy for the first half.

George Baldock: I voted for *Billy Sharp*. The goals he scored have been invaluable and he's the only player who scores the kind of goals he does.

But to be honest, it could have been one of quite a few; Enda Stevens, John Egan, Didzy, Ollie Norwood, Dean Henderson, Chris Basham... I could name anyone because all the lads have been fantastic and everyone deserves plaudits.

Enda Stevens: I picked *Billy Sharp* because he's been outstanding and broke the record but when we lost him, one man stepped up and that was Didzy.

Him, Billy and John Egan were outstanding, John in a new system in his first year... Jack O'Connell was superb. George Baldock, Kieron Freeman, Martin Cranie, John Fleck would have all been worthy winners. Ollie Norwood is like our quarterback and 'Benjamin Button', Mark Duffy, was brilliant.

Everyone played their part but Billy broke the record, scored an awful lot of goals and carried the weight of this club - his hometown club - on his shoulders. Him and Didzy are tight but I'll go for Billy's goals because when he was hot, he was so hot. A ridiculous player.

John Fleck: Because of the goals he's scored I'd have to go for *Billy Sharp.* But he's about much more than that. He's carried us over the line, not just on the pitch but off it too.

The way he controls everything is incredible, really. He does things he doesn't have to do but has done them for the last three seasons. So overall, for everything, he'd be my pick.

Jack O'Connell: I voted for *Ollie Norwood* because, after the loss of Couttsy, I think we needed someone to take games by the scruff of the neck and to be fair to Ollie, his record speaks for itself with three promotions in three years.

It could have been so many others, though. Enda was unbelievable and Deano, although he hasn't had much to do at times, was good. John Egan has been an unbelievable signing and the skipper was really good, as has my pal Mark Duffy.

Chris Basham: My choice would be between *Billy Sharp* because he nurtured the squad so well and scored so many vital goals, and *David McGoldrick*. He's an inspiration to anyone.

To come in on trial and help us into the Premier League with his goals is phenomenal but he's a real gentleman around the place as well. I couldn't choose between them.

Billy Sharp: I think *David McGoldrick* really took us over the line in the end. It was a big blow to lose me, Chris Basham and John Egan in one game against Millwall but Didzy stepped up as a leader and he did it all season. I could mention any one of the lads though, even the ones who didn't play much, like Simon Moore or Richard Stearman, because of how well they pushed the other lads.

Jack O'Connell was the most consistent, an eight or nine out of 10 every week who just gets on with his job. Didzy was a deserved winner. I scored a lot of goals but I feel like I just did my job. For him to come in and play so many games, score so many goals and be a massive part of it like he has been, all credit to him because he could easily have said 'I'm too good to go on trial'. I'm delighted for him that he's finally got a chance to play in the Premier League.

John Egan: There could be so many. I hate singling anyone out but I'd have to go for my old pal *Enda Stevens*. From day one he's been Mr Consistent, and to keep that up over a whole season is class - especially in his position where you have to be so, so fit.

He's cemented his position as the Republic of Ireland's first-choice left back, too, which is huge, and even added goals to his game late on after taking my advice and putting his laces through the ball! I think he was gutted that the season ended when it did or he'd have probably tried to go for the Golden Boot.

He's been fantastic and would be my player of the year.

Oliver Norwood: It's so tough because Enda Stevens has been incredible and John Egan has been a brick wall but I'm going to say *Billy Sharp*. The number of goals he produced is special, and leading his boyhood club to the Premier League, as captain, is the stuff dreams are made of.

Didzy has been so good too, but the skipper has really driven the standards of the football club and I think he's been phenomenal all season.

David McGoldrick: I've got two. *Billy Sharp*, because of how he always seemed to come up with a goal when we needed him, and my Irish buddy *Enda Stevens*. He was the best left back in the league all season but really came alive in the last few months.

But you can go through the team - Jack O'Connell, John Egan, Chris Basham, Dean Henderson, John Fleck, Ollie Norwood who got in the team of the year, Mark Duffy. I think there were other people who deserved it before I did, but it's difficult to single out a name because it's been a real team effort.

Mark Duffy: My player of the year would be *Enda Stevens* for his consistency. I think he's come on so much since he came here. Billy Sharp and David McGoldrick scored all the goals, but Enda's performance levels were unbelievable and for me, he didn't slip below a seven out of 10 all season.

He got stronger and stronger as the season went on and so I chose him, but any of the back five could have won it. The midfielders have been so strong and Billy and Didzy scored so many goals. Anyone could have been a worthy winner. It's been that kind of crazy season.

Official club awards

Player of the year: David McGoldrick
'David Spencer' young player of the year: Dean Henderson
Players' player of the year: Billy Sharp
Goal of the season: Chris Basham v Leeds United
Community player of the year: Dean Henderson
Golden Boot award: Billy Sharp

chapter sixteen

Through the eyes of a child

by Nick Brown

As the dust settled on a magnificent season for Sheffield United, I took the chance to reflect on the most enjoyable period I have enjoyed as a Blades supporter. Not just because of the style, panache and sheer will to win we have shown in equal measure at various points during Chris Wilder's time in charge, to get us to where we are now; but because I've been fortunate enough to enjoy it all, in its full technicolour glory, with my 10-year-old son, Harrison. I was around in the days when Dave Bassett dragged the Blades, kicking and screaming, from the old Third Division into the top flight, with a side including a certain blonde-haired right-back in Wilder and that legendary partnership and Brian Deane and Tony Agana up front. Very, very happy memories.

They sprang to mind again during the festive period after United had killed off Blackburn at Bramall Lane and the crowd was in full voice, singing about being on the march with Wilder's army and not going to Wembley. Harrison was next to me, with a beaming smile, and I whispered to him: 'Remember when I tell you about the Bassett days? These are your Bassett days. Enjoy them, son, because the Blades are going up this season'. At this point, we were half a dozen or so points behind Leeds and Norwich. And to his credit, Harrison saw a window of opportunity by making me promise to take him for dessert on London Road if and when my prediction came true.

Harrison was born in 2009, a fortnight after we had lost in the play-off final to Burnley, and his mum and I split up when he was still a baby. So in some ways, we've had more to do to enjoy the father/son bond. His first game, at three years old, was a 5-3 win over AFC Bournemouth and he soon fell in love with the Blades, in much the same way as I did when I was a small boy. The season under Nigel Adkins was his second as a season-ticket holder and, with the football dull, insipid and uninspiring, things were coming to a head. We had enjoyed fleeting success under Nigel Clough but on the whole, every game felt like disappointment after disappointment.

I remember asking him if he was enjoying it and still wanted to go - remarkably, he did - although on one occasion, he did joke about asking me to take him to Hillsborough. I promised I would one day and it would be special. Harrison left the last game of the Adkins era, the infamous Scunthorpe game and the lap of shame that followed, in tears. When Wilder came home, I met him and remember explaining about my son and how he'd cried after the Scunthorpe game. What struck me was that I was speaking to a man who understood exactly what I was saying - because he'd shed similar tears before over this club. His club. *Our club.*

I fulfilled my promise to take Harrison to Hillsborough on September 24, 2017, and he had to hold his ears because of the noise, especially when John Fleck smashed in that early free-kick. When Lucas Joao equalised he burst into tears, his dream in tatters. I remember putting my arm around him, telling him not to worry, as Hillsborough creaked under so many bouncing Wednesday fans. It seemed a lot longer than 90 seconds before Duffy scored *that* goal. For so long, Harrison had been taunted by Wednesday fans at school, telling him that the city was theirs. I turned to him after Duffy's goal, saw the beaming smile on his face and said to him: 'Son, the city is yours now'.

The disappointment of United missing out on the play-offs was intensified by one of his favourite players, David Brooks, being sold, but he quickly took to the new signings Dean Henderson, Ollie Norwood, John Egan and David McGoldrick - even though it took him three months to realise he was pronouncing McGoldrick's name wrong. I found it so endearing that I didn't have the heart to tell him. Throughout the season, we made so many great memories. I couldn't get him a ticket for Elland Road but made sure he joined in the celebrations at full-time via Face-Time. When we drew at home to Millwall I thought we'd blown it. He told me not to be so negative.

We cheered on Wednesday that night against Leeds. Sort of. We couldn't bring ourselves to do it properly so we covered their name next to the score on the TV, to say QPR instead of SW. Not that it brought us much luck. We watched the Leeds v Villa game at mine, and as the full-time whistle blew and we were confirmed as promoted, I shed a few tears of joy. Harrison asked me why I was crying, when I should have been happy. The innocence of youth. And yes, he got his dessert.

Wilder and Co. have given my son a club to be proud of. The same friends at school who used to ridicule United will be jealous of him watching Premier League football, with the same club my grandfather introduced me to in 1982. He sits next to me at every game and I have no doubt we will continue as he grows older, through thick and thin. He bombards me with questions about matches I have been to and the players I have seen.

We listen to Football Heaven or BladesPod in the car, and he continually asks me to show him what the United players have been up to on social media. He's excited about Bramall Lane being on FIFA 20. He raves about the players he meets at Billy Sharp's soccer camp and, in many ways, he sums up everything that football, and United, are about. Wilder, his staff and players have given him a team to be proud of. And for that, I am eternally grateful.

Final Championship table, 2018/19

		P	W	L	D	F	A	GD	Pts
1	Norwich City	46	27	13	6	93	57	+36	94
2	**Sheffield United**	**46**	**26**	**11**	**9**	**78**	**41**	**+37**	**89**
3	Leeds United	46	25	8	13	73	50	+32	83
4	West Brom	46	23	11	12	87	62	+25	76
5	Aston Villa	46	20	16	10	82	61	+21	76
6	Derby County	46	20	14	12	69	54	+15	74
7	Middlesbrough	46	20	13	13	49	41	+8	73
8	Bristol City	46	19	13	14	59	53	+6	70
9	Nottingham Forest	46	17	15	14	61	54	+7	66
10	Swansea City	46	18	11	17	65	62	+3	65
11	Brentford	46	17	13	16	73	59	+14	64
12	Wednesday	46	16	16	14	60	62	-2	64
13	Hull City	46	17	11	18	66	68	-2	62
14	Preston North End	46	16	13	17	67	67	0	61
15	Blackburn Rovers	46	16	12	18	64	69	-5	60
16	Stoke City	46	11	22	13	45	52	-7	55
17	Birmingham City*	46	14	19	13	64	58	+6	52
18	Wigan Athletic	46	13	13	20	51	64	-13	52
19	QPR	46	14	9	23	53	71	-18	51
20	Reading	46	10	17	19	49	66	-17	47
21	Millwall	46	10	14	22	48	64	-16	44
22	Rotherham United	46	8	16	22	52	83	-31	40
23	Bolton Wanderers	46	8	8	30	29	78	-49	32
24	Ipswich Town	46	5	16	25	36	77	-41	31

*Birmingham City deducted nine points by the EFL

About the author

Danny Hall is a sports journalist at *The Star* newspaper in Sheffield. He's a three-time winner of the 'sports journalist of the year award' and was shortlisted in the regional sportswriter category at the prestigious Sports Journalists' Association awards in London in 2019.

He has covered Sheffield United in FA Cup and League Cup semi-finals and a play-off final at Wembley, and reported home and away during both the 2016/17 League One promotion season and the remarkable 2018/19 campaign, when United reached the Premier League. 'We're not going to Wembley' is his third book, after 'He's one of our own' and 'Our Time'. Follow him on Twitter: @dannyhall04.